COLONIZING RUSSIA'S PROMISED LAND

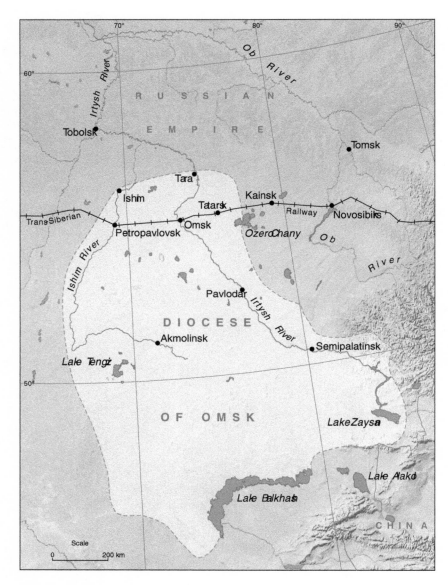

Diocese of Omsk. Weldon Hiebert, Cartographer

Colonizing Russia's Promised Land

Orthodoxy and Community on the Siberian Steppe

AILEEN E. FRIESEN

UNIVERSITY OF TORONTO PRESS
Toronto Buffalo London

© University of Toronto Press 2020
Toronto Buffalo London
utorontopress.com

ISBN 978-1-4426-3719-1 (cloth)
ISBN 978-1-4426-2474-0 (EPUB)
ISBN 978-1-4426-2473-3 (PDF)

Library and Archives Canada Cataloguing in Publication

Title: Colonizing Russia's promised land : Orthodoxy and community on the
  Siberian Steppe / Aileen Friesen
Names: Friesen, Aileen, 1980– author
Description: Includes bibliographical references and index.
Identifiers: Canadiana (print) 20190207167 | Canadiana (ebook) 20190207310 |
  ISBN 9781442637191 (hardcover) | ISBN 9781442624733 (PDF) |
  ISBN 9781442624740 (EPUB)
Subjects: LCSH: Russkaia pravoslavnaia tserkov' – Kazakhstan – History –
  19th century. | LCSH: Russkaia pravoslavnaia tserkov' – Russia
  (Federation) – Siberia – History – 19th century. | LCSH: Church and
  state – Kazakhstan – History – 19th century. | LCSH: Church and state –
  Russia (Federation) – Siberia – History – 19th century. | LCSH:
  Kazakhstan – Colonization – History – 19th century. | LCSH: Siberia
  (Russia) – Colonization – History – 19th century. | LCSH: Kazakhstan –
  Church history – 19th century. | LCSH: Siberia (Russia) – Church
  history – 19th century.
Classification: LCC BX491 .F75 2020 | DDC 281.9/4709034 – dc23

This book has been published with the help of a grant from the Federation
for the Humanities and Social Sciences, through the Awards to Scholarly
Publications Program, using funds provided by the Social Sciences and
Humanities Research Council of Canada.

University of Toronto Press acknowledges the financial assistance to its
publishing program of the Canada Council for the Arts and the Ontario Arts
Council, an agency of the Government of Ontario.

 Canada Council   Conseil des Arts
for the Arts   du Canada

 ONTARIO ARTS COUNCIL
CONSEIL DES ARTS DE L'ONTARIO
an Ontario government agency
un organisme du gouvernement de l'Ontario

Funded by the   Financé par le
Government   gouvernement
of Canada   du Canada

To my parents

Contents

Figures

Acknowledgments

I remember looking out the airplane window excited to catch my first glimpse of Siberia as I arrived in Omsk. Exploring the city, I found that I had travelled halfway around the world to wind up in the Russian version of a place I had spent my adolescence dreaming of escaping. Somehow, I had managed to substitute the gateway to the Canadian Prairies – Winnipeg, Manitoba – for another confluence of murky rivers in its Eastern counterpart. Learning to embrace the familiar landscape and climate, including the winters, taught me to appreciate the place I thought I had left behind.

Many people and institutions facilitated this journey from Winnipeg to Omsk and back again. At the University of Manitoba, the late Margaret Ogrodnick started me on this path through her kind encouragement. At Carleton University, Jeff Sahadeo, Piotr Dutkiewicz, and the late Carter Elwood contributed to my intellectual development. From the start of my arrival at the University of Alberta I've benefited immensely from Heather Coleman's commitment to her students; she truly taught me how to be a historian. I am grateful to John-Paul Himka for providing stimulating comments on my early chapters. Sarah Carter protected me from wild dogs in Omsk and I've appreciated her warmth and insight into the comparative possibilities of my work.

I have also appreciated the feedback of many colleagues during the writing of this book, including David Marples, Nicholas Breyfogle, Elena Krevsky, Victor Taki, Eugene Miakinkov, Marija Petrovic, Mark Steinberg, Diane Koenker, Eugene Avrutin, Patryk Reed, Scott Kenworthy, Vera Shevzov, Laurie Manchester, Roy Robson, Irina Paert, Daniel Scarborough, Rebecca Mitchell, Marlene Epp, Francesca Silano, David Rainbow, Mark Soderstrom, and Julia Fein. John Randolph deserves a special thanks for making my time at the University of Illinois at Urbana-Champaign so productive and enjoyable. My return to Winnipeg has been a whirlwind in the best sense possible, and I am grateful to my new colleagues at the University of Winnipeg who have welcomed me as I navigate my new position, particularly Janis Thiessen, Andriy Zayarnyuk, James Hanley, Royden Loewen, Hans Werner, and Andrea Dyck.

In Russia, archivists, librarians, and staff at the Russian State Library, the Russian National Library, the Russian State Historical Archive, the State Archive of the Russian Federation, the Historical Archive of Omsk Oblast, and the Omsk State Museum of History and Regional Studies provided essential assistance in my research. Olga Ushakova and Irina Poltavskaia gave me much-appreciated advice and help in tracking down sources in St. Petersburg. Tatiana Smirnova introduced me to Omsk for the first time and made sure that I was properly registered. Piotr Vibe made working in the Omsk State Museum of History and Regional Studies an easy experience.

A number of friends have made special contributions to this project. Elana Jakel offered editorial advice, a place to stay, and friendship (along with beautiful Lilly) while I was at the University of Illinois at Urbana-Champaign. Conversations and meals with Ruth Stoltzfus made my time at Illinois even better. Mariya Melentyeva, like a true friend, shamed me into finishing this book; I cannot thank her enough for all of her help over the years. Tiffaney Haydukewich and Alison Froese-Foster have reminded me of the richness of life that exists outside of my office. I don't know what I would do without my birthday emails from Justin Unrau. Donna Dunford and Willa Reddig have made many things possible, and Ken Reddig gave me my first job ever in an archive and is quite possibly the one to blame (or thank) for my career as a historian. Peter Letkemann offered encouragement and advice along the way and Olga Shmakina and the late Paul Toews provided lively company outside the archives and were admirable tour guides in Zaporizhzhia and St. Petersburg. Viktoriia, Karina, and the late Rita Margarita Kalinichenko gave me a home away from home in Omsk, creating memories that I will always cherish. My Omsk roommate, April French, is not only a wonderful scholar, but also an incredible friend.

Working with University of Toronto Press has been a pleasure. My sincerest thanks to Richard Ratzlaff for shepherding the manuscript through the review process and then to Stephen Shapiro, who took over the project and patiently saw the book to fruition. I am also grateful to the two anonymous reviewers who provided much-appreciated feedback on the manuscript. This type of work is an underappreciated but necessary part of scholarship, and their comments greatly improved this book. Finally, I would like to thank the copy editor, Ryan Perks, for his corrections of the many little (and big) mistakes in the manuscript.

I am grateful for the financial support that funded the research and writing of this book. Doctoral and postdoctoral fellowships from the Social Sciences and Humanities Research Council of Canada and the Department of History and Classics at the University of Alberta funded my trips to Omsk, St. Petersburg, and Moscow. A dissertation fellowship from the University of Alberta allowed me to focus on writing. In this difficult job market, fellowships from the D.F. Plett Historical Research Foundation and Conrad Grebel University College allowed me to continue to be a historian. A publication grant from the Social Sciences and Humanities Research Council of Canada helped to get this book to press. Finally, thanks to *Canadian Slavonic Papers* for granting me permission to reuse materials for part of chapter 2, which appeared as "Building an Orthodox Empire: Archpriest Ioann Vostorgov and Russian Missionary Aspirations in Asia" (*Canadian Slavonic Papers* 57, no. 1–2 [2015]: 56–75).

I owe much to my family for their love and support as I researched and wrote this book. Michael and Kim Friesen have provided good company and conversation. My niece Sara, whose birth I first heard about in an internet café in Omsk, has blessed me with countless moments of distraction with her vivid imagination and storytelling. Matthew arrived several years later, adding another reason to come back to Winnipeg. In Edmonton, Jack and Bev Edwards gave me a home away from home, and I am especially appreciative of the openness with which they welcomed me. Glenda and Murray Sloane have supported my career and taken care of my family on my many trips.

Bruce Sloane has been my anchor in life, enduring my constant comings and goings over these years with patience, love, and most of all, humour. Our beautiful tyrant, Antoshka, caused significant delays to the completion of this project, but his enthusiasm for adventure is infectious and I know that one day he will be my most energetic travel companion. Finally, my parents, Ruth and Hank Dyck, have given me their unwavering support throughout this project and beyond. Without them, none of this would have been possible. This book is dedicated to them.

COLONIZING RUSSIA'S PROMISED LAND

Introduction

Before the Bolshevik Revolution altered the trajectory of the Russian Empire, the imperial state engaged in one of its most ambitious projects. By inviting millions of settlers to Siberia, the state sought to transform this agriculturally underdeveloped region into golden wheat fields. After their 1910 trip to Siberia, Prime Minister Petr Stolypin and Aleksandr Krivoshein, whose ministry was active in resettlement, expressed their aspirations for the region under colonization, according to which agricultural settlers would be "the chief driving force" propelling Siberia into a new economic future. Even though the Russian Empire had exerted political control over Siberia for centuries, these men had decided that everything that existed before intensive colonization represented a stagnant past; only settlers could transform the region in a way that the empire's previous contact had failed to stimulate.[1]

Filosof Ornatskii, an active priest in the Russian Orthodox social gospel movement, agreed with this assessment of Siberia as a land waiting to be remade under the plough of Russia's Orthodox peasantry.[2] In a 1915 sermon soliciting support for building churches in Siberia, he spoke of the "impossibility for many of our brothers to settle down freely within the boundaries of native Russia," which pushed them beyond the Ural Mountains. In Siberia, Russian Orthodox settlers would engage with the "wide expanse of God's world." This movement of Orthodox believers created the opportunity for settlers to "fulfil their destiny ... given to the first man, 'to cultivate and preserve the earth.'" As they worked the soil, harvested the crops, and exploited Siberia's rich resources, these pioneers simultaneously "serve[d] [themselves] and praise[d] God" through their labour. Agricultural development, however, was only one part of their mission. According to Ornatskii, the construction of Orthodox churches across this land for settlers planted "fortresses of the Orthodox-Russian soul" and the cradle of

"Russian civic-mindedness [*grazhdanstvennost'*]." Despite the ongoing world war, the full development of Siberia through the movement of Orthodox settlers promised a new chapter in the history of the empire, one that placed Russia on the path toward creating "the Kingdom of God on earth."[3]

The promise of this land of plenty and opportunity coexisted with another image of Siberia as a forlorn region, a "frightening heart of darkness."[4] Stolypin and Krivoshein recorded the many challenges that awaited pioneers in this "harsh and monotonous" environment in which they were forced to engage "in a wearisome struggle with nature."[5] Western Siberia had a long-standing reputation as a religiously desolate place where one could travel the seemingly endless plains without encountering a cupola against its expansive skies. After a trip through Siberia, Anatolii Kulomzin, who managed the Siberian Railway Committee, described the region as devoid of "the native landscape so deeply thrilling to the Russian heart – when going up a hill, suddenly seeing in the distant horizon ... a stone church with a tall bell tower."[6] For state officials, the absence of parish churches symbolized the problems they confronted as they attempted to integrate Siberia culturally into the empire. Until Siberia resembled European Russia – a landscape defined by Orthodox churches filled with parishioners – the land would remain foreign, foreboding, and untamed. By remaking Siberia through Orthodoxy, its true promise would finally be achieved.

In this book, I examine the vital role performed by the Orthodox Church and faith during the colonization of western Siberia in the late nineteenth and early twentieth centuries. Instead of seeking to convert the indigenous population or engaging in the construction of grand churches to project imperial power – both techniques the church and the state had used in the past – secular and religious officials embraced Russian Orthodox settlers as the catalyst that would integrate a region that politically was under Russian authority but which remained culturally separate. To secure the success of this project, Russian state officials and Orthodox Church authorities supported the establishment of Orthodox religious practices in Russian settler communities, as they viewed Russian Orthodoxy as being synonymous with Russian culture. For these officials, Orthodoxy could be used as an anchor of stability for settlers departing from their home communities and as a tool of transformation for making this territory an indivisible part of the empire.

It was not, however, only religious and secular officials who believed in the importance of establishing Orthodox practices in Siberia. Settlers arrived in the region with the expectation that they would have access to the same religious life that they had left behind in their homeland

and they looked to secular and religious officials to support them in their efforts to recreate these customs. As settlers formed new villages, they demonstrated not only that Orthodoxy mattered; they also showed a commitment to interpret for themselves the meaning of Orthodoxy in their communities.

Ultimately, this project turned out to be more challenging than the church and state had anticipated. While they agreed that building parishes complete with churches, priests, and schools was necessary to establish functioning communities capable of perpetuating "Russian" cultural values, the process of forming these parishes highlighted the tensions that existed between and among these groups. Religious pluralism, changing social identities, the breakdown of traditional authority in the villages, the ethnic diversity contained under the umbrella of a "Russian identity," debates over the professionalization of the clerical ranks, and the standardization of religious life – conditions associated with the creation of the modern world – shaped the contours of these new communities in Siberia. Instead of a coherent, unified faith, colonization revealed underlying disagreements among these groups as to what constituted the Russian Orthodox faith and culture they aspired to transplant to Siberia.

Colonization, therefore, forced these groups to define the meaning of Orthodoxy. From the imperial centre a strongly national understanding of Orthodoxy dominated the discourse; this was a bond that stretched across the empire, joining true Russians together. For settlers, the religious practices of their home villages in European Russia, which turned out to be quite different from that of their neighbours in Siberia, continued to hold relevance. Even with the church's efforts to standardize these practices, the Orthodox faith remained highly localized throughout the empire. For others, especially among certain segments of the clergy, a regional identity grew in response to pressure from the imperial centre, the breakdown of the clerical estate, and the localized Orthodox practices of Siberian villages. Despite the competing definitions of Orthodoxy that colonization illuminated – or perhaps exacerbated – imperial authorities and Russian Orthodox officials forged ahead with the idea of Orthodoxy as representing a unified Russian culture until the end of the imperial empire. While these fractures did not directly cause the empire's collapse, they raised questions about the efficacy of Orthodoxy as a pillar for Russia's settler-driven imperial expansion.

Over the last few decades, the scholarship exploring Russia's engagement with Siberia has grown rapidly, adding new voices to the broader story of the expanding empire. Local and regional treatments of Siberian history have offered new perspectives on knowledge creation, networks, land ownership, political movements, and other themes;[7] these works enhance the numerous sweeping portraits that have been published in the past two decades.[8] Such work has shown that over the course of four centuries, the Russian state continuously rediscovered Siberia as the economic, political, social, and cultural circumstances of the empire evolved.[9] In many cases, the themes of previous discoveries were repeated, albeit with significant variations: for instance, the seventeenth-century program of Christianizing the land of Siberia identified by Valerie Kivelson, and the messianic nationalism of the nineteenth century described by Mark Bassin, emerged again in the early twentieth century in secular and religious thinking on Siberia.[10] These ideas, however, were now reinvented to be firmly associated with the movement of millions of Orthodox settlers to the region.

The addition of intensive colonization to the Siberian story mirrored the expansion of other European empires as voluntary migrants moved across the globe during the long nineteenth century.[11] Yet, for the tsarist empire, the post-1890 round of Siberian resettlement coincided with a particularly volatile period in Russian history. Often viewed as a period of "imperial anxieties," the tsarist regime struggled to establish uniformity in imperial governance over its multi-ethnic and multi-confessional empire. This was also a period of great contradictions, as the case of Siberia illustrates. Although the building of the Trans-Siberian Railway advertised the scientific advancements of the state and the intrepidness of the Russian spirit, the Russo-Japanese War of 1904–5 would reveal the Russian Empire's inability to back up its projection of power in the region. The loss of the war and the abrupt turn to parliamentary politics with the formation of the State Duma, along with the recognition (albeit imperfect) of individual religious rights in 1905, contributed to the atmosphere of transformation that was already underway. During this period, a number of visions of the empire coalesced and competed to define its future, each one pursuing a different approach to the question of nationality and nationalism.[12] For many of the actors involved in the colonization of Siberia, a shift away from the principle of estates and toward the favouring of Orthodox Russians was discernible.

This shift influenced settler colonialism as the state created new policies and structures that supported settlers in the reproduction of their own society.[13] The encouragement of Orthodox settlers to the region reflected a change in the state's perception of this land, which was now to be an oasis of agriculture amenable to the replication of the colonizers' culture. This involved the direct displacement of indigenous populations as settlers claimed moral and physical ownership over the land and nearby resources, thereby altering the local population's land use and constraining their access to traditional sources of food and water.[14] The demographic consequences of settler colonialism in Siberia was noticeable: in 1858, the non-indigenous population (Russians and other ethnicities) was over 2 million; by 1911, this number had increased to over 8 million.[15] Such a change in population altered the economic, political, and cultural contours of Russian rule. In contrast to Central Asia, where demographics and the level of religiosity among the local Muslim population persuaded state officials to pursue a more secular approach to the integration of this territory into the empire, the dominance of Russian Orthodox settlers was embraced in Siberia.[16]

A significant number of these settlers established communities in western Siberia, particularly in the territory of Omsk diocese. This diocese, established in 1895, notably straddled the imaginary line between Siberia and Central Asia as it encompassed part of the Kazakh steppe (the provinces of Akmolinsk and Semipalatinsk) and the territory north of Omsk.[17] A large indigenous population of nomadic Muslim Kazakhs inhabited the steppe provinces, initially outnumbering the Russian population significantly.[18] Upon their arrival, settlers established homes on land owned by the state or rented from the Kazakhs and the Cossacks, the latter group having settled in the region centuries earlier. As the settler population grew, the Russian state reduced the land it had allocated to the Kazakhs, hindering their movement with their herds and creating the conditions for an economic and cultural crisis in this community.[19]

A number of factors make Omsk diocese an interesting case study. This particular diocese experienced intensive settlement during the late nineteenth and early twentieth centuries as the Orthodox population almost tripled in less than twenty years, from just over half a million in 1898 to nearly 1.5 million by 1914.[20] This transformation of the territory of Omsk provides an opportunity to investigate the development of a diocese forged in the complicated environment of colonization. Established western Siberian dioceses like Tobol'sk and Tomsk had time to develop their institutional culture in a gradual, coherent fashion, whereas Omsk diocese had to be built from the ground up during the disruption of colonization.

Despite the Orthodox Church's special status in imperial Russia, scholarship on its role in the expansion and formation of the empire in the nineteenth century has been sparse. In fact, it has been mainly scholarship exploring the sixteenth to eighteenth centuries that has shown how Orthodoxy served an ideological and institutional function in the expansion of the tsarist empire.[21] In contrast, the influence of religious minority groups in the imperial borderlands during the nineteenth century has received significantly more attention.[22] While this scholarship has illuminated important themes, such as the role of missions, conversion, governance through religious toleration, and sectarian colonization in the formation of Russia as a multi-ethnic and multi-confessional empire, the contribution of Russian Orthodox settlers in conjunction with the institutional church in this process has been obscured.[23]

Such neglect of the role of the Russian Orthodox Church in empire building has hidden its intensive expansion into the imperial periphery, especially in Siberia. The institutional growth of the Orthodox Church intensified during the nineteenth century as it rapidly extended its reach into the region. In the seventeenth century, the Russian Orthodox Church established its first diocese in Tobol'sk; in the eighteenth century, it added two more, with Irkutsk and Orenburg as their capitals. A flurry of activity unfolded in the nineteenth century with 9 dioceses opening across Siberia and Central Asia, beginning with Tomsk in 1834, and ending with the dioceses of Blagoveshchensk in 1899. By the beginning of the twentieth century, 12 dioceses existed, of which 8 had been established in the second half of the nineteenth century.[24] This institutional expansion was supported by approximately 10,000 clergymen working in the region.[25]

Like other European powers, the Russian Empire used religion to justify, support, and promote the movement of settlers from the metropole to the imperial periphery. Many in clerical robes and the uniforms of official tsardom shared a similar ideological perspective, which supported this institutional cooperation. A strong belief prevailed in these circles that the planting of Russian culture through churches was necessary to ensure the success of colonization. On the ground, priests regularly relied on a narrative of cultural transformation as they described their work of establishing Orthodox outposts of settlers as glorifying both the motherland and God. Like their British counterparts, Russian Orthodox leaders also understood their work in Siberia as fulfilling the church's destiny of creating a Christian empire that would renew the world.[26] Local clergymen savoured their role in this refashioning of the wild pasturelands of nomadic Kazakhs into ploughed fields marked by bell towers and cupolas. This project also incorporated the Russian Orthodox people as a national group. By involving the Orthodox faithful in funding the building of churches, the state and church encouraged parishioners to think beyond their local identities and to envision their faith in an imperial context. Through the creation of an official space for the general public to participate in imagining colonization, the tsarist regime encouraged an expression of national identity rooted in the Orthodox faith.

Under state-led colonization, cooperation deepened between the state and the Orthodox Church in the imperial borderlands.[27] While tensions still existed, the evidence overwhelmingly shows that Siberian colonization strengthened the lines of communication and collaboration between the church and state under the banner of empire. From the late nineteenth century until the end of the tsarist empire, the building of parishes for settlers was incorporated into the state bureaucratic structure administering and supporting resettlement. For many European empires, religious institutions were a means to stabilize communities in transition and plant the culture of the imperial centre. Within this context, financial and clerical support from the metropole for local parishes shaped the religious practices of settlers, tying the centre and periphery together.[28] In the Russian case, the Siberian Railway Committee, and later a partnership formed between the Holy Synod and the Resettlement Administration (under the authority of the Main Administration of Land Management and Agriculture – Glavnoe upravlenie zemleustroistva i zemledeliia, or GUZiZ) assisted settlers in establishing the foundations for parish life: churches, schools, and access to clergymen. Especially after 1908, the technocratic approach of the Resettlement Administration aided significantly in the growth of this project. Instead of "the decade of despair" that Jennifer Hedda has identified as characterizing church-state relations in St. Petersburg, the case of Siberia illustrates how the agendas of these institutions were united in the imperial borderland.

This project, however, was one that excluded the many other non-Orthodox faiths that lived in the empire. Unlike the British case, which by the nineteenth century had embraced religious pluralism among Christian believers under the umbrella of an imperial identity, the Russian state supported an identity that assumed membership in the Orthodox Church.[29] This limited the role available to other religious groups (and other ethnicities) on the imperial periphery. Under this vision, Russian Orthodoxy was tasked with acting as a bulwark against the influence of Islam and sectarianism in Siberia. Russian Baptists and other groups, however, challenged this narrative of a divine marriage between Russianness and Orthodoxy.[30] As the Russian state aspired to a coordinated and well-organized colonization that would showcase the cultural power of the Russian Empire, these alternatives to the Orthodox faith caused great anxiety for religious and secular officials, especially in the aftermath of the 1905 revolution.

It was not only sectarians who destabilized the imperial project in Siberia. Similar to widespread urbanization happening at the same time, colonization caused disruption in the lives of settlers, exposing them to new places, experiences, and ideas without the traditional filters of rural life to soften these changes. Under these conditions, settlers understood the Orthodox Church as one of the primary institutions supporting and perpetuating the traditions of their community, particularly in grounding their youth in the village. Peasant commitment to tradition, while easily overstated, showed through strongly during the process of resettlement. Settlers travelled to Siberia to maintain their rural way of life, an option increasingly less available in European Russia as land hunger threatened agricultural livelihoods.[31]

Establishing those traditions in Siberia was challenging. Orthodox priests, like their French counterparts working on the American frontier who attempted to transform "the unsettled, unscripted, [into] a settled, scripted, and official Catholic way of life," encountered a host of issues in their newly built parishes.[32] Like on the Canadian Prairies, the settlers' former homelands shaped the ways in which they understood and interacted with their new environment religiously.[33] Orthodox settlers believed the localized practices they brought to Siberia from their original communities to be the proper way of practising Orthodoxy. This created problems for the relationship between Orthodoxy and a Russian national identity as the diversity of interpretations and practices housed under the banner of Orthodoxy – often exacerbated by social, linguistic, and cultural differences – caused tensions for settlers who were often very attached to their version of the Orthodox faith.

While settlers were invested in Orthodoxy, they showed little concern about Europeanness and Russia's Great Power status.[34] As sources written by settlers show, everyday life as defined by work, land, community, family, and faith preoccupied their thoughts more than claims to imperial greatness.[35] Nonetheless, settlers consistently referred to the territory they had left behind as "Russia," thereby illustrating that they understood their villages in Siberia as existing outside of their own homeland. And many appeared to embrace the identity of "settler." They used this term to designate a special relationship between their settler communities and the Russian state. Embedded in this awareness was the idea that they represented outposts of Russian religiosity, even if they did not live up to the expectations of state and church officials.[36]

In general, religion performed a significant role in how clergymen and parishioners created, experienced, and interpreted their new Siberian lives. Recent scholarship has explored the central role of the "lexicon, liturgy, and theology of Russian Orthodoxy" in shaping the discourse on the changing material circumstances and intellectual landscape of modern Russia.[37] Modern forms of transportation, technology, and communication not only revolutionized everyday life for inhabitants of imperial Russia, but they also transformed religious experiences, contributing to the formation of new personal, regional, and national sacred narratives that were influenced by the forces of centralization, standardization, and perhaps contradictorily, democratization.[38] In Siberia, Orthodox settlers continued to rely on their faith as a useful lens through which they could understand the changes they were experiencing. Colonization allowed them to take a more active role in defining the practices of worship that satisfied their religiosity, but it also forced them to contemplate their religious practices in the face of the religious diversity that they encountered within Orthodoxy.[39] Sometimes this contemplation led to a search for spiritual answers from other Christian faiths. For clergymen in Omsk diocese, this changing landscape challenged them to navigate standardization not only within their parish communities, but also within their own ranks, as more men from outside of the clerical estate entered into their profession.

This book relies on a variety of archival and published sources from both the imperial centre and the periphery. In St. Petersburg, the records of the Holy Synod of the Russian Orthodox Church, the office of its chief procurator, the Siberian Railway Committee, and the Resettlement Administration provide the perspectives of both the church and the state in relation to the settler movement. In Moscow, the personal papers of Ioann Vostorgov, a central figure in the resettlement story, offers insight into the breakdown of the clerical estate and the tensions it caused between European Russia and Siberia. Orthodox journals on missionary work illuminate how colonization influenced the missionary activities of the church in the region. *Church News* provides the perspective of the Holy Synod that oversaw church affairs emanating from the centre. For the local perspective, I worked with the Omsk diocesan consistory papers and the *Omsk Diocesan News*, a journal that provides in-depth coverage of the issues deemed significant by local clergy. Hidden in all of these sources are the voices of settlers as they engaged with the official structure of church and state, primarily through the form of petitions and published letters.

Chapter 1 explores the shift initiated by colonization for the Russian Orthodox Church as it transitioned from converting local indigenous populations to being preoccupied with the religious needs of Orthodox settlers. Chapter 2 focuses on how the Emperor Alexander III Fund created a space for Orthodox believers to contribute to the colonial effort through financial donations. Chapter 3 explores how the building of parish life unfolded and the challenges and compromises created by the realities of mass migration for settlers, the church, and the state. In Chapter 4, I explore the disruption that colonization brought about for Omsk clergymen as the diocese struggled with recruitment and building unity among a socially and culturally diverse set of men.

Despite the great efforts to accommodate and strengthen the Orthodox faith among settlers, cracks appeared from the outset. Orthodox settlers arrived from all parts of the empire, bringing with them the religious traditions of their home provinces. Using the concept of lived religion, chapter 5 analyses the realities of building community life as religious customs and traditions collided in the parishes of Omsk diocese. Chapter 6 explores how religious pluralism, a controversial and divisive issue in early twentieth–century Russia, influenced the unfolding of settler colonialism.

Woven together, these chapters shed light on the role of the Orthodox faith during the colonization of Siberia. They show how the economic and cultural dislocation instigated by migration did not lead to the secularization of rural communities. However, even though church, state, and settlers alike demonstrated a deep commitment to planting Orthodoxy in Siberia, colonization forced these different groups to define the meaning of Orthodoxy. The case of Omsk diocese shows the competing definitions, not readily apparent in rural European Russia, that colonization brought to the surface.

Chapter One

A Settler Diocese

In 1895, the bishop of Omsk and Semipalatinsk, Grigorii (Poletaev), arrived in Omsk to find himself without an episcopal residence. Thankfully it was late May and not January, when the cold Siberian winter air might have reduced the bishop's spirits. Finding a suitable place to live was only the first of many challenges that this sixty-four-year-old faced in his new diocese. In many respects, his former diocese of Turkestan and Tashkent had prepared Grigorii for the trials of pastoring in Omsk. Both dioceses faced many of the same issues: a shortage of priests, an absence of churches, an underdeveloped ecclesiastical educational system, meagre diocesan financial funds, and the presence of a large indigenous Muslim population. At least some of these similarities must have been apparent during his stopover in Semipalatinsk, a town across the border from the Chinese Empire that had started as a Russian fort along the Siberian line and had since grown into a centre of trade and commerce. As Bishop Grigorii passed through, nine mosques announced the religious identity of the town.[1]

From Semipalatinsk, Bishop Grigorii travelled by steamship along the Irtysh River to Omsk – a trip that took five days. By May, the ice covering the river had already cracked and floated north toward the Arctic, opening the steamship lanes between the two towns. Omsk welcomed its first bishop with the sound of ringing church bells. Despite this religious gesture, Omsk hardly had a storied spiritual, or even cultural, history. A decade earlier, the American explorer George Kennan had captured the stark functionality of Omsk as a place where "the largest building is a military academy and the most picturesque building a police station; in which there is neither a newspaper nor a public library."[2] After Grigorii arrived, the title of most picturesque building would soon belong to the Cathedral of the Assumption, a colourful, five-domed Orthodox church inspired by the fanciful design of the

Church of the Spilt Blood in St. Petersburg. Even with this architectural connection to the imperial capital, the tell-tale signs of Omsk's transitional state could be seen everywhere, particularly in the bustling railway station filled with weary settlers from European Russia passing through to unknown destinations.

The arrival of the bishop represented an opportunity to spread Russian culture across the endless steppe. In conversations leading up to the formation of the diocese, the task of missionizing the local Muslim population occupied a position of importance on the agenda of church leaders. The Orthodox Church believed that nomadic Kazakhs were Muslim in name only and therefore a fertile field for the spread of Christianity. However, the flood of Orthodox settlers appearing at the railway station had made another option possible: the Christianization of the land instantaneously through demographic transformation. The conversion of the local indigenous population, while still considered an admirable and noble pursuit, now occupied a secondary position to the primary purpose of the diocese: attending to the religious needs of the Russian settlers who now called Siberia home. The appearance of these settlers altered the priorities of local diocesan officials and offered activists in the Orthodox Church a new cause to trumpet.

People of the Steppe

Russia's political engagement with Siberia began in the sixteenth century as the wealthy and well-connected Stroganov family tasked Ermak Timofeevich and his band of Cossack mercenaries to explore the rich resources, particularly furs, of Siberia. At the beginning of the eighteenth century, the state established the first section of the Siberian line, a string of forts along the Irtysh River: Omsk (1716), Semipalatinsk (1718), Ust-Kamenogorsk (1719), and Pavlodar (1720).[3] Cossacks, groups of peasant-soldiers who provided military service for the tsarist regime in exchange for privileges, constructed and lived in these forts, from which they assumed the task of safeguarding Russian economic interests against the Kalmyks, who regularly staged incursions into this territory. Until 1809, the Bashkir Cossacks, who were Muslim, constituted a section of the Cossack guard serving to protect the empire. Eventually, the state replaced the Bashkir Cossacks with the Siberian Cossack Host, composed mainly of Orthodox Christians but still including a small number of Muslims.[4] Cossacks were, in essence, the first "Russian" settlers in the region as the state granted them large tracts of lands in perpetuity to encourage them to develop agricultural communities.[5] By the early twentieth century, Cossack communities continued to make up a distinctive portion of the parishioners in Omsk diocese.

Despite the presence of Cossacks, Russia primarily explored and exploited Siberia, instead of subduing it through intensive colonization.[6]

In addition to the Cossacks, exiles – both criminal and political – composed a significant portion of the non-indigenous population. By 1744, Russia ceased to rely on the death penalty, thereby solidifying Siberia's purpose as the primary site in the empire for the banishment of criminals and those imperial subjects that the state deemed politically suspect.[7] In the nineteenth century, the tsarist regime used Siberia as a dumping ground for groups like the Decembrists and members of the Petrashevsky Circle – most famously Fyodor Dostoyevsky, who spent time in an Omsk prison during his exile. Although the state stopped shipping criminals to Siberia in the early twentieth century, political offenders still received this punishment, with Bolshevik luminaries such as Vladimir Lenin and Joseph Stalin serving sentences in the region.[8]

The local population also grew, in part, through the exile and exodus of religious dissenters and sectarians from European Russia. Persecuted for refusing to accept the changes initiated by Patriarch Nikon in the second half of the seventeenth century, Old Believers fled to Siberia, where they could practise what they viewed as authentic Orthodoxy out of the state's reach. This established a large population of Siberian Old Believers who lived, worked, and prayed in their own communities. In the territory that would become Omsk diocese, many Old Believers chose to live off the beaten track – for instance, near the Altai Mountains.[9] Beginning in the eighteenth and extending into the nineteenth century, the state exiled apostates from the Orthodox Church, banishing members of so-called heretical groups such as the Skoptsy and Doukhobors to the region. On the one hand, state officials viewed dissenter and sectarian settlers as exemplifying strong "colonizing abilities" such as "industriousness, thrift, and sobriety." Yet, they also characterized the presence of these groups as dangerous to Orthodoxy in the region.[10] As long as Russian Orthodox settlement remained underdeveloped, this contradiction existed without causing much concern.

Finally, the emancipation of the serfs in 1861 increased the number of peasants moving to western Siberia as colonists. Freed from the bondage of serfdom, some peasants decided to take advantage of the vast tracts of land in Siberia, following the Great Moscow highway (*trakt*), which, impressively, stretched from the Urals to Irkutsk. Without a government program supporting resettlement at the time, most settlers arrived as *samovol'tsy*, or people without permission from the state to relocate.[11]

All these groups were lumped into the category of old residents (also known as *starozhily* or *Sibiriaki*), a term used by state officials, priests,

1.1 A group of escaped Siberian convicts. Library of Congress, LOT 13251-2, no. 25.

ethnographers, and anthropologists to describe the "Russian" population that lived in Siberia before the new contingent of settlers flooded
the region during the late nineteenth and early twentieth centuries.[12]
Even though this category of people lacked an official definition, the

term was nonetheless imbued with meaning. By the mid-nineteenth century, some members of the local Russian population of old residents had developed a strong regional identity. Siberian-born intellectuals argued for the territory's administrative and economic autonomy from imperial Russia as they categorized and recorded the unique history of Siberia and its inhabitants.[13] Among the general population and Siberian-born priests, the political aspect of this identity was less pronounced; however, many secular officials, church workers, and members of the intelligentsia, from both Siberia and European Russia, claimed that cultural differences existed between the old residents and the new settlers.[14] For Siberian-born peasants, the separation of the old residents from Russia had produced a distinct group of people that preserved true Russianness, unlike the new settlers from European Russia.[15]

In contrast, many state officials argued that this separation had caused the degradation of the old residents and that Siberia required a transfusion of real Russian culture through the colonization of peasants from European Russia. The lay chief procurator of the Holy Synod, Konstantin Pobedonostsev, expressed disappointment with the attitude of old residents toward the local parish, the fulfilment of Orthodox religious rites, and Orthodox holidays.[16] Even as local Omsk priests praised the old residents for not joining sectarian groups, they ruminated on how this group of people "regard[ed] the whole church with a coldness that is incomprehensible to a Russian."[17] One state official blamed their attitudes on the difficulties of early pioneering life in Siberia, arguing that old residents, surrounded by "half-wild *inorodtsy*," had to engage in a struggle with nature instead of contemplating spiritual matters, which contributed to their isolation from the Orthodox faith.[18] A British traveller elaborated on this idea, proposing that the old residents' separation from the Orthodox Church, in combination with their strong ties to the physical world, produced a faith that spiritualized nature.[19]

These lands, of course, were not empty before the arrival of the Russian settlers. In the territory that would become Omsk diocese, the majority of the population in the southern provinces of Akmolinsk and Semipalatinsk belonged to Kazakh tribes. According to the 1897 empire-wide census, the Kazakh population in this region stood at over a million people, with Tatars constituting the second-largest group. Smaller populations of Sarts, Bashkir, and Chuvash also lived in the region.[20] Economically, the Kazakhs relied primarily on livestock breeding, which their nomadic lifestyle supported, as they migrated between their summer and winter camps.[21] The Russian state considered the Kazakhs to be *inorodtsy* – a legal category of administration applied to specific groups, especially in the eastern part of the empire, "whose social structures were sufficiently 'alien' to the Russian model."[22] Since *inorodtsy* were considered to belong to a lower rung of the civilizational ladder, the legal rights bestowed upon them by the state were limited.[23]

Orthodoxy and Empire

The institutional structure of the Orthodox Church developed slowly after Ermak's initial expedition. In 1621, the first archbishop of Siberia, Kiprian (Starorusenkov), arrived in his diocesan capital of Tobol'sk. Unimpressed by the spiritual state of his diocese, Kiprian and his successors worked diligently to establish Orthodox religious practices meaningful to local inhabitants and to Christianize the landscape through the building of churches.[24] Both techniques – the invention of a locally based Orthodox tradition and the conquering of space through church building – served important functions as the church moved into pockets of the empire that were politically under Russian control, but culturally and demographically separated from the imperial centre.[25]

The conversion of local indigenous populations presented another option for Christianizing land on the imperial periphery. In the case of Siberia, the church and state's commitment to converting the local peoples to Russian Orthodoxy shifted over the course of three centuries. In the early eighteenth century, under Peter the Great, the Russian state actively pursued the idea of Christianizing the population, even sending Ukrainian missionaries to Siberia to establish churches and monasteries as well as perform mass conversions.[26] The state also encouraged missionaries to translate the Bible into local languages and to live in close proximity to their potential converts.[27] By the mid-eighteenth century, Catherine the Great would undo many of Peter's initiatives, choosing to weaken missionary activity by confiscating church lands in Siberia and rescinding many of the benefits offered to indigenous converts.[28]

To address the multi-confessional reality of her empire, Catherine relied on a policy of religious toleration. This approached influenced the development of Islam on the Kazakh steppe. Instead of supporting the conversion of the Kazakhs to Orthodoxy, she encouraged the standardization of Islam among the Kazakhs by supporting the proliferation of mosques and Islamic schools under the administration of neighbouring clerics of Tatar origin.[29] In this case, the state viewed Islam as a tool to help "transform Kazakhs into imperial subjects" by using approved imams to develop Islamic institutions, which would place the nomadic Kazakhs on the road toward a sedentary lifestyle.[30] The Orenburg Muslim Spiritual Assembly, created by the tsarist regime to administer the spiritual lives of Muslims within the empire, provided supervision over the faith of the Kazakhs, thereby allowing for the incorporation of this population into an institution linked to the imperial centre.

By the mid-nineteenth century, the state started to take seriously the integration of the steppe into the empire, which included exploring the idea of supporting Orthodox missionary work among the Kazakhs.[31] Religious and secular officials argued that, compared to Muslims in Turkestan, Kazakhs showed the least amount of "fanaticism." The scarcity of mosques and clerics in the provinces of Akmolinsk and Semipalatinsk confirmed for Russian state and church officials that the Kazakhs held their religion in little regard, which energized the idea of conducting missionary work on the steppe.[32] In the 1860s, the state removed administrative control over the religious life of the Kazakhs from the Orenburg Muslim Spiritual Assembly as a way of weakening the influence of both the Tatars and Islam.[33] Two decades later, the Orthodox Church started a mission to the Kazakhs in Tomsk diocese; another mission opened in Tobol'sk in the 1890s. In 1895, missionary posts established in the provinces of Akmolinsk and Semipalatinsk were joined to form the Kazakh mission in Omsk diocese, which would continue to operate until the end of the empire.[34]

Siberian bishops also expressed interest in missionary work among the Kazakhs and other *inorodtsy* populations. In 1885, secular officials joined the bishops of Irkutsk, Enisei, Tomsk, and Kamchatka in a conversation on church and state cooperation, particularly in the area of missionary activity in Siberia.[35] The Irkutsk Council, chaired by Archbishop Veniamin (Blagonravov) of Irkutsk diocese, explored the task of spreading Christianity among the indigenous peoples of Siberia and strengthening local Orthodox parishes. Veniamin was well versed in missionary work in Siberia, having worked for three decades in the Transbaikal region to Christianize the Buriats, who practised shamanism and Lamaism.[36] To reinforce this work among the Buriats, at the council Veniamin proposed the establishment of the Transbaikal diocese with Chita as its diocesan capital.[37]

The issue of missionary work among the Kazakhs also appeared on the agenda of the council. Bishop Vladimir (Petrov) of Tomsk argued that the provinces of Akmolinsk and Semipalatinsk formed a vast, untouched mission field for the Orthodox faith. The hundreds of thousands of Kazakhs that inhabited this land, insisted Bishop Vladimir, were only nominally Muslim. To ensure that these potential converts received the attention that they deserved from the Orthodox Church, he supported the opening of a new diocese in western Siberia.[38]

In addition to exploring proselytism, the council provided an opportunity for the bishops to discuss candidly the problems they encountered in Orthodox Siberian communities. They shared that because of the vastness of the dioceses, parishioners remained without proper diocesan oversight, which left them vulnerable to the teachings of schismatics and sectarians. In the case of Semipalatinsk, only eleven churches existed in the province, which provided little supervision over the Orthodox population. The influence of secular officials at the meeting can be discerned in the suggestion that Russian Orthodox settlers would be needed to secure Russia's border with China in the eastern part of the province.[39]

By the end of the Irkutsk gathering the bishops requested the establishment of two dioceses, Omsk and Transbaikal, from the Holy Synod.[40] The Holy Synod agreed with this assessment, approving the opening of these dioceses at the beginning of 1887. Pobedonostsev also responded enthusiastically to the agenda promoted by Siberian bishops, referring to this meeting as "an important event in the history of the national [otechestvennaia] church."[41] Pobedonostsev even informed Tsar Alexander III of this council in a short letter describing the event.[42] As a strong believer in a symbiotic church-state relationship, Pobedonostsev supported the church's work in Siberia.

Not everyone viewed this decision as a positive development, however. Tobol'sk diocesan officials appeared sceptical of the conclusions drawn by the Irkutsk Council, questioning why Omsk should become its own independent diocese. They argued that if the primary purpose of the proposed new diocese was to spread Christianity among the inorodtsy, then a vicar bishopric based in Omsk should suffice.[43] The financial cost of establishing a diocese was onerous; in contrast, a vicar bishopric was an inexpensive way of testing the waters and confirming if the region required another diocese. Such a circumspect response by Tobol'sk officials hints that they still viewed conversion as the church's primary goal in Siberia and did not foresee the monumental change on the horizon with the building of the Trans-Siberian Railway.

Launching State Aspirations

As the church contemplated its role in Siberia, the state engaged in rethinking the economic and political future of the region. For centuries, the state had understood Siberia as a source of resources, as well as a buffer zone between European Russia and its Asian neighbours. During the course of the nineteenth century this approach changed as the state slowly began to imagine Siberia as a region in which Russia could flex its imperial muscles. Especially after the humiliation of the Crimean War, the Russian state refocused its attention on geopolitical matters in the region, particularly its competition with the British in Central and East Asia.[44]

By the early 1880s, soon after his inauguration, Tsar Alexander III expressed his desire for Siberia to be integrated into the empire.[45] One suggestion that garnered attention was the building of a railway into Siberia. Sergei Witte, one of the architects of Russia's railway policy, identified Siberia's physical isolation from European Russia as an important factor in its economic and cultural separation from the rest of the empire: only a railway could bridge these worlds and offer Siberia the "access to Russian life" necessary "to bring about those very conditions of existence and development that are prevalent in the other parts of Russia."[46] State officials spent years discussing this proposal, ultimately deciding to begin construction on the Trans-Siberian in 1891.

To reflect this shift in the state's agenda, Alexander III chose Asia as the stage for his heir's introduction into state life. The epic 1890–1 trip of Tsarevich Nicholas to Egypt, India, Japan, and through Russia's eastern empire symbolized the significance of this region for the future of the empire. To prepare the young tsarevich for his journey, Pobedonostsev wrote a letter to the future tsar describing the Orthodox landscape as well as the religious and secular personnel he would encounter during his journey through Siberia. Although Pobedonostsev had never personally set foot in the region, he wrote with authority, likely relying on reports, personal correspondence, and gossip circulating through the imperial bureaucracy to educate the tsarevich.[47] The letter, written a month before Alexander III announced the project to construct the Trans-Siberian Railway, provides a snapshot of Siberia on the brink of its great transformation. Over the next two decades, two themes identified by Pobedonostsev would only grow in importance: the shortage of churches in the region and the religious diversity of the population.

Pobedonostsev's letter illustrates his conservative views on the issue of religious toleration. Highly critical of the state's legitimization of non-Orthodox faiths, Pobedonostsev offered the example of the Kazakh steppe to demonstrate the harmfulness of this practice for the tsarevich. According to Pobedonostsev, the population of the steppe had followed no religion "except crude shamanism"; yet instead of promoting Orthodoxy, the state had purposely connected the Kazakhs to "the centre of Islam in Russia," a clear reference to the placement of the Kazakhs under the control of the Orenburg Muslim Spiritual Assembly.[48] By placing these populations under the administration of a non-Orthodox religious leadership, Pobedonostsev argued, secular officials acted in ways that were contrary to the interests of the church and the state.

Russian settlers appeared only briefly in Pobedonostsev's letter. He described to the tsarevich how migrants in the Far East, who had established settlements during the mid-nineteenth century, were now in a state of spiritual decay. He argued that without churches and religious supervision these settlements had become "wild" and "morally undisciplined." To guard against such moral and cultural disintegration, settlers must have access to churches. Problematically, Pobedonostsev shared, funds were not available to accomplish this goal.[49] This dilemma would come to define Russian colonization in Siberia as the church and state agreed that church building was essential for the development of the region but struggled logistically and financially to organize and undertake such work on a large scale.

Orthodox Colonization

The opening of the Trans-Siberian Railway, one of the greatest projects undertaken by the imperial Russian state, transformed the region. As one British magazine rhapsodized, "The Trans-Siberian Railway is intended to create a new Siberia ... [Soon] people will realise with astonishment what this railway means."[50] The railway, which by 1916 linked Moscow with Vladivostok, allowed for unprecedented access to the region. Natural resources, products, and people could now be moved between European Russia and Siberia with relative ease. For American officials, this development elevated Russia to the status of a serious economic rival. They expressed awe and apprehension at both the building of the railway and the agricultural potential of Siberia, as the cultivation of new lands posed a threat to the United States' position within global grain markets.[51]

Agriculture, Russian officials believed, would be the driving force of economic growth, the engine that would transform Siberia from an Asiatic wasteland into a recognizable oasis of Russian civilization. Travellers viewing the steppe for the first time commented on the vastness of this under-cultivated land. One British journalist called the steppe region "the future granary of the whole Russian Empire, and not of that Empire alone."[52] Morgan Philip Price, a future member of the British Parliament and a tag-along on a Royal Geographical Society trip to Siberia and Central Asia in the early twentieth century, described western Siberia as remarkably similar to "entering the western prairies of Canada," another region of great agricultural promise.[53] John Foster Fraser, a British travel writer touring through Siberia, compared the southern steppes to "a billiard table" as he mused on the flatness of the land that lay before his eyes.[54] While these flatlands did not inspire

1.2 Settlers arriving from European Russia on the Trans-Siberian Railway.
Library of Congress, LOT 9917.

Fraser to poetic ruminations, the agricultural richness of the region was clear to those who touched its soil.

Even with so much potential, the Russian state was slow to open this region to mass migration. In the case of the Kazakh steppe, despite the integration of this territory into the administrative structure of the empire in the mid-nineteenth century, the tsarist regime remained apprehensive of allowing intensive settlement.[55] A general mistrust of the mass movement of peasants, in addition to the issue of how much land the Kazakhs required for their nomadic lifestyle, posed significant stumbling blocks.[56] Despite these obstacles, by the late nineteenth century, tsarist officials began to encourage colonization through the Resettlement Act of 1889, which opened Siberia (and other parts of the empire with free land) to migrants. In 1891, the state allowed pioneers to settle on the Kazakh steppe on land deemed to be in excess of the amount required to maintain Kazakh herds in an attempt to encourage both resettlement and the introduction of a sedentary lifestyle among this group. Such legislative changes transformed these lands through intensive colonization.

Peasants in European Russia took advantage of the new opportunities created by legislation and the construction of the Trans-Siberian Railway. With the average peasant land holdings shrinking significantly from the 1860s, land hunger became the norm in many parts of the empire west of the Ural Mountains.[57] The famine of 1891–2 in parts of European Russia increased the pressure to find new outlets for agricultural development. Over the course of twenty years (from 1891 to 1910) more than 3 million peasants migrated to Siberia.[58] The territories within the dioceses of Omsk and Tomsk in western Siberia received a disproportionally large number of settlers compared to other areas.[59] In the case of Akmolinsk, only 5 per cent of the population engaged in sedentary farming in 1893; seventeen years later, that number had increased to 45 per cent.[60] By the beginning of the twentieth century, the share of Siberian land under the plough had increased from 10,800,000 to 18,900,000 acres. Peasants from European Russia had transformed Siberia into fields of wheat.[61]

The majority of these peasants left from a mixture of Russian, Ukrainian, and Belarussian provinces: Kiev, Mogilev, Orël, Chernigov, Tambov, Voronezh, Ekaterinoslav, Kharkov, Poltava, and Kursk.[62] The issue of nationality and demographics, however, was complicated. Tsarist officials tended not to record the nationality of the population; rather they preserved the settlers' provinces of origin, which provides clues but does not confirm the background of the migrants.[63] The 1897 empire-wide census, which categorized inhabitants by language, gives some indication of the diversity hidden within the category of "Russian settler." According to the 1897 census, the number of Ukrainian-speakers in the province of Akmolinsk was 7.5 per cent and the number of Russian-speakers was 25.6 per cent.[64] The province of Semipalatinsk had a small population of Ukrainian-speakers (only 0.5 per cent) compared to 9.2 per cent native Russian-speakers. The number of Belarussians in these territories was small, with a population of only 114 people in Semipalatinsk and 246 in Akmolinsk. In fact, the Mordovian population was larger, with 392 inhabitants in Semipalatinsk and 8,546 in Akmolinsk.[65] By 1917, the percentage of Ukrainians in Akmolinsk had increased significantly to 29.5 per cent, while the Russian population stood at 27.2 per cent. A similar trend unfolded in the province of Semipalatinsk as the population of Ukrainians increased to 8.1 per cent and the Russian population reached 13.7 per cent.[66] Unfortunately, numbers for the Belarussian population are not available for this later period.

Although men typically outnumbered women in many villages, gender disparity was not overly pronounced. In the case of migration to western Siberia, many peasants moved as a family unit.[67] This stood in contrast to the early nineteenth-century Cossacks settlements on the steppe, in which the absence of a robust female population led to intermarriage with the Kazakhs.[68] These intermarriages, along with other factors, led state officials to critique the Cossacks as inadequate representatives of Russian civilization who, instead of Russifying the Kazakhs, had acclimatized to Kazakh culture.[69] The new wave of settlers would interact closely with Kazakhs; however, marriage between these groups happened less frequently.[70]

Upon arriving in Siberia, migrants joined or established new villages. Similar to rural communities in European Russia, local inhabitants formed a village assembly, which offered a local form of government.[71] The type of land tenure that would be followed was one of the major issues that the village assembly had to adjudicate, with most deciding to form a commune, although not all practised repartition.[72] Particularly in villages with inhabitants from different regions of the empire, establishing functioning local governance through the village assembly proved to be a difficult task. In settlers' former villages, a combination of tradition and kinship networks shaped decision-making, providing a sense of belonging and an "entitlement to the protection and benefits of the community."[73] In Siberia, it was often a struggle to establish this rapport in new villages.

Settlers also struggled to establish the basic necessities of life in their new homes. One priest described "a terrible picture of poverty: hungry, almost naked, dirty children sitting like gypsies pressed together in a cold almost dark dugout" when he visited a new settlement.[74] The governor general of the steppe, Maksim Taube, reported that settlers lived in unsanitary conditions; unclean drinking water, along with damp and crowded living conditions, created health concerns in these new villages. Access especially to clean, drinkable water on the steppe posed a significant problem for settlers – a situation recognized by many of the state officials passing through Siberia.[75] Poor harvests often compounded an already difficult situation for these pioneers, and many relied on state loans to survive. The first winter proved especially harsh, as settlers struggled with diseases such as malaria and scurvy, which caused a high mortality rate.[76] One settler, Serapion Shulgin, wrote of how scurvy had ravaged his village, making death a part of daily life and leaving children orphaned. Since the village was located thirty-two kilometres away from the parish church, the dead were buried without a funeral service. When the priest arrived, he performed the funerals without charging a fee, visited people in the community, and offered comfort to the orphans left behind.[77]

Shulgin's description of settler life offers insight into settlers' early struggles and how their presence transformed the local landscape. Originally from Perm, in 1890 Shulgin moved to Akmolinsk province with his father after a theft, a bad harvest, and the death of his mother changed his family's fortunes. Unlike many of the people who undertook this journey, Shulgin was literate, having completed a number of years of school; he would eventually find work as a teacher in Siberia. Assigned to the village of Kumdy-kul, Shulgin and his father, along with the other villagers, struggled with early crop failures caused by dry weather and the tyranny of grasshoppers. In 1894, the settlers decided that they did not want to live in a village with a Kazakh name; choosing instead to commemorate the wedding of Tsar Nicholas II, they changed the name to Novo-Nikol'skoe.[78]

Interactions with their new Kazakh neighbours brought up potential issues for colonization. At least initially, some Kazakhs appeared to welcome or at least tolerate the settlers as long as they had enough land. According to a land surveyor in Semirech'e, a neighbouring province just south of Semipalatinsk, the old residents mocked the newly arrived settlers for their agricultural aspirations and predicted tense relations between these new arrivals and the Kazakhs. The opposite proved to be the case. The settlers established functioning farms with irrigation ditches that utilized the latest agricultural equipment and opened a bazaar, which the Kazakhs frequented to sell their goods.[79]

Even with the circulation of stories depicting positive relations between settlers and the Kazakhs, it was clear that colonization constrained the Kazakhs' traditional way of life. With the growth of the settler population, Kazakhs often found that access to their traditional migratory routes and pasturelands for their cattle was restricted by the settlers' crops, causing tensions and disputes between the groups.[80] The peasants also recognized the influence of demographics on the dynamics of this relationship. As one group of settlers stated to a tsarist official, "the power of the Kazakhs lessened" as more Russians settled on the land.[81] The demographic transformation in Akmolinsk was particularly staggering, as shown through the change in the religious composition of the province's population. In 1897, the Orthodox population (primarily people of Slavic descent) was 232,401; by 1911, it had increased to 831,899 people. Semipalatinsk province experienced a more subdued growth in Orthodox settlement, increasing approximately 2.5 times from 67,620 to 183,490 during the same period. The share of Muslims (primarily Kazakhs) decreased from 64.3 to 38.1 per cent in Akmolinsk and 89.8 to 80.8 per cent in Semipalatinsk.[82] Not surprisingly, these changes in population were accompanied by the intensification of conflict and competition over land and resources.

Although Russian state officials encouraged this transformation, they expressed apprehension that settlers, who were primarily uneducated or undereducated peasants, could act as ambassadors of civilization and progress. While some tsarist elites viewed these peasants "as super colonist[s] blessed with admirable pioneer qualities, an instinct for settling new places and a knack for interacting with and influencing native peoples," in other circles the arrival of large waves of peasant-settlers to Siberia caused grave concerns as to whether this population could serve as bearers of Russian culture and promote Siberia's integration into the metropole.[83] Instead of representing the superiority of Russian culture, religion, and nationality, settlers served as a reminder of Russia's economic and social backwardness and the disputed nature of a "unified" Russian identity.[84] For members of both sides involved directly in the state planning of colonization, it became clear that simply having peasants plough the land would not "make the territory truly integrated."[85] A strong argument emerged for the state to reinforce settlers' Russian identity by supporting their religious life.

An Unofficial Settler Diocese

The opening of a new diocese in Omsk provided hope that settlers would not live outside the supervision of the Russian Orthodox Church. The first issue of Omsk's diocesan journal, published at the beginning of 1898, painted a vivid picture of the local clergy's aspirations for this territory. The opening of the diocese, attributed to the grace of both God and the tsar, laid the grounds for the transformation of this Siberian steppe from a land dominated by exiles and Muslims into a flourishing field of Orthodox parishes filled with settlers from European Russia.[86]

Yet, building Orthodox life in the territory proved difficult. Arriving in a settler parish provoked a visceral emotional reaction from priests. Omsk priests often used the term "deprived" (*lishat'*) to capture the plight of settlers without access to a church: deprived of comfort, of community prayer (*obshchestvennaia molitva*), of hearing the bells call them to church, and of fulfilling their duties as Orthodox believers.[87] Father Tikhon Korystin, the son of a peasant and newly assigned to a parish in the Atbasar district, wrote of his despair at witnessing peasants living without churches, vegetables, or *kvas* (a traditional fermented drink), and in houses without roofs. Another young priest assigned to a settler village described how the shocking poverty, the isolation, and the unforgiving climate of Siberia produced a "terrible impression." He conveyed the heartfelt reaction of parishioners, who despite – or perhaps because of – these conditions, "met [him] with tears of joy."[88]

Despite these frontier conditions, Omsk replicated the same administrative structure as every other Russian diocese in the empire. The bishop held the highest position and resided in the diocesan capital. He had the responsibility of approving the opening of new parishes and providing spiritual guidance for the laity of his diocese. Administering and governing the clergy, however, constituted his principal duty. The bishop had the authority and duty to ordain clergymen, appoint them to parishes, and look after their welfare. He also punished clergymen who had committed moral offences.[89] The church consistory worked closely with the bishop, providing him with information about the functioning of the diocese and resolutions that the bishop could accept, reject, or amend. Two main bodies helped the bishop administer the diocese: the district board (*dukhovnoe pravlenie*) and the ecclesiastical deanery (*blagochinie*).

While the institutional structure of Omsk diocese was not unique, a number of characteristics made it difficult to build and administer Orthodox life in this territory. A revolving door of bishops in the young diocese created leadership woes. In the span of twenty-two years, eight different men held this title. According to church rules, bishops should hold their offices until death; however, by the end of the nineteenth century, this practice had ceased to be the norm. Instead, the Holy Synod and chief procurator frequently advanced to better posts those bishops who performed their duties well. Some viewed this change as positive, since it rewarded those who showed real promise, while others were critical of it for breaking canon law and harming the relationship between bishops and clergymen.[90] In many ways this reflected similar changes that had taken place among governors in the empire, as a greater emphasis on merit, specialization, and expertise determined the trajectory of their careers.[91]

The situation in Omsk diocese illustrates both the costs and, to a much lesser extent, the benefits of such a system. By the reign of Nicholas II, the average tenure for an Orthodox bishop in any one diocese was 5.5 years.[92] On average, Omsk bishops served in their position for 2.75 years. With such a limited tenure, it would be unreasonable for even an experienced bishop in an established diocese to fully grasp the religious problems and spiritual geographies of his territory. The men sent to serve as bishop of Omsk reflected that diocese's junior position in the empire; it was a place to prove one's worth and move on, hence the high level of turnover. The bishopric of Omsk might be geographically close to the centre of the empire, but it was far removed from the empire's political capital of St. Petersburg and spiritual capital of Moscow. Yet the dioceses exhibiting the most undesirable traits also tended to be those most desperately in need of outstanding leadership, and Omsk was no exception. A few of the men appointed to Omsk demonstrated exceptional leadership qualities; however, almost every bishop was un-proven when he arrived.[93]

Complicating matters further, unlike most European dioceses in which secular and religious authority coincided with civil administrative boundaries, the territory of Omsk diocese overlapped with four provinces – Tomsk, Tobol'sk, Akmolinsk, and Semipalatinsk – and hence interacted with four appointed governors.[94] The governors of Akmolinsk and Semipalatinsk reported to the governor general of the steppe, who wielded ultimate authority over the provinces of Semipalatinsk, Akmolimsk, and Semirech'e.[95] Therefore, the bishop of Omsk interacted with five secular officials, all of whom had their own opinions on how civil and religious life should be organized and governed. The drawbacks of shared authority would become apparent to all sides during the early twentieth century. Governor Andrei Stankevich emphasized the complexities of this division as it related to attempts to address religious issues in Tobol'sk province, as certain administrative districts were split between the dioceses of Tobol'sk and Omsk. In his 1912 annual report, Stankevich raised his discomfort with the current system. He argued that the religious and ethnic diversity of the province, combined with the presence of settlers, required centralized and strong directives from the church. To alleviate this issue, he recommended that two districts historically associated with Tobol'sk diocese be returned to its administrative control.[96] This change, however, was never implemented.

As a young settler diocese, Omsk suffered from a shortage of churches, priests, and parishes. In his 1902 report to the Holy Synod, Bishop Sergii (Petrov) acknowledged that the number of churches required by the arrival of new settlers would only grow in years to come.[97] He was right: ten years later, the flood of settlers into Omsk continued to stretch the diocese's resources to the brink, as Bishop Andronik (Nikol'skii) concluded that parishioners could not afford to construct their own churches.[98] The chief procurator's reports provide a glimpse into the state of parishes in the diocese. In 1895, the diocese had 14 archpriests, 210 priests, 49 deacons, 221 cantors, 168 parish churches, and 226 prayer houses and chapels serving approximately 505,887 Orthodox parishioners.[99] By 1914, the diocese's Orthodox population had almost tripled, reaching 1,477,067 souls, with 519 priests, 129 deacons, and 434 cantors serving this population.[100] The number of parish churches in the diocese had grown to 429 and the number of prayer houses and chapels to 302.[101] Despite this growth, it was extremely difficult for many parishioners to interact with a priest. In 1914, the ratio of parishioners to priests in the diocese stood at 2,845:1; in comparison, the ratio was 1,921:1 in European Russia during this period.[102]

1.3 Priests travelling to visit Siberian villages. *Aziatskaia Rossiia*, vol. 1
(St. Petersburg, 1914), 491.

This shortage of priests was noticed by settlers on the ground. The
parishioners of Pokrovskoe in Tiukalinsk district waited nearly ten
years for a priest to be appointed to their parish. Desperate for help,
they appealed to Empress Maria Feodorovna with a petition in which
they explicitly self-identified as settlers: "We settlers [*pereselentsy*] arrived in Siberia in the year of 1892, settled on a state allotment ... and
like Orthodox Christians first started to work on building a church."
They had even built a home for a priest as they were "eager to fulfil
the duty of the Orthodox faith." Without a priest, they had to travel a

great distance to attend Sunday services and to perform every rite; this hardship, they complained, caused difficulties in their spiritual life.[103]

The vastness of the territory, the terrible roads, and the brutal weather of Siberia also contributed to the struggles of the diocese. The unpredictability of the weather made it difficult to travel, especially in winter, when clear skies could turn instantaneously into a snowstorm. Only three convenient transportation routes existed – the railway, the Irtysh River, and the Great Siberian road – and most parishes could not be accessed along those paths. The most important factor, however, was the expansiveness of the diocese. Religious officials writing about Omsk accurately deployed the term "vast" (obshirnyi) in their descriptions. In comparison to European Russia, Siberian dioceses were massive. Omsk diocese was over a million square kilometres, or almost twice the size of France. To offer a comparison, the dioceses of Riazan, Poltava, and Kiev spanned approximately 36,992, 43,379, and 44,730 square kilometres, respectively.[104] Even the diocese of Perm was only 291,760 square kilometres in size. The territory of Akmolinsk province alone occupied 594,673 square kilometres of territory.[105]

This problem of distance influenced the work of the deans as they performed the important task of supervising multiple parishes. They submitted reports on the state of their districts to the bishop and those reports helped to shape the administrative decisions undertaken in the diocese. On the imperial periphery, deans struggled with this task of collecting the necessary information for the consistory, as they had to complete their duties as priests and travel great distances to make their visitations to parishes under their jurisdiction.[106] In Omsk diocese, this was simply unfeasible. In 1904, only 27 dean districts existed, meaning that 27 men had the duty of supervising 293 parish churches; the situation only worsened as settlement reached a feverish pitch in the post-1905 environment. Some deans travelled over a thousand kilometres by horse to make the rounds of their parishes. Such onerous travel to visit only five to ten churches taxed the deans' energy and limited their ability to undertake such journeys regularly.[107]

Settler migration altered the spatial distribution of the population, which resulted in new parishes being opened and old parishes being reconfigured. For over twenty years, Omsk diocese was in a constant state of fluctuation. For instance, in the district of Omsk, ten parishes existed in 1900; by 1914, thirty-six had been established.[108] Keeping apprised of religious needs within the diocese was impossible, even for the bishop. In 1913, Bishop Andronik requested that deans submit a report and a map depicting the distribution of parishes in their present deaneries and their future configurations. The collection of this information by

Andronik likely stemmed from his growing frustration with the chaos caused by colonization for the church.[109] With the population of the diocese rapidly increasing, anticipating the necessary reorganization of the diocese's spatial configuration proved difficult to achieve.

The Orthodox Church initially prepared for a different type of future in Siberia. Still operating under the assumption that Orthodox missions to the *inorodtsy* formed their primary duty, Siberian diocesan officials focused their resources and attention on the indigenous populations. Omsk diocese was born out of this mindset, yet this would not be its destiny. Over the next two decades, the trials and tribulations of settlers would dominate Omsk's story as local leaders struggled to adapt to the realities of colonization, which brought millions of Orthodox settlers under their supervision.

Chapter Two

Churches as a National Project

In 1913, during Pentecost, one of the most important feasts of the Orthodox liturgical calendar, the Russian Orthodox Church asked parishioners from across the empire to donate money for the building of churches, schools, and homes for priests in Siberia. In a sermon delivered to encourage such donations, Archpriest Ioann Vostorgov described how the movement of settlers to the far reaches of the empire strengthened the state's borders and attached Siberia culturally to Russia. Settlers performing these essential tasks put their souls at risk by moving to a region without churches to care for their spiritual development. Although the Holy Synod and the state both played significant roles in addressing this need, Vostorgov called on "believing Russian people" (*veruiushchie russkie liudi*) to help their fellow Orthodox Christians maintain a fellowship with God. The sacrifices of settlers – namely, moving their families to Siberia – and of donors – sharing their financial resources – created a deep spiritual bond that united them into a people of the church.[1]

For nearly twenty years, state and church officials used the banner of Orthodoxy to elicit financial support from the public for settler churches in Siberia through the Emperor Alexander III Fund. Patrons from all walks of life, ranging from esteemed figures within the state apparatus and the Russian Orthodox Church to ordinary people without rank or title, donated to this cause. To engender support from the Russian Orthodox public, the fund not only pulled at donors' heartstrings through the image of a pitiful Russian settler alone on the harsh steppe without the comfort of the church, it also presented the resettlement of Siberia as an imperial project worthy of prayers and financial support. Such an appeal invited all Orthodox believers to envision themselves as a part of the expanding empire that would benefit the Russian peasantry through the opening of new lands and serve the interests of God and the state by spreading Orthodox Christianity and Russian nationality beyond the Ural Mountains.[2] The Emperor Alexander III Fund communicated this shift in the state's approach to colonization and provided an opportunity for Orthodox believers in European Russia to support their pioneering brethren as they served the empire.

State officials performed an essential role in pushing the agenda of the Emperor Alexander III Fund as they carried out their duties associated with peasant resettlement and the agricultural development of the region. By the early twentieth century, many state officials believed that only lands ploughed by Russian Orthodox believers would be truly integrated into the empire.[3] For these secular figures, the fostering of religious life among settlers would advance the cultural transformation of Siberia; similar to agriculture, industry, and resource extraction, they believed that the Russian Orthodox faith could serve as a conduit for bringing European values to the region. Yet religion performed a distinctive role in this process, as a consensus existed among the upper echelon of state officialdom that without religious roots in the planting of European culture, the colonial enterprise would falter. In many ways this emphasis on religion was strongly correlated with a belief that settlers would be culturally unreliable without the support of the institutional church.

Among church officials, this project also had strong ideological overtones. Vostorgov, who helped to administer the fund and publicize the plight of Orthodox settlers, portrayed this program of colonization as a sort of manifest destiny in which Russia was bound to plant Christianity in Asia.[4] While this idea of Russia's special Christianizing mission to Asia had been articulated in a variety of forms for much of the nineteenth century, the vision of Orthodox peasants as the chosen people fated to fulfil this destiny was new.[5] It communicated a belief in the colonizing abilities of the Russian peasantry with help from the church, state, and the Orthodox nation.

The Emperor Alexander III Fund

In European Russia, the building of parish churches and schools constituted a primarily local and regional affair. Church construction was locally initiated, with villages deciding on their own accord to petition the church consistory for permission to build. The decision then lay with diocesan officials, who considered whether a "need" existed for a new church. They determined this based on the criteria of "distance, size and disrepair" of the parish church.[6] If the petition met the consistory's criteria, and the community had the resources necessary to support it, then it would grant permission to build. Typically, the state only involved itself in providing wood from state lands or a salary for the clergy in cases where the "benefits package" offered by parishioners was meagre.[7] Although financial support for the building of local churches could (and did) come from external donors, church building in European Russia was largely a local undertaking and commitment.

These rules applied even in the far reaches of Siberia. To build a parish church, settlers had to petition the consistory for permission, showing both community support and the financial means for completing the project.[8] Undertaking this responsibility restricted the number of churches established in Siberia as many communities lacked the population density necessary to support a parish. Church shortages in Siberia began to concern officials in St. Petersburg; in his 1885 report, Konstantin Pobedonostsev, the chief procurator, raised this issue. Tsar Alexander III responded with a suggestion: "Need to turn the attention of donors [*zhertvovateli*] to this: here one can really donate with benefit."[9] However, the tsar's suggestion – at least initially – did not inspire any specific initiatives.

Under his son, Nicholas II, Alexander's vision of connecting benefactors with impoverished Siberian spiritual communities would become state policy. Unlike his father, Nicholas II could draw on his personal experiences in Siberia. During the tsarevich's 1890–1 trip, churches were often sites of interaction between Nicholas and the local population. In Omsk, for instance, the ringing of church bells announced the arrival of the tsarevich along the Om River. After being greeted by the governor general of the steppe, Nicholas was whisked through a crowd of people to the Church of the Prophet Elijah, where the city's clergy awaited him.[10] Such scenes happened throughout his journey, as Nicholas visited countless churches, attended services, and interacted with the local Orthodox clergy. That churches were included in the pageantry of the tsarevich's trip hints at the symbolism Nicholas would later place at the centre of his coronation and reign – what Richard Wortman has described as the "unspoken and invisible spiritual bond" that, according to Nicholas, connected the tsar with the Russian people.[11] Nicholas's own strong belief in this bond made him view the meagre number of churches for local worshippers and the impoverished state of their interiors with sympathy. At one small parish church outside of Omsk, the tsarevich made a donation to help, an act he repeated at other churches as he travelled across Siberia.[12]

Nicholas II carried memories of these crude, pitiful churches back to St. Petersburg, where he allowed them to shape how he approached his duties as the chairman of the Siberian Railway Committee. At a meeting of the committee in 1893, Nicholas advocated for the building of churches along the new railway, showing that he placed this issue at the top of his list of priorities.[13] Initially, it was proposed to use leftover funds from the building of the railway to finance this endeavour; however, in April 1894, with the approval of his father, the tsarevich began a fund to collect donations for this cause with the Siberian Railway Committee serving as the financial distribution channel. After the tsar's death later that year, the project was named the Emperor Alexander III Fund. Russia's imperial subjects would now have the opportunity to honour the late tsar by building churches, schools, and homes for clergy in Siberia.

The fund also supported the cause of Orthodoxy through the collection of money for mobile churches, or church wagons (*vagon-tserkov'*), that travelled along the Trans-Siberian line, bringing comfort to the villages located along the railway. On 11 July 1896, according to his diary, Nicholas II attended the consecration of one of these railway cars, which he described as "beautifully equipped."[14] Transforming a train carriage into a church was no easy feat; Orthodox churches, by design, should evoke God's universe by unifying heaven and earth. With their arched windows and cross-topped bell towers that called worshipers to divine services, these carriages were easily distinguished from other railcars. Inside, they were decorated with wooden panels, chandeliers, and iconostases.[15] Travelling priests had everything necessary for conducting services along the world's longest railway.

The task of managing the Emperor Alexander III Fund fell to Anatolii Kulomzin.[16] Kulomzin, who has been described as "among the greatest of [European] colonizers," was a sensible man with provincial noble roots and a Calvinist mother.[17] Through his work as the administrative secretary of the Committee of Ministers (1883–1902) and as the chairman of the Preparatory Commission of the Siberian Railway (under the umbrella of the Siberian Railway Committee), Kulomzin shaped Russia's engagement in the region. The scope of Kulomzin's work in the region is astonishing. His responsibilities included the development of Siberia's economy and the facilitation of peasant resettlement. His guiding hand touched most of the policies aimed at assisting in the colonization of Siberia – a task understood by many in the upper echelons of the Russian state as essential to the empire's political and economic standing among its competitors.

Like many other enlightened European bureaucrats of the nineteenth century working in an imperial borderland, Kulomzin viewed the building of churches as a prerequisite to transforming lands viewed as "foreign" and "barbaric" into cultural extensions of the empire. His approach reflected European notions of the civilizing force of Christianity; according to this view, churches formed a pillar of cultured society, moulding the population through a firm set of moral values. In the case of the British Empire, Anglican leaders and many conservative state officials, like their counterparts in Russia, assigned religious institutions the role of sustaining the cultural values of the imperial centre in their colonial outposts.[18] While many European state officials continued to rely on religious rhetoric to justify their empire, financial support for overseas bishoprics waned in the late nineteenth century, particularly in the British colonies.[19] In contrast, the Russian state initially left parish building primarily in the hands of the church and only later engaged in a systematic program to support the development of this institutional structure in Siberia, allotting not only attention but also financial resources to this cause.[20]

Kulomzin believed that the inaccessibility of church life along the Trans-Siberian Railway estranged Russians from civilization and that this serious threat had to be addressed with the full power of the state.[21] The stakes were high, as the absence of Orthodox churches could disrupt the goals of colonization, especially with large populations of Muslims and Buddhists in the region. He expressed joy at the planting of churches in places like Petropavlovsk, one of the main towns of Akmolinsk province, where the surrounding population was predominantly Muslim.[22] This province often occupied Kulomzin's thoughts, since he viewed the steppe as a region in desperate need of attention. In an 1898 communication with Vladimir Sabler, the deputy to the Holy Synod's chief procurator, Kulomzin discussed how the building of churches and schools could be used to promote state interests; he described Russian villages as Christian oases in a land of Muslim Kazakhs. Saving the souls of Kazakhs was not Kulomzin's goal; instead, these churches would create an Orthodox bulwark by addressing settlers' spiritual needs.[23]

Transforming towns along the Trans-Siberian Railway into bastions of Orthodoxy became part of the duties of the Siberian Railway Committee as it facilitated settler migration to the region. With financing from the Emperor Alexander III Fund, Kulomzin's commission coordinated the distribution of funds and the building of over twenty churches down the rail line from Chelyabinsk to Khabarovsk. While the railway had transformed places like Petropavlovsk, Isil-kul, and Tatarsk from outlying villages into places of trade and commerce, churches refashioned them into spiritual centres.[24] As settlements expanded north and south of the railway, the commission followed these inroads by building churches and schools in newly formed rural parishes. Western

2.1 A church built by the Emperor Alexander III Fund in Tomsk province. *Sibirskie tserkvi i shkoly* (St. Petersburg: Gos. tip., 1904), 43.

Siberia received greater attention than the eastern portion, with over a hundred new churches compared to fifty-three.[25] Under Kulomzin's direction, the state published detailed descriptions of these new churches constructed through the Emperor Alexander III Fund. Maps included in these books visually confirmed the transformation of the territory surrounding the railway into spaces of Orthodoxy.[26]

Patrons of the Fund

In St. Petersburg, donations toward the building of Siberian churches could be made at the offices of the Committee of Ministers at Mariinskii Palace, located across the Moika Canal from St. Isaac's Cathedral. The doors of the palace were open to donors each afternoon.[27] Patrons could also visit other designated sites at the provincial and district levels to contribute financially.[28] By the late nineteenth century, appealing to the general public to support causes of importance to the state and the Russian Orthodox Church was commonplace. For instance, financial contributions poured in from the public for the Slavs in the Balkan Peninsula and for the wounded soldiers of the Russo-Turkish War of 1877–8.[29] The Holy Synod also approved a yearly collection on Palm Sunday, in specific churches, for the Orthodox Palestine Society, which supported Orthodoxy in the Holy Lands.[30] Catastrophic events, such as the 1891–2 famine in European Russia, also acquainted the general public with the needs of their fellow imperial subjects, driving home a spirit of communal responsibility that manifested itself in a flurry of charity work.[31] Such initiatives expanded in tandem with the growth of social problems in the empire, capturing the attention of Russian society. Overall, however, charity work remained an underdeveloped sphere of civic engagement as the state continued to regulate and limit independent activities of this nature.[32] In the case of the Emperor Alexander III Fund, the state, and later the church, maintained control over how money was solicited and spent.

The involvement of famous religious figures provided significant publicity for the fund. Father John of Kronstadt, a deeply pious and beloved archpriest in the parish of Kronstadt, near St. Petersburg, who often facilitated the movement of money and goods from benefactors to needy churches across the empire,[33] supported the construction of churches in Siberia. Father John had the distinction of making the first donation (200 rubles) to the fund in 1894. Ten years later, he was still collecting donations for the cause, sending 6,000 rubles to build a church in the name of Saint Simeon the Receiver of God (Simeon Bogopriimets), in a Siberian village described as a place "where Orthodox peasants, encircled by dissenter hermitages, do not have the opportunity to satisfy their spiritual needs for want of a church."[34]

He was not the only religious figure to contribute donations: clergy from all over the empire collected money for building churches, including the ecclesiastical council of the famous Solovetskii monastery, which gave 3,000 rubles.[35] Some of these donations were given to mark special occasions in the royal family. For example, the bishop of Arkhangelsk gave the fund 5,000 rubles to build a church in honour of the birth of Tsarevich Alexei.[36] Priests also acted as intermediaries between donors and representatives of the fund. In one notable case, a dean from the diocese of St. Petersburg and Novgorod convinced a merchant to donate 4,000 rubles to the cause. After his donation, the merchant's wife had him committed to a hospital for the insane; she challenged the donation, threatening legal action if the money was not returned. The dean insisted to Kulomzin that the merchant made the donation when he was of "sound mind."[37] Likely, Kulomzin returned the funds to the wife.

Undoubtedly, the royal family's patronage raised awareness of this cause and made charitable giving to Siberia fashionable. Nicholas II described the fund as being of personal importance to him: "The question of building churches in Siberia, particularly in new settlements, is very close to my heart."[38] The tsar donated bells, vestments for the clergy, and complete silver sets of church equipment; he also gave financial support to assist in the building of the Cathedral of the Assumption in Omsk.[39] Other Romanovs expressed their own interest in Siberia through charity. Nicholas's mother, Dowager Empress Maria Feodorovna, helped to decorate churches in towns transformed by colonization such as Petropavlovsk in Omsk diocese.[40] Grand Duke Mikhail Aleksandrovich, the youngest son of Alexander III and successor to the throne after Nicholas's abdication, also gave to the fund on many occasions, helping provide priests with vestments.[41]

The *Village Herald* newspaper kept its readers abreast of the donations for the construction of Siberian churches and provided updates on resettlement opportunities in the empire. This newspaper, started by state officials in 1881 as a way to communicate directly with the peasantry, included short write-ups on the work of the Emperor Alexander III Fund.[42] People from a variety of walks of life made donations, and they likely enjoyed having their names and the amount they donated published in the *Village Herald*. The newspaper listed donations not only from governors and others in the upper echelon of the provincial administration, but also from ordinary people without title or position who donated small amounts to the cause, from 2 to 10

2.2 A church built through the Emperor Alexander III Fund in Akmolinsk province. *Sibirskie tserkvi i shkoly* (St. Petersburg: Gos. tip., 1904), 47.

rubles. Parishioners, priests, archpriests, deans, and consistories were also listed as donors.[43] A merchant from Tula left a little over 5,500 rubles to the cause in his will, while various St. Petersburg merchants donated 15,000 rubles in 1901.[44] Not everyone wanted their generosity to be known, as anonymous donations were viewed as more pious by Orthodox believers. Over the years, many people donated without official recognition – for instance, one anonymous philanthropist contributed the sum of 10,000 rubles. The fund also became a way to honour the dead, as the relatives of N.M. Sakharov gave the fund 2,000 rubles in his memory.[45] In his will, Major General I.F. Tereshchenko left the interest on his million-ruble estate to be spent on the construction of churches in Siberia.[46]

Although the evidence is admittedly scant, peasants did read and respond to these articles. In 1894, a man from European Russia sent a letter to the Siberian Railway Committee in which he described shedding "tears of joy" while reading an article about the committee's work building churches and schools in the province of Tobol'sk. In his letter, which is filled with heartfelt references to the monarchy, the man self-identified as a Russian (*russkii*), a loyal subject (*vernopoddannyi*), and a peasant (*krest'ianin*). He explained to the committee the importance of Orthodox churches and schools for peasants in Russia, especially for "the affirmation of the Orthodox faith and the joining of the Russian kingdom with our great Russian monarch, the Lord's anointed Alexander III." To express his commitment to the project, he asked the committee to accept an icon from him and then closed the letter by promising to pray for this "important and good work."[47] As the letter shows, by publicizing this project in Siberia, the Siberian Railway Committee captured the imagination of peasants in European Russia, who could relate to the essential role of churches and schools in their own lives and who viewed Orthodoxy as a unifying force in the empire under a benevolent tsar.

The sources also hint at the active role performed by women in this endeavour. In late imperial Russia, Orthodox women, particularly those coming from the upper echelons of society, were inspired by their faith to engage in charity work.[48] In the case of the fund, women from secular and clerical families left instructions in their wills for money to be donated to the fund. In 1917, the Emperor Alexander III Fund received the 16,800-ruble estate of a deacon's daughter. That same year, the daughter of a collegiate councillor left 5,000 rubles in her will to build a three-altar church in a remote part of Siberia. She requested that the main altar be consecrated in honour of the Nativity of the Theotokos, the right one in the name of St. Nicholas, and the left in honour of the martyrs Adrian and Natalia.[49]

Donors left little indications of their own personal motivations for contributing money to this cause. Those receiving the funds, however, readily ascribed to donors their own reasons for this generosity. In the case of Poltavskoe, a village sixty-eight kilometres from Petropavlovsk bursting with the sounds of the Ukrainian language spoken by settlers from Poltava and Chernigov, the Emperor Alexander III Fund helped to build a Russian school for more than three hundred children. To the great regret of the local district supervisor of church schools, information about the donors' identities was not provided. Nonetheless, he felt confident about their motivations, calling them "people with zeal, feeling sorry for faraway settlers, sheltered in the unpopulated and wild steppe of unfriendly Asia."[50] Nearly ten years later, a description of this parish showed that these donors had indeed helped build a thriving spiritual community.[51]

The cachet enjoyed by those belonging to the category of "settlers in Siberia" was not lost on enterprising local priests. In 1899, a sermon was published pleading for money to help build a new church in the village of Mogil'no-Posel'skii in the district of Tara. This appeal for support referred to the parishioners as settlers from European Russia – even though they had been living in the region for over thirty years. It played up both their poverty and the foreignness of their surroundings by portraying the pain of their separation from their homeland and their struggle to build a new life. The sermon, printed in Moscow, appealed to readers to send financial aid to a postal station in Tobol'sk province to the committee for church building.[52]

By providing an opportunity for people to channel their feelings of patriotism and spiritual belief, the Emperor Alexander III Fund built national awareness of the Russian state's imperial designs and fostered a sense of connection with the fate of the settlers planting Russian culture on the frontier. Over the course of twelve years (1893–1905), the fund collected more than 2 million rubles, the vast majority of which arrived from the donations made by the general public. The state only contributed 275,000 rubles to the cause.[53] Using these donations, the Siberian Railway Committee built over 200 churches and over 180 schools.[54] To commemorate donors' generosity, the Siberian Railway Committee introduced a special medallion (*zheton*). Depending on the amount they donated, patrons of the fund received either a gold or silver medallion that attached to a watch chain. Donations higher than 10 rubles received the silver and those more generous souls who gave over 50 rubles recieved the gold. The oval-shaped medallions featured a silver cross bordered by the inscription "For churches and schools in Siberia." These medallions appeared to be popular as the committee fielded donations from across the empire accompanied with requests for the keepsake.[55] The committee also produced a lapel pin recognizing those who had assisted in the building process or had provided either materials or money amounting to more than 3,000 rubles.[56] The list of people receiving this honour illustrates secular and religious officials' commitment to the cause, as pre-eminent members of both worlds received acknowledgment for their work.[57]

A New Partnership

With the closure of the Siberian Railway Committee in December 1905, the Holy Synod gained control over the Emperor Alexander III Fund. It was not, however, until 1907 that the Holy Synod publicized its acquisition and began fundraising for the cause of church building in Siberia.

It publicly appealed to Russian Orthodox believers to once again support church building in Siberia:

> Let's come to the aid of our brethren by blood and faith, not leaving them without support in satisfying the most sacred and primary need of a Christian ... Let's come to aid them in educating their children in the spirit of the Christian faith and in learning the rudiments of necessary worldly knowledge. What could be more sacred than this field of charity: an opportunity to deliver religious comfort and enlightenment to the toilers – the settlers! Good people, bring offerings according to your means for this holy work.[58]

This appeal restarted the fund and initiated the direct involvement of the Holy Synod in the task of Siberian colonization.

To help move money, supplies, and building expertise, the Holy Synod partnered with the Main Administration of Land Management and Agriculture (Glavnoe upravlenie zemleustroistva i zemledeliia, or GUZiZ). GUZiZ tasked another institution under its authority, the Resettlement Administration, with incorporating the religious needs of settlers into the plans for colonization. Officials working in these agencies relied on "technocratic knowledge" and "forms of scientized state intervention" to tackle the issue of agricultural development in a way that would combine state interests with a concern for solving the land crisis among the peasantry.[59] Settling peasants in the eastern part of the empire provided not only the state with a bulwark against the incursions of aggrandizing neighbours and a labour force to exploit the resource-rich lands of Siberia and the Far East, it also provided settlers with the prospect of a better life, since they now had access to land.

In Siberia, the state aspired to administer the resettlement in an orderly fashion, recognizing that migrants experienced an overwhelming change as they left their homes and relatives.[60] Railway subsidies, surveyors to divide the land, road construction, access to doctors, and instructions to aid in agriculture and irrigation were a few examples of the areas in which the state worked to ease the settlers' transition to a new life.[61] The building of churches and schools would be added to this long list of activities. Yet, the Resettlement Administration also recognized the contribution the clergy could make to its work. At times, state officials relied on priests to collect the information necessary for guiding official policy. They viewed parish priests as one of the most "cultured elements" of the village and therefore their best guide to local life.[62] In this era characterized by a growing reliance on statistical analysis in policymaking, the data and ethnographic descriptions produced by clergymen helped the state to categorize many aspects of village life.[63]

For nearly ten years, beginning in 1908, the Resettlement Administration and the Holy Synod pooled their resources and expertise to build churches and schools and to support the clergy in settler communities under the banner of the Emperor Alexander III Fund. This cooperation showed that both parties recognized the need to address the enormous religious challenges created by the settler movement through the establishment and strengthening of the Orthodox Church, an institution understood to be essential to the successful building of Russian communities.[64] To help coordinate this joint action, the chief procurator established a new council: the Holy Synod Special Council on Satisfying the Religious Needs of Settlers (henceforth, the Holy Synod Special Council).[65] The first meeting took place at the beginning of February 1908 under the chairmanship of Senator A.P. Rogovich and with the participation of key religious and secular representatives, including the bishop of Tomsk, the governors of Tobol'sk and Tomsk, Archpriest Vostorgov, and representatives from the Resettlement Administration and the bureaucracy of the Holy Synod. At the meeting, participants discussed how to create a general plan to build churches, assign priests, and establish schools in new settlements, and to collect information on the conditions of Siberian religious need.[66] Fulfilling the annual plans produced by this council required the collaboration of Resettlement Administration officials with various governors, the Holy Synod, the chief procurator, bishops, church bureaucrats, and priests.

The involvement of the state in the construction of Orthodox churches in Siberian settler parishes created a dilemma. While Orthodox peasants constituted the majority of settlers, other groups, including Catholics and Lutherans, relocated to the region and encountered the same issue of spiritual dislocation. An exchange in the summer of 1910 between Aleksandr Krivoshein, the head of GUZiZ, and Petr Stolypin, the prime minister of Russia and the head of the Ministry of Internal Affairs (MVD), illustrates the struggle state officials faced when it came to treating other faiths fairly while still supporting the Orthodox Church's dominant position in the empire. As Paul Werth has shown, during this period the Russian state fumbled as it attempted to conceptualize and legislate religious freedom after 1905.[67] Krivoshein reported to the MVD that Catholic settlers from Mogilev, Minsk, Vitebsk, Vilnius, and Grodno bombarded the local resettlement officials and the Catholic archbishop of St. Petersburg with petitions for help establishing their religious communities.[68] Like their Orthodox counterparts, these settlers lacked the finances to construct churches and support their clergy. In light of GUZiZ's mandate to promote the religious needs of settlers as a means to support their cultural welfare, Krivoshein asked the MVD for help in funding priests for Catholic settler villages as there was a limit to the amount of funding the Resettlement Administration could issue for such a cause.[69] Stolypin responded by acknowledging the usefulness of supporting the religious life of non-Orthodox settlers, but emphasized the necessity of following the current laws, which provided greater support to the Orthodox Church as it still occupied a privileged position in the empire.[70] Ultimately, the Resettlement Administration would help to build seven Catholic churches in three different Siberian provinces. It also assisted in sending Catholic priests and Lutheran ministers to settler communities in the region.[71]

Despite a willingness to offer limited assistance to other recognized faiths in the empire, the Resettlement Administration promoted the establishment of Orthodox communities as essential to its work in Siberia. In a 1914 publication exploring colonization in Asiatic Russia, the Resettlement Administration explicitly communicated the marriage between Russian imperial conquest and the establishment of Orthodox churches in Siberia:

> Where the golden cross of the Orthodox Church shines, [that is the place where] Russian Christian culture has firmly settled. Where there is a priest and a church for the labouring Russian people to pour out their grief and gain faith and consolation, [that is the place where] all the difficult conditions of this new life in new places will not break the spiritual forces of the Russian peasant, full of patience and hope. The building everywhere of God's Orthodox churches serves as a banner for the continuous conquest of taiga and steppes by the mighty Russian culture. And each new church is an absolute living witness to the peaceful victory of Russian labour and civilization in vast and inhospitable Siberia.[72]

Although churches had been considered a symbol of Russian conquest for centuries, this emphasis on Russian Orthodox settlers as a necessary component of Russia's cultural imperialism showed a distinct shift in attitude on the part of state officials. This reflected a change that was felt in other parts of the empire. In the Caucasus, for example, after relying on sectarian settlers to establish a Russian presence for two-thirds of the nineteenth century, state officials now strongly favoured the settlement of Russian Orthodox peasants in the region.[73]

As the Duma, Russia's first elected legislative body, debated a bill to allocate a million rubles to strengthen the Emperor Alexander III Fund in 1914, this support of the Resettlement Administration was on full display.[74] The head of the Resettlement Administration, Grigorii Glinka, explained to Duma representatives the importance of this

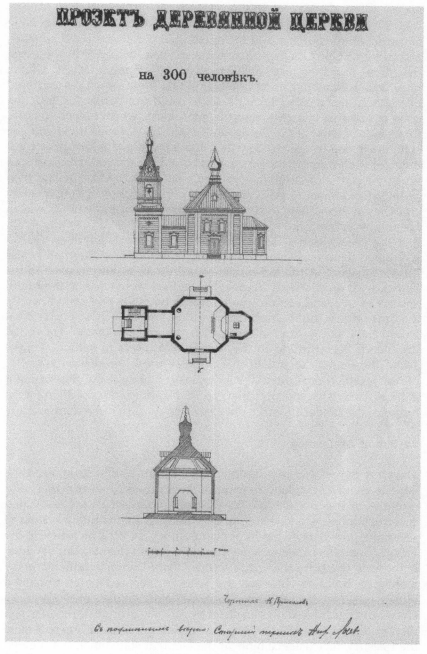

2.3 General design for a three-hundred-person wooden Orthodox church for settler parishes. Gosudarstvennyi arkhiv Tomskoi oblasti f.239, op.1, d.1170, l.1.

act for the success of colonization. He supplied three primary reasons why the Duma should approve this bill. First, the settlers requested the construction of churches and the opening of parishes; they shed tears, according to Glinka, when their requests were denied.[75] In the event that these peasants' tears failed to move the representatives, Glinka provided an economic justification: building these structures anchored peasants in the region. Since peasants could not personally bear the costs of building churches, and the noble class, which helped to build thousands of churches in European Russia, did not exist in Siberia, the state must step in to help. Finally, Glinka presented a historical argument for such support: the state helped build churches and monasteries when the centre of Orthodoxy moved from Kiev to Moscow and then again to St. Petersburg. Also, the state had funded the building of many churches in Siberia and, therefore, the allocation of more funds was in keeping with tradition.[76]

If his speech had failed to inspire Duma representatives, Glinka welcomed them to disregard his arguments and look into their hearts for the answer.[77] A million-rouble contribution, he emphasized to the Duma, was not necessary because the settlers were weak in their faith and chose to spend community resources on other projects; rather, by the time settlers could afford to build their own churches, a generation would have grown up "in mental sorrow and darkness." He ended his speech by returning to the self-defined needs of settlers. Glinka asked the Duma "to satisfy this popular need [narodnaia nuzhda] ... of our resettled peasantry."[78] As this speech shows, the Resettlement Administration was not only involved in planning and coordinating the Emperor Alexander III Fund, but also strongly supported the program.

System of Assistance

The Holy Synod and the Resettlement Administration recognized the limited resources available to manage the religious needs of settler communities. It was not feasible for them to undertake all the associated construction costs, and therefore they decided to institute a system of assistance and loans to aid local communities. In 1912, an article in the *Village Herald* described how the state envisioned this system.[79] Written in the form of a story, the article, entitled "How Siberian settlers receive money for building churches and schools," focused on an unnamed village of settlers from Pskov, Smolensk, and Mogilev provinces. The story's didactic tone shows an effort by officials to educate Siberian settlers in the bureaucratic process of obtaining a loan or support from the treasury. Its existence hints at the fact that state officials struggled to communicate to settlers the bureaucratic process by which church building would occur.

The story began with the initial arrival of the peasants. After expending tremendous energy tilling the land and building homes during the spring and summer months, settlers began to contemplate the idea of constructing their own church. In this new environment, these settlers had no idea how to achieve their goal and asking their neighbours only furthered their confusion. They knew that only the bishop could appoint a priest, that the treasury paid his salary, and that they must provide the priest with a house, but they did not know how to set this process in motion. In the midst of their confusion, the peasants approached the village elder for advice. Mitrii, the elder, did not know the answer, but he had a son in St. Petersburg who was serving in the military as a guard and who could find out the proper procedure from the Resettlement Administration.[80]

The son replied quickly to his father's enquiry. His letter described the process by which this village could achieve its dream of building a church. This description was meant to provide real settlers in Siberia with the tools to begin a similar journey for themselves. The letter also captured how secular and religious officials envisioned this bureaucratic web would function. But despite the desire to pursue an orderly and streamlined resettlement, as Mitrii's son's instructions indicated, the process was anything but straightforward. To start, the peasants needed to contact their local bishop about the possibility of opening a parish and having a priest appointed whose salary would be paid for by the Holy Synod. Every year the local bishop would provide the local resettlement official with a list of the places that had the greatest need for a church on the basis of population. Yet the settlers could not rely solely on the bishop to act as an intercessor with secular officials; they should also contact the head of resettlement through his subordinates on the ground to express their desire for a church. In other words, the village should petition both secular and religious officials. If their neighbours also lacked a church, the treasury might be able to help; however, if a church already existed in a neighbouring village, then the treasury would not provide funds.

Two options existed if the authorities chose to support the village's aspiration for a church. If the village was poor, the treasury would provide financial support that did not have to be paid back (*bezvozratnyi*). If the village had financial resources, the treasury would provide a loan (*ssuda*) to be paid back in ten years. Of the two options, villages that chose to accept a loan would receive the funds in an easy and timely manner. The treasury also did not charge interest on the money. Another

Table 2.1 Funding for the Emperor Alexander III Fund

Year	Holy Synod	Resettlement Administration	Total in rubles
1910	216,000	185,000	401,000
1911	340,000	185,000	525,000
1912	450,000	670,000	1,120,000
1913	343,000	757,000	1,100,000

Information from *Aziatskaia Rossiia*, vol. 1 (St. Petersburg, 1914), 239.

option suggested by Mitrii's son was the purchase of a portable church. These churches cost 250 rubles and arrived with everything necessary for services, including an altar and a folding iconostasis (*ikonostas skladnoi*).[81] After careful consideration, the villagers decided, given the fact that a large church stood twenty-two kilometres away, that they would build a school and a prayer house at a cost of 4,000 rubles, which would cover the hiring of a teacher and the periodic engagement of a priest. They requested the sum of 2,000 rubles from the treasury. After the delivery of the loan, this village built a prayer house and a school. A bright future lay ahead.

Although this process was rarely so straightforward, the Holy Synod and the Resettlement Administration managed to fulfil the dreams of settlers in villages from Orenburg to Vladivostok as well as in the Caucasus. As Table 2.1 shows, the budget dedicated to building Orthodoxy in Siberia increased during the early twentieth century, with the Resettlement Administration providing the majority of the capital. Using these funds, the Holy Synod Special Council helped to open 172 new parishes and provided funding for the construction of 95 churches, 28 prayer houses, and 81 clergy homes in 1909–10.[82] The next year, the Holy Synod Special Council opened 152 parishes, built 82 churches and prayer houses, 39 homes for clergy, and 46 church-parish schools.[83]

Ioann Vostorgov: Orthodox Colonizer

To better decide which settlements should receive funds, the Holy Synod and the Resettlement Administration received detailed reports on the state of religious life in Siberia and the future needs of settlers from Archpriest Ioann Vostorgov. Vostorgov was not an ordinary Orthodox priest; he was a complicated and controversial man with a strong presence in late imperial Russia. From the outset, Vostorgov's life was intertwined with the empire. Born to a clerical family in the North Caucasus (Kuban province), Vostorgov had first-hand knowledge of Russian

colonization. Many of the issues that appeared in Siberia – the resettlement of peasants, the establishment of new religious communities,
sectarianism, missionary work among non-Russian populations – he
first encountered in the Caucasus. Vostorgov developed his knowledge
of these issues by witnessing the day-to-day lives and concerns of new
settlers; through this experience, he also formulated ideas about the
roles that settlers could perform for the empire. At the turn of the twentieth century, during a speech welcoming the minister of agriculture
and state properties to a village in the Caucasus, Vostorgov extolled the
virtue of caring for the spiritual lives of newly settled Russian peasants.
If they were to "serve the Russian cause," Vostorgov emphasized, they
would need land and churches to succeed.[84]

Vostorgov's journey from the imperial periphery to Moscow, the
Russian Empire's spiritual capital, shows the possibilities available to
talented clergymen. After starting his career in Stavropol diocese, he
moved to the South Caucasus, eventually serving under the authority of the exarch of Georgia, Archbishop Vladimir (Bogoiavlenskii).
Vostorgov solidified his professional rise by gaining a reputation as a
capable liaison between the borderlands and the imperial centre. He
regularly received assignments directly from the Holy Synod to investigate issues of significance on the imperial periphery and beyond. In
1901, the Holy Synod sent him to the Persian city of Urmia to inspect
a newly established Orthodox mission.[85] At the beginning of 1905,
Vostorgov reported to the chief procurator on his inspection of parish
schools in Stavropol' diocese; by August of that year, the Holy Synod
dispatched him to survey church schools and to inspect the local diocesan school councils in seven Siberian dioceses.[86] The following year he
was transferred out of the Caucasus to the diocese of Moscow, where
he was reunited with Vladimir who had become the metropolitan of
Moscow.

In 1908, the Holy Synod Special Council again assigned Vostorgov
to travel through Siberia, only this time to gather information on the
condition of church schools and missionary needs.[87] Instead of simply
requesting reports from local bishops, the Holy Synod decided that
Vostorgov should be its representative on the ground in Siberia, keeping it abreast of the religious implications of colonization. This choice
speaks to the level of trust that the Holy Synod and the chief procurator had in Vostorgov's interpretation of the local dynamics in Siberia. Over the next five years, Vostorgov would embark on annual trips
to eastern Russia as part of these duties. In 1909, he added parts of
East Asia to his normal Siberian itinerary – namely, Japan, Korea, and
China, where he engaged with local Orthodox leaders and assessed the

missionary conditions on the ground. He submitted reports on these travels to the Holy Synod and the Resettlement Administration, helping these institutions to formulate and operationalize plans for church building, the assignment of priests, and the establishment of schools in new settlements.[88]

Through his engagement with Siberia and East Asia, he furthered developed his understanding of Russia's destiny as a great Christian empire. On his 1909 official visit to Vladivostok, Vostorgov explored this idea in a speech titled "Russia and the East." In it Vostorgov began by paying tribute to the gravity of his host city's name – Vladivostok, which means "ruler of the East."[89] After his journey through China, Japan, and Korea, Vostorgov told his audience that he remained firmly convinced of the significance of this region and of Russia's role within it. Drawing heavily on biblical history and the idea of the Israelites as God's chosen people, Vostorgov proclaimed the Russian people as inheritors of this mantle. He argued that Russia, as a result of its geographic position astride two different civilizations – European and Asian – as well as its historic calling, had a decisive role to perform in bringing Christianity to the region.[90]

According to Vostorgov, Russian Orthodox settlers had an essential role to perform in fulfilling this destiny. He firmly expressed his belief that the settlement of Russians in this territory was part of God's plan for the salvation of the region; Asia had spent too long in darkness. According to Vostorgov, God had chosen the Russian people, like the apostles, to bring the Gospel to this untapped region.[91] For Vostorgov, the hundreds of thousands of Russian settlers arriving annually in Siberia and the Far East automatically carried Christianity to the region. Settlers simply had to arrive; untrained in the vocation of preaching God's word, they would not engage in active ministry, but their spiritual lives would nonetheless inspire their neighbours. Even though settlers arrived in Siberia for their own private reasons, escaping poverty and crowded lands, Vostorgov argued that God still used them for "his holy will."[92]

In addition to transforming the religious map of the world, Vostorgov had more pragmatic reasons for encouraging the settlement of Russian Orthodox peasants in Siberia. Like state officials, Vostorgov viewed Russia's neighbours suspiciously. Convinced that the nations on the country's Asian border had designs on Siberia to ease the stress resulting from their own growing populations, Vostorgov emphasized the fundamental necessity of filling Siberia with Russian Orthodox settlers.[93] Land, according to Vostorgov, was the commodity that would protect Russia's imperial greatness. Without it, the Russian state could

2.4 Orthodox church in a settler parish in Tomsk province. *Aziatskaia Rossiia*, vol. 1 (St. Petersburg, 1914), 490.

not use Siberia and the Far East as a safety valve for unrest in European Russia, as the growing peasant population struggled to find enough land. And with enemies lurking around the edges of the empire ready to take the land, Russia had to control these territories.[94] Yet, the enemies standing on the border with Russia could one day be brothers in Christ. Vostorgov argued that if Russia "stands with Christ and with the cross, then the East, accepting Christ, would meet with us as brothers."[95] Vostorgov, therefore, understood the Christianization of Asia as a crucial step toward securing Russia's place politically, in addition to promoting peace in this volatile region.

The images and themes presented by Vostorgov in his sermons and speeches reflected the conservative branch of the Orthodox Church that embraced Orthodox patriotism, particularly after the Great Reforms.[96] These patriotic Orthodox men, as John Strickland describes, used "images, rituals, and events" to communicate and project a view of Russia and its empire that was captured in the term "Holy Rus." According to Strickland, Holy Rus was

> not a romantic "myth" describing people alienated from the state and the intelligentsia ... It was rather a model or "icon" of what the Russian people themselves must become. It was an instrument for shaping the increasingly multireligious and secularized empire into a national community that would better serve the missionary goals of the Church.[97]

This idea of Holy Rus found expression in the image of Orthodox Russia as the "New Israel." Vostorgov encouraged the public to understand Orthodox Russians as God's chosen people who would spread salvation to all nations by carrying Orthodoxy to the far reaches of the empire. By fulfilling its destiny, Russia would simultaneously secure its porous borders, particularly in the eastern part of the empire, and provide a base for missionary work beyond these boundaries.

A New Approach to Fundraising

With Vostorgov travelling through the empire promoting the cause of resettlement in Siberia, the Holy Synod and the Resettlement Administration searched for new revenue streams for the Emperor Alexander III Fund. Already by 1902, donations were less than expected, a development that caused concern among those administering the money.[98] The idea of establishing a collection during the Orthodox feast calendar for settler churches and schools had occurred to the Holy Synod in the summer of 1908; two years later, the Holy Synod Special Council officially appealed to Orthodox believers to provide financial support for this cause through a targeted collection that would occur during Pentecost.[99] For five years, the Orthodox Church held church collections for the fund across the empire. Despite Russia's participation in the First World War, in 1915 the Holy Synod decided to extend this collection for another five years. Indeed, it even expanded the donation drive by adding another major feast day, the Intercession of the Theotokos (Pokrova Presviatoi Bogoroditsy).[100]

The Holy Synod Special Council consciously modelled its fundraising efforts on other successful collections, particularly those of the trusteeship of Empress Maria Aleksandrovna and the Red Cross during the Russo-Japanese War. These initiatives had benefited from the use of local commissioners to facilitate the collection of funds and the Holy Synod tried to replicate the same system. Religious leaders expressed confidence that volunteers could be found in many towns, cities, and even larger villages.[101] Each volunteer would receive a certificate from the Resettlement Administration empowering them to act as a commissioner in a specific church.[102] Men and women from a variety of professions, including journalists, state bureaucrats, and teachers, volunteered to solicit funds in churches.[103]

The Resettlement Administration took a leading role in drawing attention to this cause. Glinka requested that the editors of Russia's largest newspapers publicize the collection.[104] An undated document produced by the Resettlement Administration showed the narrative that state officials used to promote this cause. It emphasized the sacrifices of the settlers who left their homes for new agricultural opportunities "in the severe Siberian taiga and the Kazakh steppe." These settlers required support; even the hundreds of new parishes established through the efforts of the Resettlement Administration and the Holy Synod hardly sufficed in addressing the spiritual needs of the millions of Russian Orthodox settlers crossing the Urals. In light of this grave situation, it was necessary to collect donations through an empire-wide appeal for funds. This appeal, however, was not only about settlers and their needs – it was also about asking ordinary Russians to support "the holy work" of "strengthening faith and knowledge" in the empire. The Resettlement Administration emphasized the role of settlers in securing Russia's borders and creating a distinctly Russian cultural space: a role they could only fulfil under the guidance of churches and schools.[105]

To secure a successful fundraising effort, the Holy Synod Special Council communicated clearly with local churches on how to approach and present the collection, including providing sermons in the pages of the journal *Church News* that could be read at both evening and morning liturgies. The Holy Synod Special Council emphasized that the collection for settlers should happen separately from the general church collection and that it should not only occur during the liturgy on Pentecost, but also at the evening service on the eve of the celebration. A prayer to explain the significance of the collection for supporting Orthodox believers in Siberia should be given directly before the collection.

These published sermons illuminated the efforts of church officials to employ themes that might resonate with Orthodox believers. The sermon for the evening service provided a picture of resettlement that appealed to parishioners' sense of obligation to their fellow believers, to God, and to the state by weaving together themes of sacrifice, duty, and the Russian spirit. It emphasized the sacrifices of the settlers, forced out of their homeland by land hunger, who towed their families and worldly possessions across the empire to break virgin land in Siberia. This sermon reminded Orthodox parishioners that without more people moving to these sparsely populated territories, Russia could lose parts of its kingdom to "enemy invasion."[106] It argued that Orthodox believers in European Russia had an obligation to support their "brothers by faith and blood" who travelled to the ends of the empire to serve the church and the state by securing and Christianizing the land.[107]

The sermon also emphasized that while the state took care of the basic physiological needs of settlers, Orthodox believers must have the opportunity to satiate their spiritual hunger. Indeed, this constituted one of the main obstacles for settlers who ventured into the wilds of Siberia:

> They arrive in this faraway place and there is no church, no liturgy and no priest ... Think of how great the grief of the settlers must be. And in that grief, many of them live for years: not knowing the ringing of the bell, not knowing of the holy holiday, not hearing the liturgy, not baptizing their children.[108]

The sermon ended with an appeal for Orthodox believers to fulfil their duty by donating money that would be used to build churches in Siberia. To emphasize the collective nature of the endeavour, the priest should remind the congregation that the Russian Orthodox Church, the state, and the Russian people (*russkii narod*) stood united in this cause of assisting settlers. By evoking a national commitment to the imperial borderlands, this sermon invited believers to participate in building an Orthodox empire.

These collections did not end with the abdication of Tsar Nicholas II. In 1917, the Holy Synod publicized the upcoming May collection with a supplement in *Church News*.[109] Neither did the war or the tsar's abdication undermine the partnership between the Resettlement Administration and the Holy Synod. Even with the start of the war, the Holy Synod Special Council continued to prepare plans for addressing the religious needs of settlers. As late as 1916, the council sent a telegram to Siberian dioceses enquiring about the number of new parishes they needed and whether they required candidates from the Pastoral Courses in Moscow, a program run by the Orthodox Church for training priests to serve in Siberian parishes.[110] In 1917, four days after Nicholas II stepped down from the throne, the Holy Synod Special Council detailed its plan for the year. This plan, however, was substantially less ambitious than in previous years, since it proposed only thirty-seven new parishes beyond the Urals and five in the Caucasus. It agreed to a number of temporary measures, which included increasing the number of travelling priests by eight: the dioceses of Enisei, Turkestan, Omsk, and Irkutsk received these appointments.[111] This commitment to establishing Orthodoxy in Siberia in spite of such challenging political conditions demonstrates how both church and state officials viewed their collaboration as a long-term project.

For nearly twenty years, the Emperor Alexander III Fund encouraged Russian Orthodox believers to participate in the state's national project of building an Orthodox empire. Led by Russia's royal family, the fund appealed to the general public for financial support by touting the image of the settler who served the interest of God and the tsar in the far reaches of the empire. This image held a strong appeal as priests, merchants, bureaucrats, aristocrats, peasants, and others contributed funds to the building of churches and schools in Siberia. By appealing directly to the Russian Orthodox people as a national group, the church and state emphasized the exclusive role played by Russian Orthodox believers in the building of the empire.

Chapter Three

Parishes under Construction

In the summer of 1916, as the First World War raged on the Western Front, Pavel Kirichenko, a church elder in the village of Antonovskoe, engaged in his own battle against Bishop Sil'vestr (Ol'shevskii) of Omsk diocese. In August, Kirichenko dispatched an ornate petition to Grigorii Glinka, the director of the Resettlement Administration, protesting the closure of the local parish by the bishop; the following month he appealed directly to Prime Minister Boris Stürmer. In these petitions, Kirichenko employed evocative images to convince secular leaders of the moral and social costs of this parish closure. He spoke of the hypocrisy of allowing men to die at the front "for their Orthodox faith" while their loved ones at home had nowhere to pray. Strongly hinting at the possibility of social unrest caused by growing rumours that the church was arbitrarily closing parishes in the countryside, Kirichenko showed a sophisticated understanding of the pressure points by which he might capture the attention of secular leaders.[1]

His petition, however, did not rely primarily on arguments depicting peasants as soldiers worthy of reverence or as revolutionaries in the making. Rather, he skilfully deployed the trope of "settler" to argue his case, even though the village had been established almost twenty years before by a group of peasants from the province of Poltava.[2] Appealing to Glinka as someone who cared personally about the building of Orthodox life in settler villages, Kirichenko presented Antonovskoe as a healthy spiritual community that had funded its own prayer house.[3] To Stürmer, Kirichenko communicated that he represented a group of settlers "suffering in distant Siberia for [their] faith and [their] affection for [their] church." He pleaded for help to alleviate their "intolerable grief" as they had been deprived of spiritual comfort.[4] As Kirichenko's petitions demonstrate, the notion of the Siberian "settler" had developed a robust meaning, conveying the sacrifices of the peasantry who had established new communities in this colonial environment. They viewed their migration as encouraged and legitimated by the state and this meant that the state was therefore responsible for their needs.[5] When those needs were unsatisfied, settlers readily reminded state and church officials of this identity and communicated their religious expectations.

Planting Parishes in Siberia

Peasant petitions, state reports, and church documents emphasized the need for establishing the basic elements of parish life in Siberia. Settlers persistently communicated to state and church officials that their religious communities performed an essential role in their adaptation to Siberia. Without access to churches and priests, settlers worried about the spiritual compromises that would befall the next generation. This was about saving souls, but not exclusively. Under colonization, the parish also reinforced settlers' roots as they arrived in their new homeland and planted an institution capable of supporting Russian culture. Parishes offered an accessible and familiar structure for peasants to replicate the village culture of European Russia in Siberia, allowing them to maintain their traditions in the face of the hardship and instability caused by the loss of their former communities, while encouraging them to adapt to their new environmental and social circumstances. As one of the few widespread organizing units in the countryside of western Siberia, the state and the church understood the parish, with a priest providing leadership, as both a stabilizing influence and a conduit for the dissemination of knowledge and the nurturing of peasant religious and cultural life. Especially in a region without the institutional presence of the zemstvo (elected assemblies established to provide local governance), the parish performed an essential role in organizing local communities.[6]

This notion that the parish could serve as an important institution for shaping the peasantry was not invented in the borderlands of the Russian Empire. The 1860s parish reforms, undertaken by the Holy Synod, had aspired to "revitalize the parish" as a way of addressing the material needs of the clergy and of "generat[ing] popular support and financing for charity and schools."[7] These reforms promoted the parish as a site of local engagement (albeit with limited legal and fiscal powers). Although by the late nineteenth century, the parish had not lived up to this aspiration (pressing church officials to consider new reforms) it still performed a significant role in organizing village life in European Russia.[8]

Through the Emperor Alexander III Fund, state and church officials showed a commitment to helping settlers establish parishes. This keen interest in planting parishes could be interpreted as paternalism.

3.1 Siberian village church in the diocese of Omsk. Omsk State Museum of History and Regional Studies, Omk 4052.46.

Indeed, state officials often engaged in metaphorical hand-wringing while writing about poor, hapless, and sorrowful settlers unable to build churches without assistance from the state.[9] Clergymen and tsarist officials often imagined themselves at the centre of the story of colonization, managing peasants they considered unable to organize life on their own. These officials touted their role in establishing churches and supporting proper Orthodox practice through the Emperor Alexander III Fund. Unquestionably, this fund helped parishes without easy access to capital. It also supported the penetration of the state and church into rural Siberia, connecting the settlers symbolically, culturally, and bureaucratically with the imperial centre.

Parishioners in settler communities, however, hardly waited for a benevolent state to provide for them. They actively engaged in creating, nurturing, and defining their own faith communities, often deciding for themselves what constituted an essential practice within their own understanding of Orthodoxy. While not every village adopted an activist approach or showed a strong commitment to the Orthodox Church, on the whole, settlers acted as if parishes mattered in the development of their communities. As few settler villages had deep enough pockets to pay the required costs of building churches and providing material support for the clergy, especially right after their arrival, they often relied on financial support from the state or the Holy Synod. In response to this reality, a hybrid system was created in Siberia, a sort of sliding scale according to which some parishes received full financial support from the Emperor Alexander III Fund for construction costs, others received partial support, and some parishioners paid the costs fully out of their own pockets.[10] For settlers, talking with local diocesan authorities and representatives of the imperial centre about this issue reinforced their connection to the empire's broader colonizing efforts.

Aspirations, Expectations, and Anxieties

The tsarist state managed to convince millions of people to move to Siberia; it could not, however, force them to stay. In his 1909 annual report, the governor general of the steppe, E.O. Shmit, emphasized that the Russian people would only recognize the Kazakh steppe as their homeland if they found a church and school when they arrived.[11] For Russian settlers, encountering an endless horizon without a bell tower in sight caused a sense of alienation from their environment. The minister of agriculture and state properties, Alexei Ermolov, recalled how during his 1895 visit through the region, settlers quickly turned the conversation to the question of constructing churches and schools, with many appealing to him personally in hopes of receiving building funds from the state. He identified churches and schools as two essential institutions to guarantee that these settlers established roots in their new homeland.[12]

Return migration (*obratnoe pereselenie*) caused headaches for resettlement administrators, who often watched time, effort, and money fade into the western horizon as settlers travelled back to European Russia. According to Prime Minister Petr Stolypin and Aleksandr Krivoshein, the causes of return migration were complex and individualized. These officials seemed at pains to emphasize that much return migration was caused by settlers moving outside of the state-supported resettlement program.[13] Others blamed unprepared resettlement officials for not distributing land allotments in a timely fashion.[14] Admittedly, the category of "return migration" was confusing, as it included not only those who returned to European Russia but also those who relocated to a different province in Siberia.[15] According to the numbers provided for Akmolinsk province, in 1911 approximately 13.6 per cent of settlers participated in return migration, with the majority of them moving back to their province of origin and the remaining continuing on to another resettlement village in the Far East.[16]

These numbers were sufficient to cause apprehension among representatives of church and state. Aleksandr Tregubov, a young priest with long black hair and an intense gaze, decided to take up the cause of migration when he served as a delegate to the Third State Duma for Kiev province. He proposed that the causes of return migration were two-fold: crop failure and the absence of churches. Upon his return from a visit to the Kazakh steppe, Tregubov claimed that poor harvests, which had driven settlers to Siberia in the first place, also pushed them back to Russia. In the summer of 1909, he recorded that struggles with crops, especially on the steppe, caused intense suffering for pioneers as early frost destroyed their fields in the northern part of Akmolinsk province, while the southern districts experienced drought, guaranteeing another year of poor harvests.[17] Crop failure was not, however, the only reason for return migration. Tregubov claimed that settlers' powerlessness to practise their faith contributed to their decision to return to Russia. In settlers' minds, according to Tregubov, to live as Christians entailed having a church and school: without these institutions, they would rather live in European Russia.[18]

While Tregubov's interpretation of return migration reflected his own biased understanding of the peasantry, he was not mistaken in his claim that settlers expected churches and schools in Siberia. Settlers frequently petitioned church and secular leaders for help establishing their religious life. In a petition to the governor of Tobol'sk, a group of settlers pointed out that in their former homeland they had developed the habit of praying to God in a church and that they expected to be allowed to continue this tradition in Siberia.[19] In another petition, settlers emphasized that "in Russia" they had attended services on Sundays and holidays; without a church in their new village, they now spent these times in low spirits (*unynie*) and anguish (*toska*).[20] When a priest travelling through a resettlement region asked peasants if they preferred European Russia to Siberia, many said they appreciated the agricultural land of Siberia, although they acknowledged that the region had one major problem. In the words of one respondent, "Everything is great ... but here is our sorrow: we do not have our own church of God; [we] don't have our own priest ... Here we live as non-Christians."[21] These concerns reached the desk of Chief Procurator Konstantin Pobedonostsev, who recorded in his 1902 annual report that settlers expected to find the basic elements of parish life, as in European Russia.[22] For Orthodox peasants, attending church services on major holidays, burying their dead in consecrated cemeteries, and having access to a priest for the performance of religious rites was of the utmost importance.

Settlers cited obstacles to the fulfilment of Orthodox rites as justifying state financial support for their religious communities. An application from parishioners in Tiukalinsk district for a retired priest to serve their village emphasized local barriers to the performance of rites and rituals. Twenty years earlier, these settlers had arrived from Riazan province. In their new Siberian homeland, the parish church proved difficult to access, as it was located ten kilometres away with the Om River running between the villages. In their petition, villagers wrote of their great sorrow when poor road conditions and ice floes prevented them from visiting the parish church for the Easter service. According to Orthodox tradition, Easter is preceded by forty-eight days of fasting, when believers abstain from meat, fish, eggs, and dairy products. At midnight, the priest performs the divine service, beginning with a pro-cession of icons and crosses. The priest calls out, "Christ is risen!" and parishioners respond, "He is risen indeed!" After the service, parish-ioners break their fast. Trapped on the other side of the river, these set-tlers complained in their petition that they missed "meeting the Risen Christ" and had to return to their homes to break their fast with bread that was not blessed by the priest. Even on occasions when they could attend a service at the church, the atmosphere was hardly inviting. The small church was only able to hold approximately two hundred peo-ple and those who could not fit had to stand "under the open sky." While this situation might be acceptable in the summer, during the harsh Siberian winters, when peasants had time to attend church, such a practice endangered lives.[23]

Cemeteries appeared to be almost as important as churches in the eyes of Orthodox settlers. Soon after arriving in Siberia, settlers asked state and church officials for land to establish consecrated cemeteries. In a petition from one village assembly, the request was justified with an obvious, but telling, claim that they were "mortal people" and therefore needed a place to bury their dead.[24] Another petition from a different village stated bluntly: "We arrived from Russia five months ago and still our settlement does not have a sanctified Christian cemetery."[25] In one particular case, a village petitioned to open its own cemetery; in support of this application, the parish priest sent a letter to the bishop of Omsk in which he identified the villagers as mostly poor settlers who had recently arrived from Russia in the spring. After only a few months of living in Siberia, access to a cemetery appeared to be a top priority for the community.

To open an Orthodox cemetery, communities needed permission from religious officials. Distance from the parish church constituted an acceptable reason to apply for permission, and many petitions listed this condition as their justification. Priests could not consecrate cemeteries without consent from the consistory, a lesson one dean learned after he was fined ten rubles and threatened with dismissal for consecrating a cemetery without obtaining the necessary permits.[26] Cemeteries had to abide by state regulations, which dictated their distance from the village and the quality of the soil necessary for the burial ground.[27]

Parishioners' implacability on the subject of graveyards meant that this issue often reached the agenda of the Omsk consistory. In one case, Father Semeon Belmosov struggled with parishioners over this issue, even going as far as reporting to the consistory the desire of locals at the station of Zaborovskoe for a cemetery while cautioning against the approval of their petition. As the station stood merely sixteen kilometres along a postal road from the parish church and had a small population, Belmosov recognized that it did not meet the consistory's criteria. Despite this knowledge, pressure from parishioners at Zaborovskoe station must have forced Belmosov to submit their request to the consistory; perhaps he hoped that a rejection would finally settle the matter.[28]

As the case of the village of Fominskii illustrates, official rejection did not necessarily deter settlers from pursuing their goal of having a cemetery. Parishioners in Fominskii, who hailed exclusively from the same district in Chernigov province, quickly petitioned the consistory for a graveyard.[29] The consistory denied this request as the village of Novosel'e – in the same parish and only three kilometres away along an easily travelled road – already had a cemetery.[30] After the consistory rejected their petition, these settlers attempted to find alternative means by which to achieve their objective of having a consecrated cemetery. They invited Ioann Goloshubin, a priest who was raised in Siberia, to their village under the pretext of having him bless their homes for a community festival. After his arrival, different members of the community pressured him to bless the site of the proposed cemetery. Without permission from the consistory, Goloshubin could not perform this act. According to Goloshubin, the peasants confronted him with harsh words when he refused to bend to their will. On a later visit to the village, Goloshubin had an exchange with the church elder over this issue. The elder bluntly told Goloshubin that "we will bury the dead in our cemetery," to which Goloshubin responded, "You don't have the right because you haven't received permission from a diocesan official." The elder was not convinced by Goloshubin's argument, insisting that "we wish to bury [our dead] and we will not ask anyone." To end the conversation, Goloshubin used his trump card in this relationship, stating that he would refuse to conduct any funeral services if this village disobeyed the rules of the consistory.[31] In another case, settlers began to bury their dead in a plot of land that Goloshubin had blessed for a prospective grain storage building. He reported this activity to the consistory; in the end, those peasants who participated had to pay a fine and spend twenty-four hours in jail.[32] These types of exchanges illustrate the expectations settlers brought to Siberia and the tensions that arose when local priests could not (or would not) satisfy them.

Isolation from Orthodoxy

As the church struggled to address settlers' aspirations, tens of thousands of Orthodox believers continued to pour into the borders of Omsk diocese annually. Physically separated from the Orthodox Church, settlers spoke of the vulnerability and sorrow this isolation caused in their communities. As one petition stated, "we live in the half-wild country of Siberia [k poludikoi strane Sibiri] where every non-Orthodox [inoverets] seeks to blaspheme [porugat'] the Orthodox faith."[33] In their application for a church, a village in the district of Omsk emphasized the fact that it was located "on the Kazakh steppe, far away from Orthodox villages."[34] In a letter to his parents in Poltava province, a newly arrived settler wrote that, despite the difficult emotions of leaving their loved ones behind, his family had settled safely in Tomsk province. While prayer had comforted him after this painful departure, he expressed concern that in their new home his family lived too far away from the church.[35]

Without access to a church and regular interaction with a priest, settlers worried that their faith would be in danger. As one petition described, "Among our villagers, there is already a coolness toward religion, a decline in morals." Within this lamentable environment, Baptists had already converted four families to their faith. This could have been avoided, according to the petition, with the intervention of a priest. Without spiritual guidance, these settlers felt as if they were "left to the mercy of fate."[36] Community leaders often expressed concern that isolation from the Orthodox Church could result in people searching for religious alternatives. One group of settlers, surrounded by Baptists and Old Believers, wrote of not wanting "to lose [their] good Orthodox faith" in this sea of temptation.[37] Settlers generally feared that their communities might succumb to the proselytism of other faiths or religious indifference, not outright atheism, reflecting the prevalence of religious belief and practice in rural communities during the twilight of imperial Russia.

This fear of apostasy and religious indifference had a strong generational component. After the disruption of resettlement, parents worried about losing their children to alien values in Siberia. This concern reflected a larger trend in the empire, as during the late nineteenth century priests and parishioners in European Russia also expressed disquiet with the moral state of the younger generation. Especially in central Russia, as industrial growth lured young adults to the cities, village leaders worried about the influence this urban environment might have on vulnerable young peasants.[38] In many ways, migration and urbanization shared similar social consequences as they uprooted traditional communities and forced peasants to consciously consider the elements of communal life that were meaningful to their existence.

In their petitions to state and church officials, settlers often emphasized trouble with their youth, lamenting that their children were growing up without the influence of the faith. Over the course of four years, believers in Kokchetav district delivered multiple petitions to church officials emphasizing their anxiety in relation to the younger generation.[39] One petition identified the influence of sectarians and dissenters living within the community as a factor threatening to pull their children away from the Orthodox Church. A spiritual leader (dukhovnyi nastavnik), they insisted, would protect their children from moral degeneration.[40] To respond to this concern, the Omsk consistory assigned a priest and a cantor to the village.[41]

Local clergy strongly encouraged action to address the religious commitment among the next generation. At the 1902 diocesan congress, Omsk clergymen considered how, in light of the diocese's growing population, they could support the religious development of their Orthodox parishioners, especially the youth. This meeting recognized that licentious behaviour occurred not only among adults, but also among adolescent and school-aged children (who apparently behaved especially badly at evening parties). The consistory expressed the gravity of the situation by comparing this struggle against drunkenness with the church's battle with sectarians and schismatics.[42] It appears that they made little progress, for ten years later Dean Mikhail Goloshubin engaged other priests in a discussion on the recent directive of the Omsk diocesan consistory for dealing with so-called hooliganism among rural youth.[43] This group of local priests decided to undertake six specific measures to prevent such immorality, including encouraging the youth to participate in religious services through congregational singing, opening parish temperance societies, forming a study group for energetic parishioners who wish to help the clergy attend to this issue, and teaching the youth about God's law.[44]

While this theme of impiety among the youth appeared frequently in European Russia, Omsk clergymen argued this problem was caused by colonization. A landscape without churches, the clergy argued, produced young people without any spiritual and moral foundation. Father Mikhail Mefod'ev claimed that children born in Siberia to settler families had little understanding of their faith; they could not perform simple religious tasks like making the sign of the cross or praying properly. He also portrayed young people as refusing to show deference to the clergy and displaying a disrespectful attitude toward their parents.[45] In his report on the religious conditions in the district of Omsk, Father Nikolai Lebedev claimed the youth of Omsk diocese showed an "absolute indifference to faith" – this in contrast to their parents, who managed to preserve a deep love for the services and rituals of the Orthodox Church even though their visits to the parish church were infrequent.[46] One missionary priest summarized the crisis this caused for the diocese:

> The younger generation do not have a conception of a true Christian upbringing. They have grown up without a strong or palpable connection with the church. This makes them completely unreliable for the Orthodox Church. This generation, as one can observe in settlements with sectarians, quickly and almost without any emotional hesitation, without the heavy torment and the kind of suffering usually linked with changing faiths, abandons the Orthodox faith. The youth do not value the Orthodox faith because they do not know it.[47]

For these priests, colonization allowed the youth to grow up disassociated from the Orthodox faith. This left them susceptible to the influence of alternative forms of belief or even revolutionary thought, which was seeping into communities, both rural and urban, in late imperial Russia. The Holy Synod also recognized the looming consequences for colonization if accessibility to churches and schools for settlers did not improve. Without churches and schools, the Holy Synod argued, the next generation in Siberia would grow up without "instruction in the law of Christ and without the light of knowledge."[48] This image of peasants growing spiritually wild without the intervention of the church appeared frequently in religious publications; it was used to emphasize to Orthodox clergymen and believers the importance of the church's efforts in the region.

This topic also appeared on the agenda of the top secular officials in the region. Governor A.N. Neverov of Akmolinsk identified excessive drinking among the youth as one of the many factors contributing to hooliganism in his province. He insisted that this problem could only be solved if the province had more parishes, priests, schools, and libraries to teach religious values to young people.[49] In the same year, Shmit expressed his great anxiety that youth hooliganism would spread in both urban and rural communities on the steppe. As he described the situation, "Almost everywhere can be observed complete disrespect toward elders, toward immediate superiors, wholesale drunkenness, senseless knife fighting, such wanton, groundless damage of another's property and other mischief."[50] For Shmit, a combination of the region's large, open spaces, an absence of local authority, and the low moral standing of old residents and some of the new migrants contributed to this issue.

Improvised Sacred Spaces

Under these conditions, priests had to find creative solutions in an effort to build a rich religious environment. In some cases, priests requested a portable antimins, which is a decorated cloth necessary for the celebration of the Eucharist, from the diocesan consistory. Armed with a portable antimins, priests could perform the liturgy anywhere, an important consideration when serving parishioners who could not travel to the parish church on Sundays. One priest, for example, requested a portable antimins to serve parishioners located a great distance (forty to sixty kilometres) from the parish church.[51] In villages without a church or a chapel, a portable antimins allowed priests to perform religious services in schools and even private homes. In a parish in the district of Omsk, settlers attended the liturgy in a consecrated two-room school with an altar in honour of the Dormition of the Mother of God.[52]

At times, the holding of liturgies, funerals, and other religious events in schools raised questions of appropriateness and sanitation. In one village in the district of Omsk, local state officials expressed their concern with the use of a shared space for religious services and in so doing initiated a discussion on how to regulate the church's use of the school building. Especially concerning was the holding of funerals, which entailed placing the body of the deceased in the school; this practice potentially endangered students, who could be exposed to infectious diseases. The Omsk consistory, recognizing the dangers inherent in this practice, placed four conditions on the use of schools for funerals, including that relatives should keep the deceased body at home and not at the school and that funerals had to be celebrated on weekends.[53]

While a portable antimins allowed the priest to bring the liturgy to isolated villages, not everyone viewed the conversion of secular buildings into places of worship as acceptable. Evgenii Krylov, a priest originally from the province of Penza, questioned the appropriateness of performing the liturgy in the same places where drinking, carousing, and dancing had taken place. He argued that the sanctity of the Eucharist had historically demanded a holy physical space:

> Since ancient times, Christians of all denominations sought to build a special building for the performance of the sacrament of the Holy Eucharist, not like a building for dwelling.[54]

Krylov feared that with a portable antimins, the notion of the church as a sacred space would lose "all significance." Although Krylov did not directly mention the Russian Baptists, most likely this group crossed his mind, as they often used private homes for their worship services.

Holding services in a portable tent-church also emerged as a solution for creating temporary sacred space. Although Siberian parishes had relied on this compromise since the 1870s in places such as Tomsk diocese,[55] this solution caught the imagination of state officials involved in resettlement, who pushed for its adoption in territories where the church struggled to keep abreast of the growing population.[56] A factory owned by Ivan Zheverzheev, a merchant in St. Petersburg specializing in brocade items for parishes in the imperial capital, produced these easy-to-assemble portable churches. They were contained in two suitcases and cost between 250 and 270 rubles – a far cry from the thousands of rubles necessary to construct a church.[57] While hardly an ideal setting for a service, parishioners worked with the priest to create a more familiar atmosphere by having female parishioners contribute embroidered sewing to decorate the tent-church.[58]

The Rhythm of Settler Orthodox Life

Colonization required not only compromises with regards to religious space in parishes; it also shaped the way in which rites were practised. The realities of pioneering uncoupled the sacraments from the normal peasant life cycle. Similar to settlers in Australia, migrants to Siberia placed a great emphasis on rites and rituals performed by the clergy.[59] Yet, religious services like funerals, marriages, and baptisms could not always coincide with the practicalities of burial, cohabitation, and birth in settler villages. Priests, stretched thin across the land, struggled to perform basic rites in a timely manner.[60] This situation was hardly unique to Siberia; on the Canadian Prairies, for instance, Ukrainian settlers in the early twentieth century would often visit Catholic or Protestant clergy for christenings, burials, marriage, and confession as they had arrived in Canada without priests of their own.[61] In Siberia, rites and rituals were often delayed because of distance from the parish church and lack of access to a priest. For certain rites, Orthodox parishioners met these delays with indifference, whereas the absence of other rituals caused consternation and frustration within the community.

The adaption of burial rituals to local conditions, for instance, did not appear to raise any concerns for the settler population. Instead of waiting for the priest to arrive to perform the funeral service, settlers simply buried their dead and held the service at a later date, without the body. Under normal conditions, the casket remains open during the service, as the body is blessed with holy water, and a prayer is read over the body and placed in the hands of the deceased. At the end of the ceremony the priest sings, "Come brethren, let's give the last kiss to the dead." During a funeral in absentia (*zaochnoe otpevanie*), the priest performed the same service, except without a body. This type of burial was not new to Siberia, as from the eighteenth to the mid-nineteenth century peasants often were buried without a proper funeral.[62] Priests in Omsk diocese, however, expressed their discomfort with this practice, arguing that such ceremonies had no foundation in church doctrine. Ioann Goloshubin contended that the physical body constituted an integral part of an Orthodox funeral; without the body, he argued, the ceremony was almost comical. Despite these objections, parishioners, both settlers and old residents, participated in this ceremony without hesitation.[63] Church officials expressed concern that by tolerating this behaviour, they might encourage settlers to start bypassing church funerals altogether. A decree from the consistory reminded the clergy that it was contrary to the laws of both the church and the state for parishioners to bury their dead without a proper funeral service performed by a priest. Only in the most extreme cases would the consistory permit burials in absentia.[64]

Marriage was another important religious rite that settlers tended not to reference in their petitions to church and state officials. In Siberia, villagers could live for months or even years without seeing a priest; the cycle of life continued – people often lived together before marriage, and presumably had children before a priest could sanctify the marriage. Complicating matters further, marriages were restricted by both the agricultural and church calendars. Farmers rarely married during the height of the agricultural season and Orthodox believers were not permitted to marry during major religious feasts.[65] Instead of waiting, settlers simply lived together. But while settlers showed indifference to this issue, state and church officials expressed concern. Governor General Shmit referred to this practice of civil cohabitation (*grazhdan-skoe sozhitel'stvo*) in his 1909 report as he discussed the lamentable state of religious life on the steppe.[66] The Holy Synod also communicated its fear that settlers would form the habit of substituting cohabitation for sanctified marriage.[67] Such a substitution occurred in other spaces of colonization – for example, in the wilds of Lower Canada, where in the early nineteenth century the Catholic Church struggled to convince parishioners to practise the sacrament of marriage.[68]

While sanctified marriages could wait, the baptism of infants as well as communion and confession for the sick and elderly, according to settlers, could not. Settler petitions strongly communicated to church and state officials that these two practices mattered. They regularly complained to authorities that the sick and elderly in their communities died without partaking of communion and confession because of their distance from a parish church.[69] Perhaps even more troubling, children died on the steppe without baptism, a point emphasized by clergy, settlers, and state officials.[70] The governor of Semipalatinsk reported with concern that on his travels he met children as old as three who had not yet been baptized.[71] Although settler petitions listed these sacraments to justify the opening of a parish, the building of a church, or the assignment of a priest, they did not elaborate on the importance of these rites for their communities. Scholars can provide some insight into their meaning. Christine Worobec has shown how Russian and Ukrainian peasants in European Russia considered death to be a serious moment in the lives of not only individuals, but also of the broader community. Those close to death were expected to prepare themselves through confession and communion.[72] Facing death unprepared had consequences: peasants believed "the dead sometimes remained in the world of the living, haunting them and causing calamities to befall them." Unbaptized babies were included in this category; peasants believed their souls took the form of malicious water nymphs.[73] Therefore, even though infant baptism was an Orthodox sacrament performed by priests and bishops, which conferred full church membership, its meaning within the peasant community extended far beyond that more narrow theological reading.[74]

3.2 A settler family in Omsk diocese. Omsk State Museum of History and
Regional Studies, Omk 4052.47.

Parishes Worthy of the Empire

In essence, the Emperor Alexander III Fund was supposed to help
reduce these types of religious compromises and adaptations by supporting the establishment of parish life. Through the fund, religious
and secular authorities engaged in a concerted effort to address these
issues by establishing functioning parishes as quickly as possible following resettlement. This fund allowed for hundreds of prayer houses,
schools, and homes for the clergy to be built in the diocese of Omsk.

Typically, a parish church could hold between 300 and 500 people,
although some larger villages had churches capable of holding 700 worshipers.[75] And yet, as settler parishes tended to have between 1,300 and
10,000 parishioners, these spaces could not accommodate everyone.[76]
In some places, parishioners, with help from the fund, built prayer
houses instead of churches, which were much simpler to construct, but
often resembled uninspired rectangular school buildings.

3.3 A settler prayer house in Akmolinsk province. *Aziatskaia Rossiia*, vol. 1 (St. Petersburg, 1914), 470.

State-supported church building unfolded systematically, complete with maps, reports, plans, protocols, and proposals to coordinate and supervise the process. Church building under the Emperor Alexander III Fund could be considered under the umbrella of what Willard Sunderland has termed "correct colonization," by which the state organized resettlement on the basis of "scientific principles."[77] Through church building, the state entered directly into local parishes, connecting these religious communities to the broader state project of integrating the land culturally and economically into the empire. The marshalling of the state's financial and bureaucratic resources to build churches in Siberia allowed the process to unfold quickly, across a vast space and with an intensity that could only be achieved in a modernizing empire. Nonetheless, these efforts often fell short, creating frustrations, not only for state and church officials, but for settlers as well.

From the beginning, the Emperor Alexander III Fund emphasized the building of both churches and schools. The Orthodox Church supported this approach, encouraging the construction of both institutions since it was believed that connecting religion and education provided new settlements with a strong foundation for educating and civilizing the next generation. In the eyes of church officials, education sustained and perpetuated the faith; religious education, after all, was mandatory in the empire's school curriculum. Settlers supported the opening of schools, often petitioning state and church officials for one to be established in their village. According to Governor General Shmit, in 1909 he received 253 petitions from settlers to open schools in the province of Akmolinsk.[78] In one petition to open an independent parish, settlers indicated that they happily sent their children to the village school to learn about the Orthodox faith.[79]

During the second half of the nineteenth century, access to basic education spread in European Russia; Siberia, however, still lagged behind. The flood of settlers pouring over the Ural Mountains only worsened this situation. Without the zemstvo, responsibility for primary education was assigned to the Ministry of Education, the Ministry of State Properties, the Ministry of Internal Affairs, and the Orthodox Church.[80] Out of these four entities, the Orthodox Church had, from 1884 onward, more schools (although fewer students) than the other ministries in western Siberia.[81] In the late nineteenth century, the Orthodox Church undertook an active role in establishing primary schools in the region; in 1884, only 61 parish schools existed in Tobol'sk province, and by 1914, 590 schools served the youth of that province.[82] The Omsk consistory, with help from the Emperor Alexander III Fund, opened new schools throughout the early twentieth century. In 1910, 210 primary parish schools welcomed 10,710 students in the diocese. Most of these schools were co-ed, with only 6 exclusively for boys and 14 for girls. However, more boys attended school than girls, as the female student population constituted only a third of the overall population of students enrolled.[83]

The fanfare that accompanied the opening of one parish school illustrates the importance of access to education for settlers and the degree to which schools symbolized the planting of Orthodoxy in local communities. In 1902, a new one-room parish school opened in a village in the district of Tara, constructed with money from the Emperor Alexander III Fund. To commemorate the occasion, the villagers celebrated the Divine Liturgy and then participated in a procession – complete with banners, icons, and a public prayer – that started in the church and ended in the school. The local priest reflected on the meaning of this event: "Who could contemplate ten years ago that in this dark corner of Siberia, remote from enlightenment ... encircled by ignorance and dissenters ... would be built a church of God and a school, a nursery of piety and morals?" The priest continued to emphasize how the work of the church and the school complemented each other: "The church teaches us to pray to God [and] the school explains to children the significance and characteristics of prayer."[84] From the church's perspective, schools performed the function of providing peasants with the knowledge needed to teach children the basic tenets of the Orthodox faith and morals.[85] Also, if they knew how to read, these young parishioners could learn and study the Orthodox tradition in a way not available to their overwhelmingly illiterate parents. Father Venetskii claimed that two-thirds of the young people he met on one of his pastoral trips were literate and that many had a copy of the Gospel or the Bible in their homes.[86]

At these types of celebrations, the clergy typically acknowledged the role of the state in the construction process. In the settler village of Borisovka, located eighty-seven kilometres outside of Omsk, peasants filled the church to witness the consecration by Bishop Grigorii.[87] The church had been built through the Emperor Alexander III Fund and the contributions of parishioners. During the service, the bishop gave communion to all the children, and afterward he delivered an edifying sermon on the comfort offered by the church to settlers. In the sermon, Bishop Grigorii acknowledged the role of the state in providing funds for the church and supporting settlers in creating their new community on the steppe:

> In this faraway place, where you found a second homeland [rodina], the government came to your aid: it helped not only in your farm but also looked after your soul, [and] built for you and your children this beautiful church.[88]

By reminding parishioners of their indebtedness to the state, the bishop communicated that the church represented a symbolic connection tying the community to the imperial centre.

Bureaucrats associated with the fund understood that the construction of churches and schools served not only a symbolic function in these communities; it could also be used as a teaching tool for shaping building practices in Omsk diocese, particularly when it came to adapting to the conditions of the local environment. In the steppe region, where forests were scarce, it was difficult for settlers to build traditional churches and homes from wood. Along the railway line in the districts of Omsk and Petropavlovsk settlers could find birch forests but no coniferous trees, which made better construction materials. Settlers made the best out of these circumstances, building homes from wattle, brick, and birch. These materials, however, were inadequate for more substantial structures like churches. In these cases, settler communities had to buy pinewood from state-owned timber yards, which received timber from Perm, Tobol'sk, Semipalatinsk, and the Altai Mountains.[89]

In this environment, the Siberian Railway Committee used the building of churches through the fund to teach settlers the techniques of building with air-dried bricks. The committee hoped that by witnessing the superior quality of this method, the settlers would then use it in the building of their own homes.[90] Omsk diocesan officials also recognized the importance of teaching settlers how to build in their new environments. To accommodate areas without access to forests, diocesan officials requested brochures from a Moscow engineer describing how to build cheap but fireproof dwellings using bricks. The engineer fulfilled the request, adding in a note that he hoped this technique would be useful and, in return, perhaps they would pray for him. Kliment Skal'skii, the organizer of this endeavour and also the editor of the *Omsk Diocesan News*, requested permission from the bishop to distribute these brochures through local churches to help the settler population.[91]

The construction of a church was a community affair, with the building committee comprised of the local priest, a supervisor, and representatives elected from among the parishioners.[92] In European Russia, parishes would hire local engineers and architects to help in the building process.[93] This proved difficult in Omsk diocese. For example, Tobol'sk and Tomsk provinces had only one engineer and one architect on staff; Semipalatinsk also had only one member of each profession working for the province, as well as a military engineer and a resettlement architect. These men were in charge of construction throughout the province. They gave advice and monitored the extensive construction unfolding in conjunction with colonization and the development of the region. As the diocese did not have its own architect and local building committees could not find people to hire for this task, the job of supervising construction sites often fell to those employed by the province. Building sites for churches supported by the Emperor Alexander III Fund could be located a hundred kilometres from each other, which made the duties of the engineer and the architect extremely difficult.[94] On several occasions, the governor of Semipalatinsk reported on the headaches caused by an absence of building knowledge in the region. While small school buildings were simple enough in their design not to require specialized knowledge, the construction of churches demanded supervision by people with the necessary technical skills who could guide settlers in their work. The governor complained that without the help of an architect, the churches were not built properly; yet he could not afford to distract his engineer and architect from other necessary building projects.[95]

The Siberian Railway Committee attempted to address this shortage of expertise by sending its own engineer to monitor those building sites receiving money from the fund. In 1900, Sergei Shilkin undertook a gruelling journey through the provinces of Akmolinsk and Enisei (present-day Krasnoyarsk). Travelling most likely by horse and carriage between villages and then by rail between the diocesan capitals of Omsk and Krasnoyarsk, Shilkin covered a staggering 5,200 kilometres in order to report back to the Siberian Railway Committee on the state of church building in seventy villages. In his report, he indicated very little of his general impressions as he travelled from village to village, though he did introduce his journey with the following pessimistic words: "Scattered among the vast Kazakh steppe, the settler villages of Akmolinsk province stand in the most unfavourable conditions, by their remoteness and isolation from churches."[96] He carried out his duties, noting the poverty and material shortages, as well as the hurried and haphazard techniques, that plagued church construction. This was not his first time travelling through the backwaters of Siberia, battling both the elements and the primitive road conditions on the front lines of the empire. Shilkin had also visited outposts in the provinces of Tobol'sk and Tomsk, where he performed the same duties in settler villages of supervising the building of churches, houses for clergy, and schools financed by the Emperor Alexander III Fund.[97]

In light of the complications afflicting the building process, the issue of whether Omsk diocese required a diocesan architect was raised at several diocesan congresses. At the 1905 congress, deputies contended that the diocese lacked the necessary funds to create such a position and instead recommended that clergy purchase a book of church-building plans published by the Holy Synod.[98] With the appointment of Bishop Gavriil (Golosov), this issue received more attention. Disappointed by the unattractive churches he had surveyed on his trips through the diocese, Gavriil recommended to the 1909 congress that an architect be appointed.[99] For Gavriil, churches must be inspiring – an emotion, he lamented, that was absent from his heart when he attended services in settler parish churches. In 1916, the issue of whether Omsk diocese needed an architect remained controversial. Despite the congress once again voting not to create such a position, a "builder" raised the issue in the pages of the *Omsk Diocesan News*. The author reminded readers that the diocese was still young and that many churches, schools, and clergy homes needed to be built. Problems occurred when no one on the local church-building committee understood the intricacies of construction, which led to the churches being built improperly.[100] The author argued that an architect could provide expertise unavailable locally, which would help the building process to run smoothly.

Poorly constructed churches, however, still fulfilled their purpose of offering a place for parishioners to worship and carry out their religious duties as Orthodox believers. The village of Poltavskoe in the district of Omsk illustrates how a church could simultaneously represent both the hope and piety of local believers and the failure of the building enterprise. This village was inhabited by settlers from Poltava and Chernigov provinces and surrounded by villages filled with other settlers from European Russia. Even though parishioners received funds from the Emperor Alexander III Fund, the construction of their church was beset by problems. While proper plans were used, proper materials were not. The builders used pine planks from a former railway bridge that had seen better days, and the building lacked a proper foundation. Homes for the clergymen fared no better, showing a similar level of carelessness as the church – indeed, the cantor's house had already collapsed and was deemed unsalvageable.[101]

Despite all the drama associated with construction in Poltavskoe, Bishop Sergii gave permission for the church to be consecrated. Parishioners gathered for the Divine Liturgy, along with the local clergy. The priest chose the book of Kings for his sermon and spoke to the congregation about God's kindness to King Solomon during his temple-building efforts. This contradiction – of glorifying an almighty God in a shabby church – did not go unnoticed. As one observer of the event put it,

> During the consecration of the church of God, among parishioners prevailed the following dual feeling – on the one hand, a great joy that they finally live near a church of God and that they have the opportunity to attend services often without having to travel over fifty *versts* [53 kilometres] to baptize their children and to perform the other Christian duties. On the other, [they experience] a hidden grief that too much inattention and carelessness of the builders is reflected in the structure of this church of God. As [they] gradually decorate the church, the latter feeling will be eliminated – but it will continue for a long time because as recent settlers, the parishioners are poor people.[102]

Given the many dreadful reviews of church building published by secular officials, it is likely that more parishioners throughout the diocese experienced such grief. Likely such buildings caused embarrassment for state officials, who sought to visually communicate the technical prowess of Russia's colonization efforts through churches constructed under the Emperor Alexander III Fund.

Unintended Consequences

This fund created the expectation that the state would provide financial support for the construction of churches in settler parishes. This expectation, however, complicated settlers' relationship to their churches. In his 1904 report, Bishop Mikhail (Ermakov) expressed concern to the Holy Synod over a phenomenon he noticed on both of his trips through the region. In places where the fund helped to build churches, Bishop Mikhail claimed that parishioners' attitude toward the church was cold (*kholodno*). In those villages, parishioners refused to maintain and decorate their churches, which traditionally was the duty of the community. Instead, parishioners responded, "We have a government church ... The treasury built the church, the treasury must repair and decorate it. Why would we spend money on someone else's [church]?"[103] According to Bishop Mikhail, this reaction stood in contrast to the attitude of parishioners who had used their own funds or had support from donors to build a church. Ten years later, Bishop Andronik described the same attitude, commenting that settlers – Ukrainians in particular – showed indifference to repairing their churches by shouting "Let the treasury repair it" at local gatherings.[104]

Tsarist official T. Tarasov, who was involved with the fund before 1905, elaborated on this phenomenon. He commented that settlers differed greatly in their willingness to participate in the building process and in their attitude toward caring for the local church, which appeared not to correlate with the economic welfare of the village or the province of origin of the settlers. Peasants from the same province could demonstrate either enthusiasm or indifference to church repair. According to Tarasov, indifferent settlers understood the assistance they received from the state as payment for their participation in colonization and, therefore, as something they had a right to receive. Since peasants felt entitled to such support, they did not understand why they should use their own money to maintain the church, as this was the duty of the state. Similar to Bishop Mikhail, Tarasov identified the local priest as performing an important role in convincing settlers of their obligation to care for the parish church. He criticized priests for preferring to solicit money from outside sources, like the Emperor Alexander III Fund, instead of teaching the peasants of their "moral duty" to maintain their parish churches.[105]

It is difficult to assess, however, whether settlers perceived this as a widespread problem. Evidence does exist that settlers showed a strong sense of pride when they paid for their prayer houses and churches through their own communities.[106] And the financial contribution of

3.4 A settler village on the Kazakh steppe. *Aziatskaia Rossiia*, vol. 1
(St. Petersburg, 1914), 547.

parishioners in Siberia was significant. In many settler communities, parishioners supplemented contributions from the fund in the building of their local church.[107] In villages without churches, parishioners often paid for the building of prayer houses as a substitute place of worship until a church could be constructed. For example, in one village in the district of Pavlodar, settlers from the provinces of Chernigov, Samara, Riazan, Mogilev, and Poltava constructed a prayer house to hold services as they waited for an opportunity to build a church.[108] Many believers, therefore, did not wait for the state to provide financial support; instead they organized locally to address the spiritual needs of their communities.

Settlers arrived in Omsk diocese with the expectation that they would have access to the same religious life they had left behind in their homeland. For settlers, the church represented a continuation of their previous lives despite the change in location, environment, and neighbours. They relied on the church to preserve their religious traditions and to integrate their children into the community's moral economy. As settlers established their religious practices, they showed agency in deciding what had meaning for them as a community. In some cases, they showed a willingness to adapt certain religious rites in response to the local environment, while in others they demanded that secular and religious officials fulfil their self-defined religious aspirations. As both church and state officials recognized the stabilizing influence of the parish, they were supportive of this cultural institution, which would simultaneously protect the souls of settlers and serve the aims of colonization.

The process of creating communities capable of representing and reproducing Orthodox culture, however, proved difficult. Even parishes in European Russia had not lived up to the expectation that they would stimulate local initiative; in Omsk diocese, many parishes barely managed to provide the basic conditions for proper Orthodox practice. Nonetheless, the process of building churches and schools through the Emperor Alexander III Fund created a connection between St. Petersburg and villages in Siberia, with these structures serving as a physical reminder of this relationship. Even churches built through parishioners' own funds contributed to the integration of these lands into the empire, as celebrations of the consecration of an Orthodox church seemed to confirm settlers' ability to Russify "foreign" and "untamed" spaces.

Chapter Four

The Politics of Pastoring

In 1912, a public battle of wills erupted between the bishop of Omsk, Vladimir (Putiata), Archpriest Ioann Vostorgov, and members of Omsk's diocesan clergy. The combatants traded barbs in official church publications, private letters, and internal church correspondence, accusing each other of slander and un-Christian behaviour. The fight hinged ostensibly on the graduates of the Pastoral Courses in Moscow, which opened in 1909, and the pernicious influence they were alleged to have on diocesan life in Omsk. These courses, organized and administered by Vostorgov, sanctioned by the Holy Synod, and based in Moscow, trained men for pastoral service in Siberian settler parishes. Lasting just over a year, this spat could easily be portrayed as a clash of egos initiated by Vladimir, a former aristocrat who as bishop provoked the local clergy into joining a personal vendetta, and reciprocated by Vostorgov, a polarizing archpriest with grand designs. Yet beneath the hyperbolic tone cultivated by these two larger-than-life figures lay deeper institutional, social, and cultural tensions in the church that were exacerbated by settler colonialism. The arrival of millions of settlers intensified the problem of the recruitment of Orthodox clergy into Siberian parishes – a challenge that existed across the empire. This crisis of numbers offered not only the opportunity for experimenting with alternative forms of training such as the Pastoral Courses in Moscow, but also for reconsidering the type of training necessary for Orthodox priests to address the growing complexities of their parishes. In Siberia, the notion that priests must not only embody pastoral attributes but also act as missionaries, took hold and inspired initiatives aimed at producing priests capable of forming a front line in the battle against sectarianism on the imperial periphery.

Across European empires, recruiting priests and ministers for colonial churches proved to be a difficult task. The Church of England, for instance, struggled to provide enough clergy for its churches in the British Empire – by 1925, only Newfoundland was self-sufficient when it came to producing local clergy. Although the Church of England managed to engage some ministers from local populations, most colonial churches relied on clergymen born and trained in England to supply their parishes.[1] Recruitment issues in colonial churches produced variations on two responses: the recruitment and training of clergy in the imperial centre specifically for the empire, or the development of local infrastructure to train clergy in the imperial periphery. In the British case, both techniques were employed to address this problem of recruitment during the nineteenth century.[2] In the Russian Empire, the idea of training priests specifically for the imperial periphery only materialized in the early twentieth century in response to the pressures created by the agricultural resettlement then underway in Siberia. With only six seminaries to provide priests for twelve Siberian and Central Asian dioceses, a shortage of priests was inevitable.[3] The establishment of the Pastoral Courses in Moscow offered a partial solution, by recruiting and training priests from outside of Russia's traditional seminary structure.

Without clergy to perform services in newly constructed churches, to consecrate graveyards, and to protect parishioners against the teachings of religious competitors, the cooperative parish-building work of secular and religious officials would be rendered meaningless. The Orthodox clergy had an essential role to perform in facilitating and guiding settlers' adaptation in these new locations and in preventing them from losing the cultural identity thought to be embedded in their faith. Within ecclesiastical circles, a debate arose over the type of priest best suited for church work under the conditions of colonization: whether men from European Russia possessed special knowledge of the spiritual essence of settlers that a priest born, raised, and trained in Siberia might struggle to acquire. Such discussions were not confined to European Russia, as priests in Omsk diocese also ruminated in conversation with the imperial centre on the necessary characteristics of those men entrusted with the souls of Siberian Orthodox parishioners. These conversations demonstrated the struggle faced by the Orthodox Church when it came to responding not only to the disruption caused by colonization, but also to the opening of the clerical estate.

The Role of the Pastoral Priest

The 1840s marked the beginning of the pastoral care movement in which Russian Orthodox publicists encouraged an expanded understanding of the duties performed by priests. Instead of focusing primarily on providing religious rites and preparing parishioners for the afterlife, priests were now charged with improving the earthly existence of their parishioners and with modeling pious living. These social roles added to the expectations placed on priests for service within their parishes. As Jennifer Hedda has highlighted, church scholars in the late nineteenth century started using the term "pastor" (*pastyr'*) as opposed to "priest" (*sviashchennik*) as a way of emphasizing this "new way of understanding the clergyman's role and responsibilities."[4]

Education, according to church leaders, was paramount in the pursuit of this task: priests should be well versed in both secular and religious matters and should devote their energy to the spiritual and material care of their flocks.[5] Only seminary-educated clergymen could explain the tenets of the Orthodox faith, engage in polemical conversations with schismatic and sectarian groups, and provide an example for the woefully undereducated peasantry to emulate. This emphasis on education mirrored not only a broader trend in Russian society, but also followed – albeit at a slower pace – developments in Western Europe in which, starting in the eighteenth century, Catholic and Protestant authorities showed a strong commitment to training priests and ministers for their vocation through access to seminary education.[6] By the mid-nineteenth century, the Orthodox Church had achieved significant success in raising the educational levels of its clergy. Many dioceses could boast that over 90 per cent of their priests had graduated from a seminary.[7]

Before the Great Reforms of the 1860s, the clerical population belonged to a closed estate, meaning that only the sons and daughters of clergymen could be trained in clerical schools and only clerical sons could be ordained. These sons and daughters also married each other, thereby perpetuating the insularity of this community and securing the financial future of clerical families. Such a system produced a distinct clerical culture, which supported the world view of even those who left religious service to enter the secular world.[8] Reforms to seminary education resulted in a slight opening of this closed clerical estate, as the sons and daughters of clergymen could now pursue careers outside of the church. Although members of other social groups could attend clerical schools, even as late as 1914 these groups constituted only 16 per cent of seminarians.[9] This change was intended to improve the overall quality of the Orthodox clergy by providing opportunities for motivated individuals who desired to serve the church. Although clergymen's sons still dominated the ranks of the empire's clergy, representatives from other estates also found their way into the fold.

Yet, opening the estate created new problems. Even with the seminaries full of students, many sons of clergymen chose secular professions instead of ordination.[10] As statistics from 1911 show, approximately 73 per cent of graduates from Russian seminaries decided against entering church service.[11] This situation concerned church officials, who feared the "intellectual and moral" decline of Russia's parish clergy as many of their best candidates for ordination opted to apply their talents outside of the church.[12] Such an exodus also caused a shift from a clerical surplus in the 1860s to a shortage by the early twentieth century.

A Portrait of Siberian Priests

Even before the construction of the Trans-Siberian Railway, priests from European Russia had crossed the artificial boundary of the Ural Mountains to lead Orthodox flocks in Siberia. The surplus of clergy in European Russia created a scenario in which, by the mid-nineteenth century, serving the church in the borderlands held an allure for men who struggled to find work in the imperial centre.[13] For some, embracing activism on the periphery also allowed them to make a positive contribution to society. The obituary for Father Shestakov, originally a teacher from the province of Kaluga in central Russia, illustrates these motivations. For this priest, Siberia offered the prospect of both a permeant clerical position, which he could not find in his home province, and a chance to bring God's graces to the far ends of the earth. His eulogist, Father Aleksandrov, reminded readers of the atmosphere and ideals that permeated post-emancipation Russian society, reflecting on how Siberia offered an outlet to fulfil these aspirations:

> In the 1860s, everywhere in print and in society could be heard talk that it was time to turn serious attention to this rich region of Russia; Siberia needed education people, intellectuals for connecting this region to the general cultural life of Russia. Educated representatives of the civil and church administration in Siberia zealously called to those from Russia desiring to serve the church and fatherland in the work of promoting orderliness in the ecclesiastical and civil life of Siberia, which suffered from the weak development of the principles of churchness [tserkovnost'] and civic-mindedness [grazhdanstvennost']. Many young people responded to this call with the fervent desire to bring their contribution of the light of knowledge and of good to dark and severe Siberia.[14]

With encouragement from state and church officials, Siberia became a place where able men could transform the local population through the strengthening of Russian culture. And whereas a posting in the boondocks had perhaps previously implied personal mediocrity, it could now communicate the strength of one's character and a commitment to being useful.[15]

The petitions of men like Father Shestakov to Siberian bishops for pastoral positions were welcomed in a region suffering from insufficient numbers of clergymen. Even before settlers flooded the region, Siberian seminaries simply could not produce enough priests.[16] Exacerbating this problem, graduates of seminaries increasingly decided not to serve the church.[17] For instance, out of thirty-nine graduates from Tobol'sk seminary in 1844, twenty-five applied to enter into state service.[18] In a region eternally desperate for well-educated secular officials, seminary graduates had many alternative employment paths available to them. After intensive colonization started in the late nineteenth century, opportunities in the secular world proliferated, which worsened the church's recruitment prospects. In places without a seminary, like Omsk, this shortage was acutely felt as diocesan officials struggled to convince graduates of Tomsk and Tobol'sk seminaries to join the priesthood in their diocese.[19] At any given time, Omsk diocese had between fifteen and forty vacant priest positions. Desperate to find candidates, diocesan officials there attempted to poach seminary graduates from other dioceses in the empire through advertisements placed in diocesan journals.[20]

As Bishop Sergii noted in his report to the Holy Synod, the recruitment of priests from other dioceses generated its own perils. Gathering information on applicants' moral characters – including any serious transgressions – from their former superiors proved difficult. Bishop Sergii complained to the Holy Synod that countless times he only later learned that a newly appointed priest was fleeing from sins committed in European Russia. Hoping to start anew in faraway Siberia – where his indiscretions might remain hidden – the priest continued working in the church and escaped bearing responsibility for his actions. In many cases, these transgressions were eventually revealed, or, if the priest continued such behaviour in Siberia, new charges would be lodged. This was the reason, Bishop Sergii claimed, that he had to administer a disproportionately high number of punishments among the clergy despite the small clerical population of the diocese. The sins of Omsk priests resembled those across the empire: drunkenness, charging high fees for rites, and various acts of immorality.[21]

The moral character of newly arrived priests was not the only problem the bishops of Omsk faced as they dealt with clerical staffing. Most bishops highlighted two problems in their reports to the imperial centre: that clergymen originated from different parts of the empire and that they were undereducated. Each of Omsk's eight bishops expressed distress with the educational background of their clergy. In 1903, only

158 out of 314 priests had finished their seminary education.[22] A few years later that number had declined, as according to Bishop Gavriil only 43 per cent of priests in Omsk diocese had graduated from a seminary.[23] The remaining 57 per cent had a variety of educational experiences, ranging from self-taught to completing teaching college, and every option in between.[24] Bishop Gavriil lamented the fact that many of the priests demonstrated lethargy when it came to bettering themselves through reading and studying, especially in the field of anti-sectarian missionary work. For Gavriil, these priests' disinterest in anti-sectarian literature was of great concern, as they had to lead the struggle against the "enemies of Christianity" produced by religious pluralism.[25] The expectation that priests would not only tend to their flocks but also actively engage in the struggle against sectarianism through self-education demonstrates the pressure placed on priests to perform greater duties, which would be quite difficult without the foundation of a seminary education.

This emphasis on education hid another significant division within the clerical population of Omsk diocese: priests' social backgrounds. While over half of Omsk's priests were from clerical families, at least 25 per cent originated from other social backgrounds, which included merchants, townspeople, Cossacks, bureaucrats, peasants, and other groups. The remaining quarter of Omsk priests were from an undetermined social background.[26] Therefore, although men originating from the clerical estate still dominated the ranks of Omsk's priests, peasants and other non-clerical social backgrounds were strongly represented in the diocese. This shows that in settler dioceses like Omsk, the closed ranks of the clerical estate had opened significantly.

A priest's social background also influenced whether or not he had received a seminary education. People from outside the clerical estate tended not to have seminary training. They had a variety of other educational experiences, including from district, city, primary, or catechism schools, teacher training institutes, or the Pastoral Courses in Moscow.[27] Only a minority of priests from non-clerical backgrounds had completed any type of seminary education in the diocese. In contrast, most priests from a clerical background had some form of seminary training. Therefore, the division in seminary education also reflected a divergence in social backgrounds, which likely added to tensions between the groups. Clergy from non-clerical backgrounds could not rely on their professional training nor did they have access to a family tradition of clerical work to provide guidance in their parish duties.

Finally, at least half of Omsk diocesan priests were educated (and likely born) in European Russia. Most of these men arrived from the

Volga and from provinces in central Russia. Fewer men originated from the western borderlands, the northwestern provinces, and the south of the empire.[28] Such diversity in education, social backgrounds, and place of origin was unheard of in European Russia. In Siberia, this reality had implications for the development of clerical culture in the region.

A Seminary in Omsk

The absence of a seminary raised serious questions about the educational opportunities available to the sons of clergymen in Omsk diocese as these young men historically had represented the pool of labour from which the church could pull for its next generation of clergy. To receive an education, these men trained at either Tobol'sk or Tomsk seminaries, both of which were located over eight hundred kilometres away.[29] This affected the local church's ability to retain not only the labour of the sons of clergymen, but also their cultural experience of growing up in clerical families, which provided a comprehensive experiential learning environment in which to prepare them for church work.[30]

Solving this problem by building a local seminary had been on the diocesan agenda for years. At the 1899 diocesan congress, local clergymen unanimously agreed that Omsk diocese required a seminary, arguing that its absence placed their sons' education in a precarious position. They asked the bishop to petition the Holy Synod to financially support this project. Bishop Grigorii agreed to this request, adding "for a long time [I] have worried about this."[31] But despite the united position of the bishop and the clergy, little progress was made. In 1909, Bishop Gavriil approached the Holy Synod with a proposal to build a seminary in Omsk, going so far as to create a commission to organize the project. The resulting plans revealed the importance placed on establishing a seminary that was responsive to local needs. In particular, the commission stated that Omsk diocese required priests with missionary training to deal with sectarians, dissenters, and Kazakh Muslims. Despite these special needs, the commission supported the position that creating a normal type (*normal'nyi tip*) of seminary, with a few tweaks, would suffice. It provided the example of Kazan seminary to demonstrate the possibility of strengthening the missionary component of training while still maintaining the traditional seminary structure.[32]

In Omsk diocese, Kazakhs constituted the largest non-Orthodox and non-Russian population, and the proposed seminary would train missionaries to proselytize successfully among this group. To this end, the commission proposed that seminarians be taught the Kazakh language, along with enough Arabic that they could translate the most important passages from the Koran. Not only must seminarians understand the Kazakh language, they also needed to be familiar with Kazakh social, cultural, and religious life through the study of the ethnography of the Kazakh people and the history and doctrine of Islam. By instilling a firm understanding of Islam, the seminary would prepare priests to convince the Kazakhs of that creed's fallacy. Similarly, students were to be taught the doctrines of sectarian and schismatic groups to ready them for polemical debates.[33] To make room on the schedule for these types of courses, Bishop Gavriil suggested either reducing the hours dedicated to the traditional subject of Latin, or indeed excluding it altogether.[34]

The Holy Synod expressed its support for the project and approved Gavriil's request to establish a seminary, but it did not agree to provide full funding for the structure.[35] This did not dampen Bishop Gavriil's resolve. Through negotiations with the City Duma of Omsk, Gavriil managed to obtain a plot of land for free on which the seminary could be constructed.[36] Gavriil also proposed that the clergy help to fund the seminary's construction through a one-time fee. While not rejecting the idea outright, deputies at the 1909 diocesan congress noted the impossibility of such an undertaking that year as the expense of building a candle factory and a diocesan women's school had exhausted the local coffers.[37] Also, the deputies did not have a mandate from the deanery councils to discuss this issue. It was agreed that a decision would be postponed until the seventh general diocesan congress. In the meantime, the clergy showed its reticence by asking the bishop to petition the Holy Synod once again to fund the construction of the seminary. The bishop responded to this resolution with the following words: "I am sorry that the deputies declined my energetic wish to open a seminary in Omsk."[38] Bishop Gavriil had good reason to be upset; conditions applied to the land allocated by the Omsk Duma stipulated that building had to commence within three years or else the consistory would lose the property. Gavriil pressured the clergy to speed up their local consultations and agree to contribute funds to the construction of the seminary.

The responses from the deanery councils communicated a deep support for improving the accessibility of education and an acknowledgment that a better-educated clergy could address key problems within their diocese. Mikhail Orlov, the chairman of one deanery council as well as a diocesan missionary, emphasized how seminary training would allow Omsk clergy to respond properly to the Baptist leaders who had migrated to the steppe in recent years.[39] Without educated and capable men, Orlov feared that the "false" propaganda of the Baptists and other sectarian groups would find fertile ground in the region's towns and villages. Nonetheless, Omsk clergymen still maintained the position that the Holy Synod should pay the full amount for the seminary. Ksenofont Petrovskii, a dean of the district of steppe churches in Akmolinsk province, claimed that the coffers of the consistory were "becoming depleted" and he emphasized the difficulty of finding a new, local source of funds to pay for the seminary.[40]

This issue of finances was not resolved when the Romanov dynasty collapsed in 1917. Countless documents were exchanged over the years, but as the financial circumstances of the Holy Synod and the Russian state declined, particularly after the start of the First World War, it seemed less likely that Omsk would receive positive news that full funding was available for this project. In 1915, fed up with the Holy Synod's foot-dragging and desperate to save the plot of land the city had allotted for the seminary, diocesan representatives petitioned the Holy Synod to allow the consistory to build a temporary wooden structure and open the seminary in a limited capacity. This request was denied by the centre, as such an act was viewed as being unproductive and a waste of money and materials. In 1916, diocesan officials received official word that construction would be postponed indefinitely until "a more favourable time."[41]

The Pastoral Courses in Moscow

This foot-dragging on the part of the Holy Synod should not be interpreted as indifference by the church (or the state) to the issue of clerical training in Siberia. The recruitment of priests caused consternation among St. Petersburg's church and secular elite. In 1908, the Holy Synod envisioned addressing this labour shortage by encouraging monks and other potential clerical candidates to serve in Siberia and the Far East. To promote this solution, the Holy Synod published a description in its journal Church News of the opportunities available for men with the stamina and fortitude necessary for working under the challenging conditions of colonization as itinerant priests performing rites and rituals within a specific area. Since these were paid positions – including funds for travel – such men would not have to rely on parishioners for their daily bread.[42] While the advertisement generated some interest, Chief Procurator Sergei Lukianov acknowledged to Resettlement Administration officials that the applications would never produce enough candidates for the hundreds of parishes then waiting for a priest; European Russia could not fill its own empty clerical positions, let alone provide Siberia with the priests it needed.[43] Another option, however, had appeared on the agenda – the establishment of special courses to train priests for Siberia, to be based in

Moscow and administered by Vostorgov. To get such an initiative started, Lukianov enquired whether the Resettlement Administration would pick up half of the costs.[44]

State officials involved in colonization embraced the idea of creating such courses. After being directed by his boss, A.V. Krivoshein, to assist in this endeavour "without fail," Grigorii Glinka entered into correspondence with Vostorgov to establish how the Resettlement Administration could support the courses and work to ensure that the Duma approved this budget line.[45] The Resettlement Administration's support for this plan arguably showed that its officials understood the presence of priests in the region to be integral to the success of colonization. In a draft GUZiZ report to the Council of Ministers, religious motivations appeared at the centre of the ministry's argument in favour of Vostorgov's courses; however, the tone of the document indicates that it was likely influenced by the Holy Synod. The report lamented that the lack of priests abandoned settlers to an unfamiliar environment, surrounded by "*inorodtsy*, Muslims, Buriarts, and even different sects," without pastoral leadership and without church rites. Settlers continued to practise Orthodoxy, but not necessarily properly – for instance, officials witnessed an Easter celebration that included a procession and a service led by someone other than a priest. Such events, GUZiZ argued, threatened the purity (*chistota*) of Orthodoxy in the region, presumably by the embellishments or omissions that unsupervised services or rituals might produce.[46] Providing priests for settler parishes therefore fulfilled the religious needs of settlers and protected the integrity of the Orthodox faith in this zone of colonization.

According to Vostorgov, the idea for the Pastoral Courses was born on his first trip to Siberia as he witnessed the difficulty of retaining clergy and populating parishes with strong, well-educated priests gifted in pastoral work. He proposed that the church approach teachers from parish schools with at least nine or ten years of experience for the opportunity of serving as priests in Siberia. Emphasizing candidates' teaching background had two advantages, according to Vostorgov: experienced parish teachers had a well-developed mind and sense of self-discipline; and ten years of service allowed the teacher an opportunity to observe and study "the pastoral and spiritual life among the common people [*narod*]." In fact, Vostorgov viewed experience among the common people in areas such as missionary work, preaching (both "in the church setting and outside of it"), and leading church choirs as highly desirable traits.[47] This elevation of practical experience over educational credentials – most strikingly, seminary education was not required for enrolment in the courses – reflected Vostorgov's position that the ability to communicate and teach ordinary parishioners was the most important consideration when selecting priests. He aimed to find the hidden talent of imperial Russia by targeting capable people who had a strong connection to the church, but who thus far had limited opportunity to serve.

Vostorgov did not tout this initiative as a training institution for colonial priests, yet neither did he present this plan as a temporary solution. In many ways, the early twentieth century was a transitional moment for the church as the system of clerical education and recruitment needed to evolve; however, a consensus on a new system had not coalesced.[48] While Vostorgov presented the Pastoral Courses as an easy way to address the crisis in Siberia, in reality it was a new training method aimed at producing priests competent in church doctrine who could also speak the language of the people and engage in serious missionary work in the face of a growing sectarian crisis. In essence, he wanted to train men who could address the conditions plaguing modern parishes.

To be eligible for the program, candidates had to agree to eight conditions. These conditions revealed both what was required of the participants and what they could anticipate from the courses. For example, participants were expected to pay their own way to Moscow: those needing financial assistance would receive only three kopecks per kilometre to the nearest train station and the cost of a third-class ticket to Moscow. Once in the spiritual capital, participants would receive shelter, food, heat, light, and linens for free. There was also the possibility of a stipend for participants' families of up to fifteen rubles a month. (It should be noted, however, that course administrators preferred unmarried men – this in sharp contrast to the general expectation that Orthodox parish priests be married.) In exchange, once they had completed the courses, participants were expected to travel to a diocese chosen by the Holy Synod to start their five years of service. To facilitate their travel beyond the Urals, graduates would receive a second-class ticket from their last place of service to the capital of their new Siberian diocese. From the treasury, they would receive a salary of between 300 and 600 rubles a year, and in most parishes, although not all, a home would be supplied for them.[49]

The first instalment of the courses lasted only four months, beginning on 15 October 1909 and ending on 15 February 1910. This time frame proved too short, and the following year it was extended to eight months. Participants in the courses received training in theology, church sermons, church discipline and regulations, pastoring, the doctrines of sectarian and schismatic groups, church songs, basic hygiene, and church architecture.[50] Although Vostorgov's name dominated the press coverage of these courses, in reality an entire team of Orthodox clergymen taught the Moscow participants, with Vostorgov's individual efforts focused on theology, church sermons, church regulations, and practical leadership for pastors.[51]

The courses proved extremely popular. For the 1910–11 course, Vostorgov received over 2,000 applications from all over the empire. Only 177 representatives from 54 dioceses were admitted. Of those accepted, 27 were deacons, 32 were cantors, and 111 were teachers. The courses also admitted people from backgrounds often thought unlikely to produce a parish priest; these included a military officer, a doctor, a police officer from St. Petersburg, a bureaucrat, an official from a railway station, and even a former Old Believer. The majority of the participants – 159 – were "Russians," a term that did not distinguish between Russian, Ukrainian, and Belarussian backgrounds. Other ethnic groups, however, also attended, with 18 participants from various groups, including 5 Chuvash, 2 Koreans, a Tatar, a Mordvin, a Zyrian, a Kazakh, a Cheremis, an Iakut, and a Moldavian, among others. Six of the "Russian" students also had knowledge of languages spoken by a minority group in the empire.[52]

State officials showed interest in evaluating Vostorgov's initiative. In 1911, Semen Bondar, an official in the MVD specializing in the study of the Baptists, filed a report on the Pastoral Courses in Moscow. As Vostorgov had left the city on one of his many trips, Bondar was unable to witness the powerful orator in action. His report was nonetheless filled with praise for Vostorgov's methods of moulding students into priests with a missionary and pastoral focus. Indeed, these courses presented a new model for training priests as Vostorgov aspired to produce "zealots of pastoring." In particular, Bondar appreciated that Vostorgov established a practicum for his students to develop their preaching skills. At the evening service on Saturday night and at the liturgy on Sunday morning, students preached in sixty Moscow churches. This type of practicum, Bondar noted approvingly, was also favoured by the Baptist Seminary in London.[53]

In addition to these events, Vostorgov had initiated evening gatherings called "popular missionary lecture halls." At these gatherings, held during the week, students from the courses engaged with the congregation. For example, at Novospassky monastery, interlocutions (*sobesedovanie*) were held three times during the week. On Sundays and holidays, students conducted edifying readings; two days a week they led choir practices, which typically drew between 50 and 80 people. On average, attendance for the other nights garnered between 400 and 500 people. According to Bondar, the audience consisted of people from the "lower classes."[54]

Bondar attended one of these interlocutions, in which three Moscow pupils preached to approximately five hundred people. Bondar described the course participants as speaking "simply and unpretentiously and holding the lectern firmly and confidently." He appeared impressed that such simple and enthusiastic words held the congregation's attention. At these events, parishioners were encouraged between speakers to participate in worship through the singing of hymns. Vostorgov had a pamphlet published of the most common chants of the Orthodox Church, which cost five kopecks.[55] The entire evening projected the values Vostorgov sought to cultivate in his priests: engagement in worship and not simply the performance of rites. Bondar recognized that an essential quality of Vostorgov's program was its training of priests who understood the lives of the common people and would be prepared for the hardship of service in Siberia. As he wrote, "[These participants] are people ... accustomed to living in an atmosphere of intense labour. Besides, the majority of them come from the common people, and know their life [and] their needs."[56] Bondar left this experience impressed by the educational system that Vostorgov had created. It differed so resolutely from the "soulless mechanism" of other spiritual schools that he proposed that it should be held three or four times a year as a "preaching school" under the tutelage of the metropolitan of Moscow. Such a development, argued Bondar, would "bring significant benefits to the Orthodox Church."[57]

Despite Bondar's recommendation, the Pastoral Courses in Moscow continued to serve only the settler communities in the eastern borderlands of the empire. After completing the courses, priests received assignments to new parishes in Siberia. This proved to be a confusing time for graduates, as many priests remained uninformed about the characteristics of their parishes. One graduate, Ivan Mel'nichenko, wrote a note without an addressee in which he enquired about the state of his assigned parish. He had no idea, for instance, if his new parish had a church or a school; he also did not know how to get to his destination.[58]

This note landed on the desk of a bureaucrat at the Resettlement Administration in St. Petersburg, who was unable to answer such questions without help from local officials in Semipalatinsk. A telegram arrived in St. Petersburg from the province, providing the details that Mel'nichenko required.[59] In less than two weeks from Mel'nichenko's original letter, M. Chirkin, from St. Petersburg, had responded to the incognizant priest, relaying to him the most pertinent points. He was assigned to the village of Malorossiiskii (which was in the middle of nowhere, located approximately three hundred kilometres from the far-flung city of Ust-Kamengorsk), and while the village had a school, the church and the home for the priest were still under construction. The parish was small, with only 1,385 parishioners of mainly Ukrainian descent. Chirkin also advised the priest on the route by which he would travel: he should catch the Trans-Siberian train from Moscow to Omsk, where he would board a steamship to Semipalatinsk, and he should present himself to the local officials upon arrival.[60] They would, apparently, look after the details of taking Mel'nichenko the rest of the way.

Training Missionary Priests

Vostorgov created courses not only to produce more priests for Siberia, but also to educate local clergymen in the fight against sectarianism. In 1912, the Holy Synod granted Vostorgov permission to lead two Pastoral Missionary Courses in the cities of Khabarovsk and Tobol'sk, in addition to his other Siberian duties scheduled for that summer. Although some Siberian dioceses had already organized short training events to educate the clergy on some of the key questions of faith at the heart of the battle against sectarianism, Vostorgov's Pastoral Missionary Courses were substantial events in which participants gathered for three weeks to learn how to fight against the propagation of sectarian and schismatic groups.[61]

The reaction to the courses was overwhelmingly positive. The governor of Tobol'sk, Andrei Stankevich, praised this system of educating priests, reporting to St. Petersburg that it taught them more about sectarianism than "any books [or] treatises."[62] The Holy Synod's missionary council applauded the courses and Vostorgov's work, expressing the desire that more be organized for the next year.[63] On the final day of the Tobol'sk courses, Bishop Aleksii (Molchanov) expressed his gratitude to Vostorgov. After thanking him for presiding over the courses, the bishop addressed the controversy surrounding the archpriest and his work in Siberia. In light of the "terrible anger and envy" directed toward Vostorgov's activities in Siberia, Bishop Aleksii felt compelled to highlight how these initiatives had helped to alleviate some of the strain caused by colonization. He praised the archpriest for the complementary work of both sets of courses, which tackled key issues arising in Siberia. Bishop Aleksii ended his speech by assuring Vostorgov that he would have an honoured place in the history of the religious life of Russian settlers to Siberia.[64] Despite his kind words praising Vostorgov's diligent work in Siberia, Bishop Aleksii's comments also acknowledged that not everyone viewed Vostorgov's activities as uncontroversial.

The Qualities of a Settler Priest

The "terrible anger" referenced by Bishop Aleksii flowed fiercely and publicly from the diocese of Omsk. During his brief tenure as Omsk bishop, Vladimir engaged in a concerted campaign to establish a local seminary and to stop the flow of graduates of the Pastoral Courses in Moscow (known as *Vostorgovtsy*) into his diocese. He challenged the suitability of recruits sent from these courses, contending that Omsk diocese would prosper if he could train priests locally. The bishop even placed the growth of sectarianism in Omsk squarely on the shoulders of Vostorgov and his pupils. These men, complained the bishop, were completely unprepared for pastoral work and they corrupted the Orthodox population with their negative personal characteristics, which included "ignorance, crudeness, arrogance, non-recognition of authority, stubbornness, [and] especially self-interest."[65] With such men leading Orthodox flocks, argued Bishop Vladimir, Baptist preachers found fertile ground in the diocese. Bishop Vladimir claimed to have a stack of cases proving the disruption and harm caused by Vostorgov's pupils. However, he directed his harshest judgement at Vostorgov, calling him a half-educated archpriest who had done irreparable damage to the dioceses beyond the Urals by wasting tens of thousands of rubles on the Pastoral Courses in Moscow that could have been used to train clergy locally.[66] Bishop Vladimir asked the Holy Synod to withdraw financial support from Vostorgov and the courses.[67]

An aristocrat by birth and a former member of the Preobrazhenskii Regiment, Bishop Vladimir had a keen intellect and a reverence for female company.[68] Despite his association with the highest echelons of Russian society, including Tsar Nicholas II, Vladimir renounced the secular world in 1899 and entered the Kazan Theological Academy.[69] After graduation, he received a position in the Russian Orthodox Church serving the Russian embassy in Rome, but his tenure was cut short by scandal. After engaging in similar salacious behaviour in the Russian embassy in Paris, Vladimir returned (or was returned) to Russia. In 1907, he became the bishop of Kronstadt, a vicar bishopric under the authority of the metropolitan of St. Petersburg. Vladimir remained in this position for four years until his posting to Omsk in 1911. His career in Omsk was lively but short-lived: two years later, the Holy Synod transferred him to Polotsk as a vicar bishop. He would eventually land in Penza, where he was defrocked by the Holy Synod in 1917. This development, however, did not end Vladimir's career, as he started his own "Free People's Church" and emerged as a favourite of the Bolshevik regime after joining the Renovationist movement.[70]

It is difficult to pinpoint exactly when hostilities began between the two men. By the fall of 1911 Bishop Vladimir had submitted a complaint to the Holy Synod against the archpriest, citing Vostorgov's interference in a diocesan matter pertaining to a graduate of the Pastoral Courses in Moscow, Ioann Kislovskii. Vladimir accused Vostorgov of flouting the power of the local diocese and breaking canonical law (one of Bishop Vladimir's favourite accusations against Vostorgov) by personally presenting Kislovskii's petition to the Holy Synod.[71] After revealing that Bishop Vladimir had declined to meet with him during his summer trip to Siberia, Vostorgov defended himself to the metropolitan of Moscow, Vladimir (Bogoiavlenskii), denying that he had communicated with the Holy Synod about Kislovskii's dispute with Omsk diocesan authorities. Furthermore, he claimed that graduates from the program understood that his authority ended with their assignment to Siberia. He reminded the metropolitan that 286 men had completed the courses and none of them had broken the rules in their postings.[72]

The feud went public in 1912 with a speech given by Vostorgov to the graduates of the third Pastoral Courses in Moscow. The speech, published in the Holy Synod's widely read *Supplement to the Church News*, received its title – "Whom shall I send?" – from Isaiah 6:8, in which Isaiah answers God's call to be a prophet. In the speech Vostorgov painted a dreary picture of Siberia. For Vostorgov, Siberia was a land without churches, devoid of the religious culture found in European Russia. It was also a place inhabited by criminals and political exiles, many of whom preached socialism and atheism. Finally, he presented Siberia as a region with a history of isolationism vis-à-vis Russia, which bred a local spirit of separatism.[73]

Vostorgov also noted that historically, Siberian parishes had developed with only a few churches spread out thinly over vast distances. This geographical reality had limited the contact between priests and their parishioners, creating an environment in which parishioners only saw their priests during the performance of rites. While he acknowledged that performing rites in such an environment was indeed a great feat, in reality Russian settlers could not live under such conditions as they needed to engage in a host of religious activities on a regular basis, such as the liturgy, services for the dead, public and private prayer, Akafist hymns, religious conversations, and sermons. Siberia's history of political instability demanded that settler parishes have strong leaders who could connect these pioneers to European Russia. According to Vostorgov, graduates from the Pastoral Courses in Moscow served this function well: they would carry their experiences of the spiritual history of Russia and of Orthodox piety to Siberia, helping the settlers to maintain these ties.[74]

Vostorgov recognized that tensions between local clergy, church administrators, and the Moscow graduates would exist. Using the metaphor of scorpions, Vostorgov warned his students about the new environment and people they would encounter. Even local diocesan officials, according to Vostorgov, had the potential to sting the Moscow graduates: "Sometimes you will be stung poisonously [*zhalit' iadovito*] even by church figures [*tserkovnye deiateli*] who themselves grew up and were educated in the old Siberian conditions of life."[75] Without providing any concrete evidence, he claimed that many local priests, while they did not themselves want to serve in settler parishes, would nonetheless be indignant if Moscow graduates received these assignments. As well, the innovative training graduates received in church work would show the faultiness of local methods and would lead to "poisonous bites." Reminding the graduates that their training had prepared them for this duty of serving settler parishes, Vostorgov encouraged them to view these tensions as another hardship that they should meekly endure.[76]

Vostorgov's speech, in combination with Bishop Vladimir's dislike of graduates from the courses, briefly opened a window for Omsk clergymen to express publicly their grievances with this system. In reality, the themes of Siberia and Siberian priests appeared sparingly in Vostorgov's article. Yet, these small references to the Siberian clergy took on a life of their own, and their interpretation at the local level revealed deep-seated anger among Omsk priests toward the policies instituted in their diocese from the imperial centre. Public responses to Vostorgov's article appeared in two places: an anonymous article by "a Siberian Priest" (who had arrived six years ago from European Russia) in the unofficial section of the *Omsk Diocesan News* as well as in the proceedings of the seventh Omsk diocesan congress. In these forums, the Omsk clergymen challenged Vostorgov's conclusions on all fronts: from the ability of local clergy to work in settler parishes and the characteristics of Vostorgov's trainees to the legitimacy of the Pastoral Courses in Moscow. Strikingly, all three of Vostorgov's detractors were priests originally from European Russia and two had confirmed clerical family backgrounds. These men's responses appear to indicate a willingness among European Russian priests living in Siberia to adopt a Siberian regional identity when speaking to the imperial centre.

The clergymen in Omsk diocese interpreted this article as an attack on priests in Siberia in an official church publication. The local clergy expressed their disappointment at the thought that educated people in European Russia would base their impression of Siberia on this portrayal.[77] Father Aleksandr Troitskii, originally from Tver province, accused Vostorgov of slander (*kleveta*) against the clergy of Omsk and repeatedly called Vostorgov's words "lies."[78] According to Father Ioann Vinogradov, a transplant to Omsk diocese from the province of Simbirsk (present-day Ulyanovsk), Vostorgov had gravely offended the Siberian clergy with his mockery of their work.[79] These men wanted to set the record straight when it came to the graduates of the Pastoral Courses in Moscow and local religious conditions in Siberia.

The criticisms levelled at Vostorgov's pupils can be divided into two categories: ability and attitude. In terms of ability, Omsk clergymen argued that fast-tracking these priests for Siberia left them untrained and unprepared to do the work of a parish priest. Omsk priests claimed that it was impossible to learn how to competently perform the liturgy and pastor parishioners in such a short period of time.[80] Instead of sending highly prepared, well-educated, and innovative priests trained in homiletics, catechism, and missions to Siberia, as Vostorgov claimed, the graduates of these courses were ineffective teachers who did not know the rites of the Orthodox Church and had to be taught how to perform the liturgy by local priests.[81]

In terms of attitude, the Omsk clergymen claimed that Vostorgov's priests displayed an arrogant disregard for diocesan authority. As one priest remarked,

> For them, the local diocesan administration does not exist, because they consider themselves subject to the Holy Synod and their teacher, Vostorgov. Pride, unsociability, arrogance, roughness, and many other [traits] adorn the majority of alumni of the Moscow Pastoral [Courses].[82]

These priests also appeared not to care that they did not understand the spiritual regulations governing their position. Instead of following the rules of the ecclesiastical administration (*dukhovnoe vedomstvo*), they simply used their own personal judgement (*lichnoe usmotrenie*). For example, Omsk priests accused the *Vostorgovtsy* of performing marriages without the proper documentation required by the consistory.[83] For the Omsk clergymen, the *Vostorgovtsy's* lack of knowledge of Orthodox rites, combined with their arrogance and disrespect of local diocesan structures, should have disqualified them from being appointed to the position of parish priest.

Local priests further objected to Vostorgov's negative presentation of the local clergy and the state of Russian Orthodoxy in Siberia. According to representatives of Omsk clergymen, by describing Siberia as a land "without churches," Vostorgov created the impression that the local population lived without faith. They also accused Vostorgov of planting in the minds of these graduates the idea that Siberian church figures might "sting" them, which "instigated his pupils against the native Siberian clergy."[84] Vostorgov's trusted position meant that his students took these provocative images literally, arriving in Siberia with preconceived negative perceptions of local life and of the ability of local clergy. To challenge this picture, one priest from European Russia contended that the local clergy had not "stung" him upon his arrival and that most other European Russian clergymen had similarly positive experiences in the diocese.[85]

Omsk clergy also took offence at the portrayal of Siberia as the home of a separatist and revolutionary spirit that desired to free itself from the monarchy and from Russia. In reality, according to Father Vinogradov, it was in European Russia, not in Siberia, that a "terrible revolutionary fire" burned. Instead of being incited by the political teachings of the exiles, old residents reacted with laughter to their propaganda. In fact, Siberian priests witnessed the puzzlement (*nedoumenie*) of their parishioners in the face of these ideas.[86] Only local clergy, they argued, could understand the political mood among the local population – not priests trained in Moscow or an archpriest who only viewed Siberia from the "windows of railway cars and the deck of a steamship."[87] In the eyes of Siberian priests, the mood sensed most often in their parishes was patriotism and loyalty to the tsar.[88]

They also objected to how Vostorgov presented the Siberian laity as devoid of spiritual culture. To draw attention to the misleading representation of Siberian religious life, one author noted that old residents showed a greater willingness to support their church and clergy with their own funds, in contrast to the settlers – Ukrainians in particular[89] – who sometimes even converted to sects in order to avoid paying for parish life. This situation stood in sharp contrast to parishes of old residents, who, despite "living without churches," held firm to the faith of their ancestors in the face of sectarian preaching.[90] These priests expressed concern over religious life in settler parishes, commenting that many had been "infected" (*zarazhennyi*) by sectarianism.[91]

Finally, the clergy of Omsk connected the existence of the Pastoral Courses in Moscow to the absence of a local seminary. At the seventh diocesan congress, the clergy requested that the bishop once again appeal to the Holy Synod to build a seminary in Omsk and to stop sending priests trained in Moscow. They insisted that these priests fostered "animosity and hatred" in the diocese.[92] The courses, one priest argued, were not created to respond to the needs of Siberian parishioners; rather, they owed their formation to ego and politicking in European Russia.[93] Instead of sending these people to Omsk diocese, members of the local lower-ranked clergy should be promoted as they had proven to be better candidates for the priesthood.[94] Local clergy, it was argued, had the added advantage of wanting to stay in Siberia, in contrast to the graduates from Moscow, who travelled to Siberia for material gain and would return to European Russia after their mandatory five-year terms had ended.[95]

In this tense atmosphere, Dmitrii Karneev, a graduate of the first Pastoral Courses in Moscow and a priest in the district of Pavlodar, wrote a defence of the Vostorgov-trained priests.[96] In this article, which was submitted to the diocesan journal, Karneev admitted that he could not stop the barrage of slander thrown at Vostorgov, and despite his great loyalty to his mentor, he quickly moved on to assess the accusations against the Moscow graduates. One of the main criticisms aimed at this group was their lack of experience and knowledge of religious rites. Karneev admitted that the first cohort of graduates could have been better trained; however, he argued that very few graduates showed the level of incompetence assigned to them. Admitting that a few might fall short of expectations, Karneev nonetheless questioned why the unpreparedness of a minority should taint the reputation of the majority. And he astutely raised the point that most Siberian priests had never met a graduate of Vostorgov's courses, as the majority of priests in Omsk were not from the program.[97]

Karneev freely admitted that many men relocated to Siberia for the opportunity to improve their material circumstances. However, he accused all European clergymen, not just the Moscow graduates, of choosing Siberia to escape their impoverished lives. Karneev reminded readers that the author of the *Omsk Diocesan News* article also left his parish in European Russia six years earlier. If this author could accuse priests trained in Moscow of being motivated by "Siberian gold," could the same accusation not be made against him? He proposed that those who had found "the good life" in Siberia were hostile to any new arrivals, viewing them as competitors. Criticism and hostility became their weapons against the new clergy who threatened their material livelihoods. Karneev experienced this directly at the first deanery council he attended, where he had to endure abuse from local priests, who even refused to take his hand.[98] These virulent attacks on the Moscow graduates, argued Karneev, created an inhospitable atmosphere for these men serving in Siberia. Instead of being judged by their actions, they were being judged by their origins. Under such difficult circumstances, graduates had a legitimate reason to want to leave Siberia, and yet they stayed, remaining committed to serving Siberian parishes in their adopted homeland.[99] Karneev's article, however, would not be published. Word arrived from his dean that diocesan officials considered it "one-sided." Instead, Karneev sent a copy of his defence to Vostorgov, thereby preserving it for the historical record.

At the beginning of April 1913, during his speech closing the fourth Pastoral Courses in Moscow, Vostorgov attempted to thaw relations with clergymen in Siberia. He acknowledged that his speech from last year's graduation had been misinterpreted as a critique of the Siberian clergy. To clarify his position, Vostorgov warned this next batch of young priests not to enter their new dioceses in Siberia with pride or self-conceit. He praised Siberian priests for their commitment to their parishes and for the work they had achieved under such strenuous conditions. He called on the graduates to learn from the clergy living in Siberia who understood the conditions and particularities of local life in the region, as these men had flourished in conditions that priests from European Russia simply could not comprehend. The speech gained wide circulation after it was published in the *Supplement to the Church News* in early May.[100]

Likely Vostorgov's words reached the ears of the new bishop of Omsk before the article appeared in print. At the end of April, Bishop Andronik petitioned the Holy Synod for permission and funds to establish a short missionary course for July. In light of Bishop Andronik's request, the Holy Synod assigned Vostorgov to hold his Pastoral Missionary Courses in Omsk, allocating 3,000 rubles to the event.[101] One hundred and seventy Omsk clergymen, along with fifteen from Tobol'sk and fifty from the diocese of Tomsk, attended the courses for three weeks in July, which garnered coverage in local and national church publications. An article in the *Omsk Diocesan News* described Vostorgov's final lecture as "produc[ing] a deep impression on the audience" through the lively way he presented the materials.[102]

At the end of the courses, an Omsk clergyman presented Vostorgov with an icon of the Mother of God (*Bogomater'*). An address delivered by the clergyman emphasized the difficult road ahead for the Russian Orthodox Church as it struggled with the enemy of sectarianism. According to the speaker, the growth of sectarianism in Omsk necessitated measures like the training of priests to engage in pastoral-missionary work. Vostorgov's leadership in this area was much appreciated, as the speaker acknowledged:

> Believe, dear leader, that your words and instructions, speeches and living example of pastoral zeal and missionary work will never be erased from our memory. In the far and neglected villages of our diocese, we will keep in mind everything that we learned in the courses under your leadership.[103]

The speech made no mention of the tensions of the past and instead focused solely on fighting sectarianism in Siberia.

Despite the controversy surrounding the graduates, the Pastoral Courses in Moscow continued to be operated until the end of the empire. These men were strongly supported by state officials. Prime Minister Petr Stolypin, who met these priests on his journey across Siberia, wrote of the favourable impression that these graduates had made on him, describing them as demonstrating "deep faith" as they undertook their work with an ardent commitment.[104] The governor of Semipalatinsk referred to the "selfless" and "useful" work performed in his jurisdiction by these priests.[105] Aleksandr Kologrivov, an MVD official who visited the Omsk region to investigate the growth of sectarianism, also spoke positively of these graduates, although he noted the negative view that diocesan officials had of them. Even though their fellow clergymen levelled criticisms against these priests, Kologrivov stated that parishioners liked these men and admired their "selflessness [and] readiness at any time to assist with good advice in spiritual and solely worldly matters." He viewed these qualities as important for priests under modern conditions (*sovremen-nye usloviia*) and he believed these men would help, not hinder, the state of Orthodoxy in the region.[106]

And yet, even with these words of praise, Vostorgov was abruptly removed as course administrator in 1913. His supporters blamed Chief Procurator Sabler for removing Vostorgov after pressure from "the Left in the Duma," as that body was stalling the release of 53,000 rubles to pay for graduates' travel expenses to Siberia.[107] Aleksandr Tregubov reprehended his fellow Duma delegates for their critique of the Pastoral Courses in Moscow, pointing out that Siberian dioceses needed priests and that the majority of graduates from the program were good people and fine priests.[108] Even with Vostorgov's exit, state administrators continued to support the courses. In 1915, GUZiZ officials expressed their support by calling the courses both "desirable and useful," noting that the approximately 560 candidates that had finished the program only placed a small dent in the problem of clerical shortages in the borderlands.[109] Aleksandr Naumov, who became the minister of agriculture in late 1915, described the continuation of these courses as "extremely necessary."[110] Even Siberian dioceses with seminaries could not solve their priest shortage; they, too, relied on the Pastoral Courses in Moscow to provide candidates to fill settler parishes. In 1916, the Holy Synod assigned sixty-three graduates to eleven dioceses.[111]

Even without control over the courses, Vostorgov continued to be intimately involved in the expansion of the church in Siberia until the collapse of the empire, travelling to the region to monitor the spiritual needs of settlers for the Holy Synod.[112]

With the advent of colonization, dioceses in Siberia faced the deepening challenge of recruiting educated men to fill the vacant priest positions in their parishes. Palpable concern existed among the church elite that such vacancies would aid in the spread of sectarianism across Siberia, particularly in Omsk diocese, where Baptists had already demonstrated the effectiveness of their message in reaching Orthodox believers. With settlers arriving daily, action, not debate, was needed. Instead of encouraging local solutions – the most logical and traditional being the establishment of a seminary in Omsk diocese – the Holy Synod decided to support Vostorgov's innovative yet unproven idea of training lower-ranked clergy, teachers, and others from diverse, non-clerical backgrounds as special priests for settler parishes. Foregoing the traditional seminary curriculum, Vostorgov aspired to produce missionary pastors who could inspire and connect with their predominantly peasant audience. The Pastoral Courses in Moscow represented a new approach for recruiting and training the empire's clergymen.

While it is doubtful that graduates of these courses were as incompetent as the dissenting members of the Omsk clergy claimed, they nonetheless became a lightning rod for a general sense of discontentment among certain segments of the local clerical population who resented the imperial centre's interference in local diocesan life. These factors encouraged the formation of a regional identity in protest against the imperial centre, even among priests originally from European Russia. However, the discord in the clerical ranks cannot be solely attributed to tensions between the centre and the periphery. With the weakening of the clerical estate in Siberia, the diversity of social backgrounds among Omsk's clerical population contributed to these tensions as clergymen struggled to find unity within their own ranks.

Chapter Five

Living and Dying among Strangers

On 30 August 1914, Andrei Semenovich Soltanovskii died from the hardship of being a priest in Siberia. While that was not his official cause of death, Soltanovskii's obituary in the *Omsk Diocesan News* nevertheless characterized his tenure as a priest in the district of Kokchetav as a formidable experience. For this son of a deacon born across the empire in Bessarabia, it was not easy shepherding seven thousand parishioners living in scattered villages over a span of fifty-three kilometres.[1] According to his obituary, Soltanovskii's spiritual talents had gone unrecognized in his homeland, and in 1900 he joined the great Siberian migration, travelling to this "far away and cold" land. Soltanovskii struggled to adapt to "completely new conditions of life and work" as he cared for this sprawling parish, regularly rushing from village to village over rough terrain in severe weather to tend to the needs of his parishioners. In one instance, the poor priest waded through frigid water during the spring melt with his sacred equipment held above his head as he endeavoured to arrive in time to bless his parishioners' food, allowing them to break their Easter fast and properly greet the risen Christ.[2]

Difficulties related to weather, distance, and inadequate roads could hardly have surprised Soltanovskii. Unexpected, however, was the absence of a spirit of religious unity among Orthodox settlers in Siberia. Ioann Savel'ev, Soltanovskii's eulogist who was also a transplant from European Russia, described how these parishioners from "immense mother Russia" engaged in disputes and disagreements over differences in habits, customs, and religious rites. Many of Soltanovskii's parishioners arrived from the Ukrainian-speaking province of Chernigov, while the rest had migrated from various villages in European Russia.[3] As different types of lived Orthodoxy collided in his parish – especially Ukrainian and Russian traditions – Soltanovskii faced the challenge of bringing spiritual unity to these settler communities.

This obituary unintentionally raises a variety of themes related to the role of lived religion in the formation of migrant communities on the imperial periphery. Across Omsk diocese, settlers established thousands of new villages, in addition to transforming the villages of old residents (also known as *starozhily* and *Sibiriaki*), which grew in size. Settler villages were composed of a number of groups from various parts of the empire; sometimes one group constituted a majority while other times settlers from fifteen different provinces inhabited the same space. Even if the population of a specific village was relatively homogenous, the parish in which it was located likely contained representatives from several different provinces. Colonization brought people together from various backgrounds who almost overnight became neighbours, fellow villagers, and parishioners.

As the vast majority of the millions of pioneers to Siberia belonged to the Russian Orthodox Church, ostensibly this faith should have provided a firm foundation on which to recreate village life. From the outset, however, divisions appeared in these settlements. For example, neighbours often spoke Russian with local inflections and sometimes even spoke a different language altogether.[4] They wore clothing and followed the customs, both religious and secular, of their home communities in European Russia.[5] Such outward displays of difference sometimes created hostilities. Although some scholars have argued that colonization created a "project of the 'great Russian nation' in which ethnic lines did not prevail" and in which settlers "acutely felt their Russianness ... stripped of local particularities," an intimate portrait of parish life shows that the dissolution of former identities required both time and effort.[6] At least initially, Russian Orthodoxy, one of the strongest pillars of this empire-wide identity, continued to be shaped by particularities imported from local communities in European Russia.

As Russian colonization was predicated on the idea of strengthening the empire through the transplantation of a unified Russian culture, the appearance of dissonance in the ranks of Orthodox settlers raised questions about the efficacy of Orthodoxy as a cultural tool for transforming Siberia. State officials in St. Petersburg showed little concern for this issue, as they focused their attention on the broader project of funding church building rather than the nitty-gritty realities of daily life in parish communities. Save for a few priests, even the Omsk clergy, at the forefront of this local drama, struggled to articulate the challenges they encountered pastoring in these composite communities. Nonetheless, the steady appearance of references to tensions over religious practices

5.1 An old-resident village in western Siberia. *Aziatskaia Rossiia*, vol. 1 (St. Petersburg, 1914), 184–5.

in sources produced by settlers, the clergy, and state officials reveal the depth of this issue.

One of the main recorders of the tensions found in Siberian settler villages was Ioann Goloshubin, a congenial man with a bushy beard who belonged to a growing contigent of local priests who viewed themselves as experts and keepers of local customs and knowledge in the Russian Empire.[7] Born in 1866, Goloshubin was originally a priest in Tobol'sk diocese, but he found his parish reassigned with the formation of Omsk diocese. He pastored his flock with vigour until he retired (or was removed for his outspokenness, according to Soviet sources) from his parish in 1913.[8] Later, he was elevated by the Soviet regime on the basis of his regular contributions to regional newspapers as a talented native Siberian writer and folklorist. In the local diocesan journal, Goloshubin authored intimate ethnographic portraits of religious life in rural Siberia, particularly in the series "From the Impressions of a Village Priest," in which he described the trials and tribulations of shepherding a parish community of old residents and settlers.

5.2 Father Ioann Goloshubin. Omsk State Museum of History and Regional Studies, Omk 14962.

Lived Religion under Colonization

For many years, scholars of Christianity have viewed the parish as a battleground between official and popular belief, with the institutional church fighting against parishioners' ignorance of the tenets of their faith. Beginning in the 1990s some scholars challenged this dichotomy, arguing instead that the term "lived religion" better captured the realities of daily religious belief. These scholars have shown the need to "take seriously believers' own assertions that what they were doing was Christian even if their practices may appear to differ substantially from official teachings."[9] In breaking down this boundary, they recognized the role that priests played in sustaining beliefs and rituals outside the realm of formal theology. Working under the realities of parish life, a flexible approach to theology and ritual practice on the part of the priest could help to strengthen or expand religious communities.[10] Priests, however, not only participated in negotiating the boundaries between official and unofficial rituals; they also performed an essential role in reinforcing localized religious traditions.

As a heavily ritualized faith, Russian Orthodoxy required a tremendous amount of religious infrastructure to be practised properly: consecrated churches and access to priests were vital for Orthodox parishioners. Clergymen performed an essential role since both liturgical and many extra-liturgical rituals required their participation. The general structure of religious practice was replicated across the empire, and the liturgy, the sacraments, veneration of icons, processions, feasts, and the church stood at the heart of these religious traditions. Yet as a faith practised in a predominantly rural country whose population was restricted in its mobility, Russian Orthodox rituals acquired embellishments and ornamentation in local settings.[11] Peasants were physically tied to the village of their ancestors because of the organizational structure of the commune, which gave the community regulatory control over the land.[12] This created highly localized practices that rooted Orthodox communities in a particular place.

Despite pressure to standardize and unify religious rites and rituals during the long nineteenth century, the heterogeneity of practices within Christian confessions was staggering. Many studies have called into question the notion that "religious belief ... represented a unified 'cultural system' of coherent, mutually reinforcing symbols promoted by ecclesiastical institutions."[13] Gregory Freeze was one of the first scholars to recognize the full diversity of Russian Orthodox belief and the important role that localized popular practices played in the formation of Russian Orthodox identity for rural communities. He showed that investigations into religious life in the countryside by parish clergymen and ethnographers uncovered "a mind-boggling kaleidoscope of what was ostensibly a common faith and common ritual."[14] By the late nineteenth century, this "kaleidoscope" of customs, so vividly demonstrated during the colonization of Siberia, continued to shape the countryside despite the church hierarchy's efforts to reform the parish and to harmonize Orthodox practices.

In Omsk diocese, local priests encountered all sorts of variations on Orthodox rituals that peasants demanded be practised. In turn, these settlers also experienced the diversity of Omsk's clerical estate. Although these men had chosen the same calling, they brought different backgrounds and experiences to their position as pastors in Siberian parishes. Customs that appeared normal to a priest raised in Poltava province might seem strange, or even abhorrent, to a priest born and raised in Siberia, and vice-versa. The diverse social backgrounds of parish priests added another layer of complexity to the local dynamics as priests with a peasant background might understand the practice of these rituals differently than those born into clerical families and trained in the seminary. In Omsk diocese, when the priest hesitated to perform a particular ritual, the decision about whether to acquiesce often depended on various factors, including his own background, whether the demand was thought to be egregiously against church doctrine, and competing definitions of appropriate Orthodox practice among his parishioners.

Cracks in Community Life

As settlers began building their villages along simple dirt roads, arguments quickly arose over agricultural, religious, and cultural customs. In a letter to the *Village Herald*, a new settler from Akmolinsk province, Fedor Korban, wrote: "Our main trouble is that the population is from twenty-three provinces and we cannot 'sing in unison' with each other; hence, disorder in community affairs."[15] A clerk from Akmolinsk province, Gerasim Tsybenko, living in the settler village of Donskoe, complained in the same publication that the *moskal'* (Muscovites or Great Russians) from Samara province often neglected to observe restrictions on working during holy days and Sundays as they cultivated their fields during the summer months. Tsybenko, who self-identified as a *khokhol* (a term for Ukrainians), viewed this and other of the Great Russians' customs as impermissible and sinful behaviour according to the laws of God. In his eyes, such transgressions angered God, who responded by punishing the village. Tsybenko interpreted the poor harvest experienced in Akmolinsk province as judgement for these sins.[16] In a community with strong divisions – as illustrated by Tsybenko's use of the terms *moskal'* and *khokhol*, which, depending on their use, had both pejorative and complimentary connotations – tensions between groups only worsened under the strain of an agricultural crisis, a frequent occurrence in Siberia.

Divisions existed not only among settlers, but also between settlers and old residents (*Sibiriaki*). Tikhon Bobylev, a peasant living in Tomsk province, began his letter to the *Village Herald* by clarifying that he was not an old resident: "Although I live in Siberia, I am not a *Sibiriak*." Instead, he was a settler who had travelled to the region from western

Russia after hearing a land scout praise the richness of the land. Instead of finding the promised garden of Eden, however, Bobylev discovered a religious wasteland. The neglected and dilapidated churches in his region did not evoke the glory of God, particularly in his own parish church, with its faded icons and horizontal cross, which had been knocked over by the wind. When the community attempted to raise funds to repair the church, Bobylev wrote, it encountered difficulties, with settlers unable to contribute out of poverty (*bednost'*) and *Sibiriaki*, even though they were wealthy, displaying an unwillingness (*nezhelanie*) to contribute.[17] Despite their shared "Russian" and Orthodox heritages, settlers characterized *Sibiriaki* as miserly, inhospitable, and ignorant of how religious life should be properly organized.

Old residents, in turn, harboured their own prejudices against their new neighbours. They often preferred their own relatives and friends to the waves of settlers arriving on their doorsteps. Some resented the reorganization of their parishes to accommodate this influx of people, as in the case of the village of Zotinoi in the district of Tiukalinsk. In a petition protesting the transfer of their village from the parish of Kulikovskoe to that of Potaninskoe, parishioners listed a number of objections, including the size of the proposed church, which would leave women and children to freeze on the porch; the necessity of crossing the Om River at an inconvenient spot to attend church; and the close relations between the villagers of Zotinoi and their old-resident neighbours in Kulikovskoe. As the parish of Potaninskoe was filled with settlers, the old-resident inhabitants of Zotinoi questioned whether the two groups would have amiable relations.[18] This animosity, however, could change over time. Five years after this petition, the village of Zotinoi once again appealed to the Omsk diocesan consistory to break these ancient ties and join them to the settler parish of Bogdanovich, composed primarily of pioneers from Poltava, Chernigov, Kiev, Kherson, Samara, and Tula. Zotinoi became the only village of old residents in the parish.[19] In this petition, the Om River now constituted a barrier to their continued membership in the parish of Kulikovskoe, which partially justified the transfer of Zotinoi to a new parish.[20]

Even the bishops of Omsk observed the disharmony between settlers and old residents within Siberian parishes. On a trip through the diocese, Bishop Mikhail gave a sermon in a village that directly touched upon the absence of unity within the community. Having heard from the dean that tensions existed between the old residents and the new settlers in the village, he communicated to parishioners the importance of living in Christian peace with each other.[21] The animosity between the old residents and new settlers was nonetheless displayed when

Bishop Mikhail asked the congregation to sing a prayer (*molitva*) while he performed a blessing. Silence greeted the bishop's request. The priest explained to the bishop that general congregational singing in the parish had yet to be established because of disagreements among parishioners as such discussions created strife between different factions. Turning to the crowd, the bishop admonished them for such in-fighting, and since no one would sing, he refused to continue blessing them. The parishioners responded with lamentations as they begged the bishop not to stop. Most likely mortified by this scene, the local priest invited the bishop to visit his home. Bishop Mikhail declined and continued on his journey.[22]

Under these conditions, events traditionally reaffirming community identity in European Russia could lead to displays of division in Siberia. For example, Orthodox village feasts and their accompanying processions (*krestnyi khod*) offered a space for local residents to explore a communal identity. In addition to several empire-wide celebrations, each locality had its own schedule of processions. Historian Vera Shevzov has presented feasts and processions as moments when parishioners gathered for the common purpose of worship, such as the blessing of ground wells or fields, as well as the remembrance of local events that had meaning for the community, which could then be added to the local church calendar for generations to come.[23]

In Siberia, such events could reveal cracks in the community, as different factions attempted to hijack the proceedings to satisfy their own religious proclivities. During a procession in the village of Mikhailovskoe, the local priest witnessed just such a disruption when one group demanded that the icon be carried down a certain street and another insisted on a different route. In the end, one group stood victorious while the other grumbled, swore, and finally simply left the event and went home.[24] In all likelihood, those involved relived the conflict in the subsequent days and instead of binding the community together, this procession only served to reinforce its divisions.

In many ways, Orthodox parishes were spaces of negotiation, both between parishioners themselves and between parishioners and the parish priest.[25] One source of conflictual relations was the dual role of the rural priest within the parish, who was simultaneously "the main liturgical celebrant and bishop's representative ... [and] part of a local rural community that had its own order, customs, and rules for solving disputes and organizing activities."[26] While Siberian parishes shared many characteristics with their counterparts in European Russia, the Siberian context altered how the relationship between parishioners and priests developed. Unlike parishes in Voronezh diocese, for instance, where different groups were either for or against the priest, religious factions in Siberia primarily developed according to the parishioners' place of origin.[27] This created a dilemma for the priest, who had to balance the interests of different groups in a way that did not exacerbate these deep-seated divisions. For example, Ukrainian and Russian peasants shared the custom of ringing the church bells to announce a death; *Sibiriaki* did not.[28] In the village of Syropiatskoe, Goloshubin refused to perform this custom as he did not wish to offend the local *Sibiriaki*. Yet, in the village of Novosel'e such a refusal would have incurred many complaints from his parishioners; he therefore allowed them to follow this "Russian custom."[29]

Priests also struggled with requests from settlers asking them to perform Orthodox rituals just like the priest back in their home village in European Russia. To communicate this desire, settlers from all over the empire frequently used the phrase "Back home in Russia" (U nas v Rossii) in their discussions with their local priests. Such a phrase denoted a separation between the priest and his parishioners and the rigidity with which peasants held to certain practices. By using this phrase, parishioners implied that the priest was unversed in how to perform these rituals properly; their choice to correct and edify the priest shows that the peasants understood their version of a given ritual as an authentic expression of Orthodox belief.

Some priests proved to be more amenable than others to the idea of performing rituals "like they do in Russia," creating conflicts among the clergy. These men faced the scenario of either performing the ritual or losing out on the fee paid to them if other priests from neighbouring parishes proved more willing to undertake this work. A petition from Father I. Grushetskii to the Omsk consistory asking that a fellow priest, Aleksandr Miroshnichenko, be prohibited from administering rites in his parish illustrates the territorial nature of pastoring. Unfortunately, the details of this case are sparse; the dean investigated the accusation and found that Miroshnichenko only performed baptisms when the infant's life was in danger.[30] Despite his exoneration by the consistory, the case of a priest originally from Kiev province administering rites in a village named Novo-Kiev (New Kiev) raises questions about the possibility of different approaches to religious requests. Sometimes, these rituals did not even reflect the home traditions of parishioners. For example, Goloshubin recalled how a priest from the Caucasus or the Don district introduced a new ritual into funeral services that Ukrainian peasants appreciated and soon began to request. This ritual involved the priest reading from the Gospel and intermittently placing the book on the mouth of the deceased.[31] Even though such an act had no foundation in Orthodox theology or Ukrainian religious customs, according to Goloshubin, both settlers and this priest had incorporated this act into the sanctity of Orthodox funeral services.

Since most priests did not grow up in the same geographical locations as their parishioners, demands for the performance of "strange customs" by parishioners often startled them. Goloshubin wrote of what he labelled the absurd and inexplicable customs that accompanied settlers to Siberia, identifying Ukrainians from Chernigov and Poltava as the worst offenders in comparison to those from the Russian provinces of Riazan and Samara. For instance, Goloshubin recalled how his first visit to his parishioners for the celebration of the Theophany (Epiphany) turned into a lesson on celebrating the holiday like "they do in Russia." Along with a cantor, he walked from house to house, singing hymns, sprinkling icons with holy water, and making the sign of the cross. At one particular house, the peasant asked him, *"Batiushka* [Father], why didn't you draw us a sausage [*kolbasa*]?" Goloshubin, understandably confused, asked, "What sausage?," to which the peasant responded in Ukrainian, "The same we draw in Russia." Peasants had made this request several times that day. As a native of Siberia, Goloshubin, had no idea what it meant "to draw a sausage," so he enquired with a prominent settler from Chernigov who had recently married the widow of a priest. The settler explained that the peasants wanted the cantor to draw a cross on the wall with "Jesus Christ" at the top of the cross, a spear and sponge on the sides, and the shape of Calvary at the bottom. The cantor should then turn to the peasant and say, "And here is your sausage." For his work, the peasant typically paid the cantor either two or three kopeks or a sausage.[32] Goloshubin, an experienced priest trained at Tobol'sk seminary, found himself re-educated on how to celebrate the Theophany.

Even when priests decided to indulge peasants in their native customs, the results could be unexpected. One Russian priest thought that he understood the customs of Ukrainian settlers in his region. During the same ceremony that Goloshubin described, this priest directed a young boy, filling in for the cantor, to draw a cross on the wall of a wealthy Chernigov settler.[33] The settler, confused and outraged by the boy's actions, cried out while the priest was still singing. The priest continued with the ritual and, after it was over, responded to the peasant: "Why didn't you let him draw the cross? Isn't this your native custom?" To which the peasant, from Chernigov, replied, *"Batiushka*, at home in Russia the cantor draws a prayer on the wall, not a cross." The exchange illustrates how even sharing the same provincial homeland did not mean that peasants performed rituals in the same way. Even though both examples of "drawing the sausage" involved peasants from

Chernigov, the actual performance of the ritual was slightly different. These differences, while seemingly small, held great importance in the eyes of the peasants. As demonstrated by the emphatic reaction of the settler from Chernigov, the slightest change altered the ritual's meaning.

While the practice of "drawing a sausage" confused Siberian parish priests, it did not in their eyes result in the grave offence occasioned by many other practices. Indeed, some caused the local priest to pause and ponder whether he could perform such an act in good conscience. At the funeral for a young boy, a peasant handed Goloshubin an iron spade and said to him, "*Batiushka*, seal my boy for me." Not knowing what to do, Goloshubin completed the Orthodox service for the dead (*panikhida*) and used the shovel to sprinkle dirt on the grave, saying, "The earth is the Lord's and the fullness thereof." After the peasant informed him that this action was incorrect, Goloshubin learned the art of sealing an Orthodox grave. In the ceremony, which is still performed in contemporary Ukraine, the priest uses a spade to make a cross at all four corners of the grave.[34] Ukrainian peasants believed that the act of sealing the grave kept the deceased in the ground. As historian Christine Worobec has shown, Ukrainian peasants were concerned about the dead walking the earth and even, from time to time, opened graves to drive a stake through the heart of the deceased.[35] While Goloshubin made no reference to a belief in the walking dead, he did express his apprehension with performing this ritual; however, he noted that "Russian priests" (presumably referring to priests from European Russia) appeared not to share his concern.

As frustrations mounted within newly constructed parishes, the clergy of Omsk searched for ways to support each other. In 1902, at the congress of the clergy of Omsk, a resolution was put forward to establish an annual gathering at which deans could discuss the "unprecedented incidents and puzzling questions" caused in local parishes by the "enormous flood of settlers into Omsk diocese from different places in Russia."[36] As the resolution implied, Omsk clergymen often observed occurrences during the celebration of rites that required deliberation, presumably to decide what was acceptable and to share experiences and tips on how to handle tensions in their parishes.

But it was not only the performance of rituals and rites that divided Orthodox communities in Omsk diocese; for settlers, outward displays of difference could be just as important. The distinction between the spiritual (religious rituals) and the secular (accents, clothing, and customs) in settler villages is artificial as parishioners regularly conflated the two categories. Accents and customs marked one's authentic membership within the community as much as the "proper practise" of religious rituals.[37] Father Ioann Vostorgov witnessed the tension that diversity in language and customs created in settler parishes; he commented that these tensions caused local communities to split into factions and henceforth avoid each other. When interactions did occur, quarrels (*ssory*) would break out as they laughed at other groups' pronunciation of Russian words and ridiculed the customs of their neighbours. Vostorgov recalled one settler village in which Russian peasants from Voronezh engaged in a battle with Belarussian peasants from Vitebsk. By engaging in these conflicts, he noted, the villagers "spoiled one another's lives." During one of his trips to Siberia, he witnessed the humiliation of a Mordvinian family as they endured the jeers of their Russian neighbours because of the clothes they wore and their accented pronunciation of Russian words.[38] Such hostility, Vostorgov argued, poisoned both the social and religious life of the village.

Common language arguably created the intimacy necessary for the formation of strong communities. Father Nikolai Venetskii claimed, likely exaggerating for effect, that settlers in one of his parish villages had roots in twelve different provinces and spoke twelve different dialects (*narechie*) of Russian.[39] As he travelled through his parish, Venetskii also saw how the differences between the Ukrainian and Russian languages exacerbated tensions between these groups. Venetskii provided an example of a peasant from Poltava trying to interact with her neighbour from Olonetsk province (in the Far North) in Ukrainian. Her strange phraseology, according to Venetskii, elicited a look from the Olonetsk neighbour that would cause anyone to laugh. Even though both shared a peasant background and were members of the Russian Orthodox Church, these commonalities were not enough to produce a basic understanding, let alone the bonds of friendship. Venetskii, who travelled through the villages of his parish, recalled how after hearing him speak Ukrainian, one peasant woman and her mother from Poltava province opened up about the difficulties of settlement.[40] The women's reaction shows the immediate kinship that a common language created. While language alone did not cause an insurmountable divide between people in Siberia, it did much to influence the initial level of goodwill between neighbours, as well as between parishioners and priests.

Echoes of the Union

The task of imposing standards, of fighting against popular beliefs, was not a straightforward process. While priests effortlessly formed judgements on the acceptability of specific practices, in reality, the line between theologically sound and erroneous practices was oftentimes not clearly demarcated. In settler parishes, priests showed their own biases, demonstrating both acceptance and intolerance of the same religious customs – particularly among the large number of Ukrainian settlers in Omsk diocese, who drew the most attention from clergymen in the region – as they contemplated the curious and troubling customs witnessed among these peasants.

For these clergymen, the practices of local peasants were shaped most directly by the religious context of the Ukrainian-speaking provinces from which the settlers came. In the late nineteenth century, the issue of the Uniate Church – or Greek-rite Catholics – deeply concerned Russian Orthodox leaders. The church, which emerged at the end of the sixteenth century, followed Catholic doctrine while performing Orthodox rites. Priests in Siberia, aware of this fact, watched Orthodox peasants from Ukrainian provinces closely for any signs of Catholic influence in their religious rituals.[41] They understood icons as one potential indicator of this influence. In one settler home, Father Venetskii recalled seeing a primitive icon of the death of Jesus, which he identified as showing signs of its Catholic theological origin.[42] Peasants also requested variations to liturgical rites that priests regarded as being influenced by Catholicism. While baptizing a child, for example, Goloshubin noticed how the people gathered around the basin reacted fearfully to this act. Upon further investigation he learned that these spectators had come to watch "how the priest bathes [*kupat'*] the child." Goloshubin's performance of the rite elicited great astonishment among the settlers; they explained to him how, back home in Russia, the priest poured (*oblivat'*) water on the child instead of immersing (*pogruzhat'*) the child, as Goloshubin had done.[43] In Orthodox tradition, the priest baptizes the child by full immersion, naming each part of the Trinity as he submerges the child. Immersion baptism symbolizes "a mystical burial and resurrection with Christ" and only a severe illness can justify the priest pouring the water instead.[44] In contrast, Catholic tradition requires only the pouring of water over the infant's head. Initially, Goloshubin had difficulty believing the peasants; however, comments from other members of the clergy confirmed the veracity of this claim.

The ringing of church bells after a death among settlers from Ukrainian provinces also caused alarm among the clergy of Omsk diocese. While ringing the bell is also Russian custom, Goloshubin's Ukrainian settlers requested that the bell be rung not only at the time of death, but also as the coffin was carried to the cemetery and for a few more days afterwards. Goloshubin argued that this was unacceptable.[45] He was not the only priest who deemed these demands excessive. The clergy of the diocese – so disturbed by this custom – placed it on the agenda of the 1909 Omsk diocesan congress. The congress heard descriptions of these "offensive" burial rituals. To promote unity (*edinstvo*) in the practices of Orthodox believers, members of the congress asked the bishop to restrict the ringing of church bells in association with death rituals and prohibit burial processions.[46] Most likely, these clergymen had raised this issue at the congress because it had created problems in their own parishes. By taking a collective position, these men supported religious uniformity within the community – and indeed, a ruling on this problem at the congress encouraged priests to stand united against any deviation in practice.

Embellishments incorporated into other rites startled many Omsk clergymen, who questioned the appropriateness of altering the sacraments to accommodate the customs of peasants from Ukrainian-speaking provinces within the empire. For Goloshubin, the marriage custom of binding the hands of the couple with an embroidered ceremonial linen towel was particularly puzzling.[47] He labelled this practice an "absurd demand," an assessment shared by Father Nikolai Kudriavtsev, who also saw this custom as an indictment against the impiety of settlers from Ukrainian provinces. Listing a number of other transgressions, including indifference to the church and attending confession only out of habit, Kudriavtsev identified settlers from Ukrainian territories as particularly susceptible to the influence of sectarianism and prone to misunderstanding Orthodox practice.[48] As Kudriavtsev wrote, "There are many other rituals [*obriady*], especially among settlers, which do not agree with church liturgical practices."[49] In his description of the hand-tying ritual, Kudriavtsev used the term "the sacrament of marriage" to emphasize the impropriety of such an act. He offered the example of settlers' treatment of communion to further illustrate how they viewed rites "not as a sacrament, but as a ritual." Kudriavtsev complained how a young Ukrainian settler (he used the term *khokhol*) arrived after the liturgy to ask him for communion before undertaking a trip back to European Russia. Kudriavtsev refused the request, to which the peasant, clearly irritated, responded in Ukrainian, "Are there different laws in Siberia, *Batiushka*? We have communion at any time."[50] For Kudriavtsev, this request embodied the flippant religiosity of this group of people.

Not all clergymen agreed with this assessment of Ukrainian settlers. Father Afanasii Liasetskii, for example, took umbrage at the way Kudriavtsev criticized Ukrainian piety. In his article "In defence of Ukrainian settlers," Liasetskii reminded readers of the long historical struggle waged by Ukrainians in the western borderland of the empire against the Catholic Church – a battle fought on behalf of Orthodoxy. He acknowledged that Ukrainians had been affected by this struggle, writing, "Many customs and rites of the Little Russians have remnants and echoes of the union [*uniia*]. But if they in any way harmed Orthodoxy, the holy Church would have long ago adopted proper measures to eradicate this 'evil.'"[51] As for these alterations in the performance of rites, Liasetskii failed to see the harm. He argued that acts like ringing the church bells during the procession to the graveyard or binding the hands of wedding couples had religious meaning for settlers. For instance, the custom of ringing the church bells proclaimed the death of a fellow believer and reminded people that one day they, too, would have to face the judgement of God. To dispel Kudriavtsev's argument that Ukrainians viewed the sacraments lightly, Liasetskii wrote:

In Little Russia, when meeting a priest carrying the sacraments, everyone drops to his knees, bowing his head to the ground, without looking at what type of ground is under his feet: dry or mud or snow. He remains in that position until the priest has taken a few steps from him.[52]

In Liasetskii's eyes, Ukrainian settlers demonstrated a deep commitment to the Orthodox Church and therefore they should be allowed to keep their religious idiosyncrasies.

In part, the priests' various positions can be explained by their own personal experiences of Orthodoxy. Liasetskii, a former student of the Podolsk ecclesiastical seminary, located in the western borderlands, had an intimate knowledge of Ukrainian communities before his arrival in Siberia.[53] In contrast, Goloshubin only encountered Ukrainians for the first time – outside of the novels of Nikolai Gogol – in Siberia. Kudriavtsev, for his part, was a graduate of the Vologda seminary, located north of Moscow, in a region with few Ukrainian-speakers.[54] Even though all three had been educated in ecclesiastical seminaries, they originated from different parts of the empire and their definition of tolerable peasant religiosity reflected their backgrounds. What appeared to Goloshubin and Kudriavtsev as absurd (and perhaps superstitious), Liasetskii interpreted as reasonable and meaningful to settlers' practise of Orthodoxy.

Remembering the Lost Homeland

The obstinacy shown by settlers in relation to their religious practices can, in part, be explained by their tremendous sadness at leaving their home villages. The physical and economic sacrifices brought about by the trek to Siberia paled in comparison to the emotional hardships caused by leaving family, friends, and the familiarity of life in their former villages. Ioann Petrov, who worked as a travelling priest, commented that it was not only poverty and hunger that contributed to the abject state of settler communities – it was also the separation from their homeland and their close relatives.[55] Petrov was not the only priest to raise homesickness as a significant factor influencing settlers' adaptation to their new lives.

Memories of what they had left behind coloured the way settlers interacted with their new surroundings as they sought to keep their former homeland alive through their religious practices. This was not unique to settler culture in the Russian Empire. In the case of the Canadian Prairies, settlers nurtured ties to the Old World while laying claim to their new land by sacralizing their villages with references to their former homelands in cemeteries, churches, shrines, and place names.[56] Similar processes took place in Siberia. For example, the villagers of Mikhailovskoe in Petropavlovsk district, the majority of whom arrived in Siberia from Chernigov province, wanted to commemorate their homeland by commissioning an icon of the newly canonized bishop of Chernigov, Feodosii (Uglitskii). Instead of choosing to have the icon written in Siberia, the settlers placed an order in the city of Chernigov; this would allow the icon to be blessed with the relics of Saint Feodosii. Upon its arrival, almost the entire village met the icon in a procession.[57] The villagers now had a physical reminder of their spiritual homeland.

Settlers' celebration of religious rituals could serve as a stark and painful reminder of the community they left behind. Duma representative and priest Aleksandr Tregubov travelled through settler villages in the district of Pavlodar, performing the liturgy, consecrating graveyards, and blessing wells, crops, livestock, and homes. For Tregubov, meeting settlers in villages so far away from their homelands created a sorrowful picture – he emphasized how, despite their initial happiness at meeting, a sense of sadness saturated his interactions with them.[58] Particularly during holidays, memories of joyous religious celebrations in their homeland contrasted sharply with their current spiritual isolation, causing despondency among the faithful. In one village, parishioners described how their Easter celebration turned mournful as they remembered the life they had left behind in European Russia. Even the risen Christ could not alleviate their grief. As they told Tregubov,

> When midnight came, we sang "Christ has risen" but we could not finish – everyone burst into tears. We remembered our native villages, the call of the bell to vespers, the joyful sounds of voices hurrying to church, an illuminated church, the solemn liturgy, and here we are abandoned, forgotten by all, and deprived of the joy of the great celebration.[59]

These occasions caused settlers to remember what they had left behind and how much they had sacrificed to journey to Siberia. The poignancy of these people's loss remained strong: to forget the customs and traditions of their former communities constituted a betrayal of their family, ancestors, and friends.

Consequences of Difference

Many priests became convinced that if conflicts over religious customs continued, settlers would lose their faith. As the missionary priest Pantleimon Papshev summarized, "Having become accustomed from their birthplace to well-known customs, they cannot get used to new ones. They consider these new customs as something less holy and less worthy of veneration than their native practices." Papshev, a graduate from the missionary seminary in Ardon (in the diocese of Vladikavkaz), observed that settlers "all have different customs and religious rites, which sometimes seem to others not only ridiculous, but also reprehensible." Disputes between the practitioners of these different rites caused both sides to feel "some sort of unpleasant, bitter aftertaste in their souls and annoyance that what earlier seemed so pure and perfect to them is now condemned and ridiculed." This unpleasantness eventually turned them away from the church, into the arms of sectarians or down the path toward religious apathy.[60] Therefore, disenchantment with Orthodoxy was caused not by the rationalization of religious beliefs, but rather the disruption brought about by colonization, which challenged the communal aspect of faith that traditionally bound parishioners together through a tapestry of liturgical and extra-liturgical practices. Mockery by members of their own community – even if that community was newly formed – constituted a bitter pill for peasants to swallow. It caused feelings of shame for peasants, who suddenly had to face accusations that their traditional way of practising the Orthodox faith was wrong.

Not all settlers, however, meekly submitted to the judgement of others. Local priests told stories of peasants stubbornly clinging to the traditions of their home communities in European Russia, in spite of criticisms from the clergy and other settlers. In all likelihood, the strength of one's faction within the community contributed to that individual's ability to hold tenaciously to the religious customs of one's homeland. Those who settled in communities with a sizable population from the same region stood a better chance of protecting their religious customs.

Signs of Compromise

Religious leaders hoped that with time and with strong leadership from the clergy, these differences would disappear. The Akmolinsk governor argued that engaging local children in formal education was crucial for developing a common identity among the next generation. Through their interactions in schools, children had an opportunity to create a sense of community that otherwise eluded their parents.[61] Vostorgov cited the Caucasus and the Volga region as illustrative examples of Russian resettlement in which original difference no longer mattered after ten to twenty years of living and worshiping together: settlers in these regions spoke like each other and practised the same Orthodox customs and rituals. According to Vostorgov, the priest was at the heart of this process as he could establish unity in church practices.[62] Only under the leadership of the parish priest could settler peasants be reassured in their faith and joined to their neighbours under the shared identity of Orthodox belief.[63]

But despite this faith in the capabilities of Orthodox priests, these men were limited, in terms of both training and in resources, in how they could respond to the challenge of creating religious unity. Orthodox leaders had developed strategies for priests to address issues like alcoholism or sectarianism in their parishes; however, it appeared that priests received little guidance on how to create solidarity in settler communities. Instead, settler priests improvised their responses as they became acquainted with their parishioners. Some engaged in the most basic form of community building: the construction of churches. The village of Pokrovskoe was truly in the middle of nowhere, located almost nine hundred kilometres from the diocesan capital on the Kazakh steppe.[64] In this settlement, Father Vasilii Peshekhonev understood church building as a means of creating a sense of community where none previously existed.[65] Despite the difficulties of working in a settler parish in which parishioners originated from different provinces and divided into factions based on these local identities, Peshekhonev persevered in his objective of building churches. Parishioners initially resisted these initiatives. One village in the region refused a church on the grounds that it would be a financial burden. When it finally relented, the parishioners offered only minimal support. Undaunted, Peshekhonev travelled from Ust-kamenogorsk to Semipalatinsk, raising funds for church building in his region; he also found experienced workers who could build inexpensive churches. The four churches built in his parish were a testament to Peshekhonev's labour. This feat was noticed by the governor of Semipalatinsk, who praised Peshekhonev and the energy he brought to church building on the steppe, even requesting that Grigorii Glinka reward these efforts with the Order of St. Anna (third class), an honour given to those who served with distinction in either the civil service or the military.[66]

To encourage community events, priests travelled regularly in their parishes to perform religious services and meet with parishioners. Father Nikolai Venetskii provides a glimpse of the religious improvisation that took place under the difficult conditions found in the province of Akmolinsk. Travelling through his parish, Venetskii performed services and rituals for his parishioners under makeshift tents. In the village of Sofievka, young and old villagers helped to ready the tent and old women decorated the inside. During one service, Venetskii gave a sermon on forgiveness because he had heard of hostilities between Ukrainian (Little Russian) and Russian (Great Russian) villages; during another service he witnessed the powerful singing of Ukrainian tenors and performed baptisms and prayed for the deceased. These events, and the socializing that occurred afterward, provided an opportunity for the priest to interact with parishioners over tea and to hear about their daily lives as settlers. In this particular village, Kazakhs and grasshoppers were the focal point of villagers' complaints, with the former stealing horses and the latter ruining crops.[67] Venetskii listened sympathetically to these concerns and worshiped with the parishioners, thus reminding them of their spiritual connection to the Russian Orthodox Church, and indeed to each other.

The influx of settlers created opportunities for the reinvention of village life in old-resident parishes, especially as many of these villages lacked churches. New settlers helped with the financial burden of building a church and supporting a priest, as well as strengthening the village's application for permission to build from the Omsk diocesan consistory. Settlers could also stimulate a community's enthusiasm for the project. For instance, the arrival of settlers in the old-resident village of Paletskii invigorated the village's efforts to build a church. Despite the consistory's initial rejection of their petition for a government-funded church, the villagers continued to push forward, contributing their own money to the cause. Finally, seventeen years after the arrival of the settlers, a church was consecrated in the parish.[68]

The consecration of churches illustrates one way in which parishioners could show communal unity. In 1901, the parish of Potaninskoe, in the district of Tiukalinsk, celebrated the consecration of its church. This village of more than one hundred fifty households contained representatives from over fifteen Ukrainian and Russian provinces. The local priest, a graduate of Tobol'sk seminary, Pavel Kuznetzov, acknowledged that despite establishing their new home in Siberia, these settlers maintained the customs and rituals of their native homelands in both their religious and domestic lives. These differences, however, did not hinder the local community from organizing quickly and effectively to build a church when a neighbouring village failed to meet its obligation to open a parish. The inhabitants of Potaninskoe petitioned to collect wood from a state forest for this purpose and secured financing from the Emperor Alexander III Fund.[69] The consecration ceremony for the church allowed parishioners a moment of pageantry mixed with a form of worship distinctly different from that seen in their daily lives. Three priests performed the service with two choirs in a church lit with candles. The powerful and expressive sound of their voices inspired awe among the parishioners. For the old residents, who never dreamed they would have access to a church, this was also a moment of reflection. One old resident summarized this feeling as follows: "Who would have thought that in this place we would have a church of God!" The appearance of a church in the land of Kazakh herdsmen was a symbol of unity for its peasant inhabitants.[70]

The promotion of Siberian saints constituted another technique for building a sense of community that transcended local practices. In 1916, the Omsk diocesan brotherhood, with support from Bishop Sil'vestr, proposed a biography of saints and other faithful who had lived in Siberia. The brotherhood argued that such examples of piety would educate Orthodox settlers in Siberia.[71] The campaign to canonize the former bishop of Irkutsk, Sofronii Kristalevskii, which originated in Siberia in the early twentieth century, likely started this search for local holy men and women. Sofronii gained a reputation for helping downtrodden new arrivals in their transition to life in Siberia. In 1918, his would be the last canonization approved by the Orthodox Church until the post–Second World War period.[72]

The history of Siberian colonization shows that settlers told their own stories about their faith and how to practise it. The speed with which peasants attempted to rebuild their religious lives demonstrates that the proper practice of the Orthodox faith remained essential in their eyes. Moving across the empire – and in particular, the necessity of building communities with strangers – challenged their faith. Parishioners struggled to look past the different accents, clothing, customs, and religious rituals of their neighbours. Such differences proved difficult to overcome, in part, because religious rituals and customs provided peasants a way of remembering their homeland. Only time would sever these settlers from the past as they learned to live and worship together. As life in the diocese of Omsk illuminates, the unified "Orthodox culture" that the state and the church hoped settlers would transplant to Siberia was itself a sort of illusion, even in European Russia. By contrast, lived Orthodoxy retained local and regional characteristics throughout the empire into the early twentieth century.

Chapter Six

An Anthill of Baptists in a Land of Muslims

Although colonization created many problems for the Orthodox Church, none of these dilemmas was quite as disquieting as the growth of the non-Orthodox Slavic population in Siberia. In 1913, Andronik (Nikol'skii) lamented his new position as the bishop of Omsk to his mentor Archbishop Arsenii (Stadnitskii). He would have preferred "quiet Tobol'sk," he said, instead of his assignment to this "anthill of sectarianism."[1] Local missionaries agreed with the bishop: they compared the growth among settler communities of other Christian denominations, especially the Baptist faith, to an infectious disease spreading through the diocese.[2] By the late nineteenth century, many officials in the church and state used membership in the Orthodox Church as a shorthand for membership in the Russian nation; it was implied that settlers who shed their Orthodox identity had ceased to be "loyal" and were therefore politically unreliable.[3] In the case of the Baptists, the prominent role played by German-speaking communities in that faith's proliferation led many to equate Baptist converts with German culture.[4] Under this assumption, church and state authorities interpreted the arrival of ethnic Slavs who practised non-Orthodox faiths in Siberia as a religious and political threat to the region's integration into the empire.

Despite the language adopted by Bishop Andronik, in reality, the largest non-Orthodox faith within the boundaries of Omsk diocese was Islam, with close to a million adherents. Historically, the tsarist state had relied on Islam as a tool of imperial administration; however, the situation had shifted in late imperial Russia.[5] Although the tsarist state continued to practise a policy of religious toleration vis-à-vis Islam within the empire, by the early twentieth century, some secular officials had grown increasingly suspicious that Islamic leaders, influenced by pan-Islamic and pan-Turkish ideas, held political aspirations that could threaten the security of the empire.[6] In this discourse, the Kazakhs occupied a special position. Unlike the Muslims of Turkestan and the Volga region – labelled "fanatical" by many tsarist officials because of their commitment to their faith – church and state officials considered the Kazakhs only nominally Muslim and therefore "non-fanatical."[7] Such a benign label, however, did not imply trust on the part of the imperial centre. The Kazakhs' religious identity still placed them under suspicion in the eyes of tsarist officials, who expressed concern that a politicized version of Islam might deepen its presence on the steppe.[8]

Under colonization, this politicization of religious identity saw the issues of Orthodox resettlement, sectarianism, and Islam become firmly intertwined. In Omsk diocese, state and church officials considered Orthodoxy as a necessary stronghold (*oplot*) in the effort to secure the imperial regime's cultural and political interests in the region. In his reports, the governor of Semipalatinsk, Aleksandr Troinitskii, argued that Orthodox churches and settlers constituted the most effective way to proclaim Russia's control over this territory in the face of external and internal threats. The presence of settlers, for instance, would serve the political function of protecting Russia's borders by discouraging the Chinese Empire from encroaching on Russian territory.[9] On the cultural front, according to Troinitskii, Orthodox churches and monasteries could serve a similar function against internal religious competitors who had designs on this land. Local clergymen articulated this vision in their descriptions of church building in the region. For example, in 1910, nine years after a fire ravaged the Orthodox church in the town of Pavlodar, church officials celebrated the laying of the cornerstone of a new cathedral that would stand as an Orthodox barrier against the tides of Islam and sectarianism.[10]

Such celebrated bulwarks of Orthodoxy, however, were not without their challenges. Bishop Andronik was not alone in his fear that sectarianism could overshadow the work of the church. Ioann Vostorgov expressed his concern that instead of symbolizing the strength and power of the Orthodox Church, the dioceses of Omsk, Tomsk, and Blagoveshchensk might each be lost forever as "a sectarian stronghold" (*sektantskaia tsitadel'*). As he wrote, "I am ... afraid of the responsibility for my silence before the stern judgement of God and before the judgment of history."[11] Such a development could pose a serious threat not only to the church, but also to the integrity of the empire. Vostorgov blamed the disintegration of the Byzantine Empire on its religiously diverse borderlands of Egypt, Syria, and Armenia, which weakened the power of the imperial centre. Although he did not accuse non-Orthodox religious believers in Siberia outright of being traitorous, Vostorgov argued that only Russian Orthodoxy could attach this borderland to St. Petersburg, thereby securing its future in the empire.[12]

After 1905, this issue became more pressing. To quell the revolutionary fervour rising in the empire, Nicholas II not only created Russia's first parliament, he also approved a number of fundamental changes to Russia's religious laws. Russians could legally leave the Orthodox Church (although they could only join another Christian faith) and religious groups who were formerly persecuted by the state could now hold meetings in prayer houses or homes. Inhabitants of the empire had the right to freedom of conscience; this was a concept that the state never fully articulated, but it offered ordinary people a sense of control over their own religious identities.[13] While the Orthodox Church still held its position as the established church and it maintained the exclusive right to proselytize, this change nonetheless profoundly altered the religious landscape of the empire. In Omsk diocese, Muslim converts to Orthodoxy petitioned to become Muslims once again and Russian Orthodox believers asked to leave the church for another Christian denomination. Freedom of religious conscience increased the fear among Omsk clergymen and provincial governors that Russian Orthodox colonization, which was demographically Russifying the provinces of Akmolinsk and Semipalatinsk (albeit at a much slower rate), could be undone through the conversion of these settlers to the Baptist faith. Instead of the transformation of this land of Islam into a bastion of Orthodoxy, colonization could lay the foundation for the growth of sectarian groups whose loyalty to the Russian state could not be guaranteed.

Converting Kazakhs

Omsk diocese, similar to other locations in the empire with a large non-Orthodox population, established an external mission dedicated to converting people who had never subscribed to the Orthodox faith. The Kazakh mission served this purpose, attempting to convert Kazakhs, many of whom identified as Muslim, to Orthodoxy. With the establishment of the diocese in 1895, missionary posts from both Tobol'sk and Tomsk dioceses were joined to form the mission, which included sites in the provinces of Semipalatinsk and Akmolinsk, as well as two monastic communities (Kara-Obinsk in Petropavlovsk and Znamenskii near Semipalatinsk).[14] The mission's Orthodox congregation was composed of 13,133 people, with approximately 12,837 Russians and 296 baptized Kazakhs. Nearly 2,000 Russian settlers also lived in villages or farmsteads close to the missionary posts.[15]

As historian Robert Geraci has shown, contact between Kazakhs and Russian settlers created challenges for church leaders interested in missionary work. His analysis demonstrates that settlers complicated any attempts to present a coherent, unified faith to the Kazakhs as the set-tlers themselves – according to the missionaries – often had to be edu-cated in the faith.[16] This lack of religious knowledge, combined with an absence of churches and schools, inspired initial concern among church and state officials that settlers would be vulnerable living among the Kazakhs. In his 1894 report, the governor of Akmolinsk expressed his fears that the separation of settlers from their homeland, in combina-tion with their contact with the local indigenous population, might lead Orthodox settlers to imitate their Kazakh neighbours.[17] According to the 1899 report of the Kazakh mission, the missionary stationed at the Atbasar post focused his efforts on "unsteady Christians" from both the local Kazakh and Russian populations, who showed spiritual weakness in this ocean of Islam. The mission post reported only fif-teen conversions to Russian Orthodoxy from among the local Muslim community; in the other direction, the Islamic faith gained two Russian apostates.[18] As is clear, despite the expressed fear of some missionaries, the conversion of ethnic Slavs to Islam in the steppe rarely occurred. This stands in contrast to other parts of Central Asia in which church officials claimed that the absence of religious support and the inter-mixing of Russians and Muslims – including Muslim men and Russian women – had led some to convert to Islam.[19]

Despite the relative rarity of this occurrence, settlers used the fear of this possibility in their petitions to church leaders. For instance, in 1908, a petition from a group of Orthodox settlers requested help opening a church and school; in so doing, they insisted on the importance of edu-cating their children in the faith as the village was situated among the Kazakhs, whom the parishioners had "started to imitate [*podrazhat'*]."[20] This statement, however, should perhaps not be taken too literally. This particular village was located in the district of Petropavlovsk, one of the most intensely settled areas in the province of Akmolinsk during the twentieth century. While Kazakhs still lived in this territory, the Russian population constituted a solid majority in this district.[21]

After the changes to religious rights in 1905, conversions to Orthodoxy slowed to only a handful each year.[22] The missionaries working with the Kazakhs struggled to adapt to these new conditions. Almost imme-diately after the introduction of freedom of conscience in the empire, Kazakh converts petitioned the Semipalatinsk governor to allow them to leave the Orthodox faith and return to Islam, claiming they had been converted by force or fraud. This changed the dynamics between the Kazakhs and the missionaries, causing frustration for the latter as they claimed that the laws gave an advantage to Muslim preachers who planted hostility toward Christianity.[23]

6.1 Muslim Kazakhs living on the steppe. INTERFOTO/Alamy Stock Photo.

Some officials believed that the settlement of Orthodox colonists in this region could help "civilize" the local population by encouraging them to adopt a sedentary lifestyle. In 1902, the governor of Akmolinsk identified this goal as one of the roles of the diocesan Kazakh mission.[24] Five years later, Governor Troinitskii expressed support for this idea, advocating for the movement of Russian settlers to his region as a way to gradually settle the Kazakhs.[25] He also praised the establishment of a new female monastery in Semipalatinsk as a "reliable stronghold of Orthodoxy among the Muslim population" and a cultural centre from which the Kazakhs could be encouraged to acculturate to the agricultural practices of the colonial state.[26] This idea gained greater traction after a trip made by one Duma representative, Father Aleksandr Tregubov, through Semipalatinsk and Semirech'e provinces in 1909. Tregubov took up this cause, convinced as he was that if the Kazakhs embraced a sedentary life, they would be open to conversion to Orthodoxy. He argued that this process would unfold only if Kazakhs lived among Orthodox believers, since this would persuade them of Orthodoxy's "superiority" over Islam.[27] He argued that the

Kazakhs never truly believed in Islam and that they showed greater openness to Russian influence through schools and churches than other Muslims in the empire.[28]

Initially the Holy Synod hesitated, preferring to delay a decision on this issue by sending it to the council on external and internal missions for further investigation.[29] By 1912, members of the Holy Synod decided to support this idea, and the chief procurator communicated their decision to the Ministry of Agriculture and State Properties; however, the Holy Synod stipulated that Orthodox believers should always form a majority to safeguard Orthodoxy's advantage over Islam.[30] Officials from the Resettlement Administration supported this decision, communicating to the governor general of the steppe that this could serve as a way of "introducing the indigenous population of the steppe provinces to the Russian state and Russian culture."[31]

The local Kazakh population reacted negatively to this initiative. A petition to the empire's Council of Ministers from a village in the province of Turgai protested this proposal and called for the Russian state to respect its own laws on religion. It accused GUZiZ and the Resettlement Administration of violating these laws by promoting the settlement of Muslim Kazakhs in villages with a majority of Orthodox believers and admonished these tsarist officials to act like civilized people by respecting the rights of others. The idea of using demographics as a tool of conversion and sedentarization highly offended this group. Instead of "civilizing" the Kazakhs, the petition argued that such a measure would corrupt them as Russian settlers were known to have issues with drunkenness – a problem not shared by their abstinent Muslim neighbours.[32] While this petition was clearly written by "an insider" with a vast knowledge of the laws and structure of the Russian imperial regime, it is important to note that by the early twentieth century the Kazakh intelligentsia had grown increasingly vocal about their political rights and the problems caused by Russian settlers' intrusion into their lands.[33]

Although the idea of Christianizing the Kazakhs through settlement was not new, the aggressiveness of this specific proposal reflected a growing divide in the empire. Despite the tsarist regime's historic reliance on religious toleration, by 1910, as historian Paul Werth has demonstrated, officials had adopted a less cooperative tone with their foreign confessions, such that many leaders of non-Orthodox faiths now felt a strong sense of hostility from the state.[34] In the case of Islam, concerns over pan-Islamic thought influenced this tone, with Prime Minister Petr Stolypin adopting "strident rhetoric" in relation to the Muslim population in the empire.[35] On the steppe, Governor General

E.O. Shmit warned the imperial centre that Tatar agitators had been propagandizing pan-Islamic ideas among the Kazakhs. These activists cleverly tailored their message to the Kazakhs' situation by linking the community's economic crisis with peasant resettlement and calling on the Kazakhs to unite with other Muslims to defend their interests. While Shmit argued that the Kazakhs could not comprehend the idea of belonging to a unified national and religious group, he reported that he would monitor the situation and take action if necessary.[36]

Omsk missionaries, for the most part, did not adopt a politicized tone in their work among the Kazakhs. Official reports on the Kazakh missions focused on the everyday problems of this work rather than on where the missions fit into a grand imperial project. Through her analysis of these reports, historian Yuliya Lysenko has shown that although missionaries in Omsk diocese had initially presented a strong sense of optimism about their work, after 1905 they began to accept the futility of their activities among the Kazakhs.[37] Even conversions from Islam to Orthodoxy were interpreted under the rubric of religious salvation, not politics. For instance, the *Omsk Diocesan News* reported that Alekberov Samakhuddin, a thirty-three-year-old Muslim man, had become "Mikhail" after his baptism into the Orthodox Church. The short article praised his individual act of conversion but did not draw any wider cultural or political conclusions from this event.[38]

In many ways, Muslim Kazakhs served a symbolic function for the local Orthodox authorities in the diocese. In their discussions about settlers, church officials often connected negative terms such as "foreign" (*chuzhoi*), "backwoods" (*glush'*), or "desolate" (*glukhoi*) with the indigenous Kazakhs and the local landscape.[39] During his trip to villages through the eastern part of the province of Akmolinsk, Bishop Andronik interacted with local children, questioning them about prayers, the lives of saints, and holy days. During these visits the bishop blamed the children's lacklustre performance on their parents, scolding local mothers with the following words: "The children do not know their prayers, which means that you, mothers, also pray poorly. If this continues, then your children will live like the Kazakhs, not knowing the Christian prayers."[40] With this comparison, Andronik used the Kazakhs as a rhetorical device to chastise the "uncivilized" behaviour of Orthodox settlers.

Russian Orthodox clergymen also used the image of Kazakhs and Islam to emphasize the transformation of the region initiated by settlement. In his welcome speech to the bishop, Father Simeon Petrov spoke of the steppe as a desolate land filled with Mongolian tribes practising their Muslim faith; only with the arrival of Orthodox settlers could the light of Christianity shine.[41] Andronik responded by praising the local parishioners for their role in this process:

> Twenty years ago, this space was inhabited by Kazakh nomads and predatory animals. Now your diligence has created a beautiful church, topped by a cross. This cross, shining on the church and visible from afar, serves as a symbol – a sign that here dwells Orthodox believing people honouring the cross of the crucified Christ – the Giver of Life.[42]

Especially in the province of Akmolinsk, where Orthodox believers already formed a majority, church officials often used Kazakhs as a symbol of the land's untamed past and its ultimate subjugation with the arrival of settlers.

Keeping the Faith

There is a long history of people considered by the state to be of questionable religious character finding shelter in Siberia. Since the seventeenth-century schism in the Orthodox Church caused by the reforms of Patriarch Nikon, Old Believers had found sanctuary in the region. They produced thriving communities with their own leaders, traditions, and culture outside the immediate gaze of the Russian state, and by 1911 this population had reached approximately 21,865 in Omsk diocese.[43] The majority lived in the Bukhtarma region.[44] Surrounded by mountains and located in the far reaches of the diocese, near the Chinese border, the geography and topography of this region offered Old Believers a certain amount of natural shelter from Orthodox missionaries. While the Orthodox Church considered Old Believers to be less of a concern than Baptists, the strength of their presence in Siberia still caused apprehension.[45]

Old Believers would be joined by Baptists, Molokans, Doukhobors, and others. Although the categories were not standardized, the term "dissenters" (raskol'niki) tended to refer to Old Believers who claimed to practise the true Orthodox faith, while "sectarians" (sektanty) referred to those who had left the Orthodox Church, such as Baptists or Molokans. Native Siberian priests held firm to the position that before the arrival of Russian settlers, Siberia "was absolutely free and clean from any rationalistic sect."[46] Another clerical author articulated a similar position in the Omsk Diocesan News: "Ten years ago native inhabitants of the city of Pavlodar ... had no idea about Molokan sectarians and shtundo-baptists and now these and others appear not only in Pavlodar, but also in the district ... Mother Russia [matushka Rossiia] awarded them to us Sibiriaki."[47]

According to the old residents, sectarianism – viewed almost universally by church and state leaders as a force corrupting Orthodox souls in Siberia – was caused solely by settlers.

Omsk diocesan leaders adopted a fatalistic tone in their references to sectarians, as if an unstoppable evil had been unleashed among the settlers. In his 1907 report to the Holy Synod, Bishop Gavriil claimed, "At present time, sectarianism grows and multiplies, so to say, not by the day, but by the hour."[48] The sectarian population of the diocese grew, in part, because the state did not pass legislation to limit the settlement of non-Orthodox believers; as a result, sectarians were free to travel to the steppe. As one priest complained,

> In the resettlement stream pouring into the boundaries of the diocese, there are a great number of ready, radical sectarians, propagating their sect everywhere: along the journey in the carriage, at transfer stations and after settlement in new places. Every year, the resettlement movement grows, increasing the general population of the diocese. At the same time, the number of sectarians increases through migration and there is no possibility to fight against this growth. No one can forbid them from arriving and settling in Siberia. And dissenters clearly understand all the benefits of life here and do not miss using them to their advantage.[49]

State officials discussed the desirability of controlling the type of settler undertaking the journey; however, in reality restrictions based on ethnic or religious background would have been difficult to enforce. The metaphor of infection, used to describe the spread of the Baptist faith, implied that only the isolation of Slavic settlers from those confessing a faith considered heretical by the church could offer a cure.[50] At least some officials in the Resettlement Administration agreed in theory on the desirability of separating sectarians from Orthodox settlers, supporting the position of Governor General Shmit, who wrote to the imperial centre about isolating Baptists from Russian settlers during colonization.[51] However, instituting such a policy, even if desirable, proved difficult: Resettlement Administration officials in Akmolinsk province noted that information on confessional status was not properly collected and that Baptists often misrepresented their religious identity.[52]

As church officials debated and discussed which conditions helped religious dissenters to propagate their faith, they identified the railway as a particular point of vulnerability for the Orthodox Church. As the church soon realized, the railway provided a path from which sectarians could spread their alleged heresy across the empire, from Moscow to Vladivostok.[53] At the Chelyabinsk station, sectarians opened a Bible society to supply settlers passing through with religious literature.[54] Towns with railway stations in Omsk diocese gained a reputation throughout Siberia as being hotbeds of sectarian activity. Clergymen identified three main railway stations – two of which were located in Omsk diocese – as "landmark posts of sectarianism." In these towns, sectarians settled and established well-organized networks where leaders and their supporters worked diligently to propagate their faith.[55] Orthodox missionaries often mentioned visiting villages near the railway line in their activity reports.[56] The Baptist leader Gavriil Mazaev recalled a number of organized and accidental meetings with Orthodox missionaries involving the railway. In one case, he met with an Orthodox missionary in a public meeting close to Petropavlovsk station to discuss differences between Baptist and Orthodox positions on the baptism of children.[57] During the encounter, Mazaev recognized Omsk missionary Dimitrii Nesmeianov, who was accompanied by another priest, as he waited for a night train in a station along the Trans-Siberian. The missionary, the priest, a young woman, and a gentleman joined Mazaev around a table, where they debated religious issues.[58]

Finding reliable statistics for the number of sectarian groups in Omsk diocese is difficult; we know, however, that it was not facing a demographic crisis related to this issue.[59] According to the numbers provided for the Irkutsk missionary congress in 1910, Omsk diocese included a total population of 8,474 sectarians.[60] Statistics for Akmolinsk province specifically provide another window onto the demographic landscape of Omsk diocese. According to the 1913 report of the Akmolinsk governor, Baptists constituted only 0.67 per cent of the population; in fact, the total number of rational sects (groups who relied solely on reason in their interpretation of the Bible) in the province only made up 1.35 per cent. In contrast, Orthodox believers made up 57 per cent of the population, while Muslim believers constituted 38 per cent.[61] Unfortunately, the number of sectarians in Semipalatinsk is not available; nonetheless, in the twilight years of the empire, Muslims still made up the vast majority of the province's population, with Orthodox believers constituting less than one-fourth.[62]

Within Orthodox dioceses across the empire, religious leaders established internal missions dedicated to reclaiming people who had left the Orthodox faith and preventing future apostasies. During the 1899 clergy congress in Omsk diocese, the deputies approved the establishment of two positions dedicated to missionizing the Old Believer population and two positions to stem the spread of sectarian faiths; they also agreed to create a library filled with publications to aid in missionary work. To help cover the cost for the two positions, the congress approved the allocation of money from the sale of candles in the diocese.[63] By 1910, Omsk diocesan officials had requested another missionary position be created. Citing the growth of sectarianism and the expansiveness of the diocese, Bishop Gavriil asked the Holy Synod for the necessary financial support to hire a missionary to work in the province of Semipalatinsk. Calling the request "extremely necessary," Bishop Gavriil emphasized the spread of the Baptist faith in his appeal.[64]

Secular leaders appointed to the region played a discernible role in shaping how the imperial centre viewed the borderlands. In 1910, Governor General Shmit caused a stir in St. Petersburg when he stridently placed the issue of sectarianism in Siberia on the imperial agenda. In his report, Shmit argued that the state must support Orthodoxy in his region and stop the spread of sectarianism perpetuated by the Baptists, Adventists, Shtundists, Molokans, and Mennonites, who preached their faiths among Orthodox settlers. Shmit's experience travelling through this region had convinced him that the Orthodox Church's inadequate resources and its lack of spiritual leadership each contributed to this situation.[65] Shmit emphasized the "unpreparedness" of local priests, who, he claimed, were "often indifferent spectators of the victories of militant Baptists." These priests failed to provide settlers with a sense of comfort, turning them into easy prey for Baptist ministers who spoke the language of the village and attacked the Orthodox faith convincingly and clearly.[66]

According to Shmit, the state's new acceptance of freedom of conscience only served to weaken Russia's imperial presence in the region. As he made clear in his report, Shmit believed that the strength of the Russian state and of its imperial efforts was directly tied to the health of Russian Orthodoxy in the empire. As he wrote, "so long as the Russian *muzhik* [peasant] has not lost his Orthodoxy, Russia will remain strong and powerful, but with its loss, the dangerous cosmopolitanism, which the enemies of our motherland so energetically sow, will take root."[67] He described settlers as being awash in a world of heresy, of Kazakhs, Tatars, and sectarians. In this dangerous environment, Russian peasants needed the support of the state.[68]

Having read Shmit's report in horror, Tsar Nicholas II mobilized the imperial bureaucracy to provide answers to this crisis.[69] Under Stolypin's initiative, collegiate councillor Aleksandr Kologrivov from the Ministry of Internal Affairs was sent to assess Shmit's claims about the state of the Russian Orthodox faith in Siberia. Expanding on many of the themes raised by Shmit, Kologrivov shared the same perspective that sectarianism was not purely a religious matter, but rather an issue of national importance. Although Kologrivov acknowledged that many Russians who converted were seeking to better themselves spiritually, he argued that it was not possible for these peasants to keep their nationality (their "Russian soul") and reject Orthodoxy. According to Kologrivov, as these peasants deepened their commitment to their new faith, they showed an "indifference to their homeland and the protection of its interests." With the loss of their nationality, they became more susceptible to anti-militaristic views; they even started to adopt a German accent as they showed belligerence toward church officials and their own Orthodox neighbours. This should cause the state concern in Siberia, he argued, because much of Akmolinsk and Semipalatinsk provinces had been infected by Baptists. And the number of adherents would only increase with the continuation of colonization.[70]

Kologrivov admitted that problems existed among local religious and secular officials. While there were a number of bright lights within the clerical ranks, in general, these men were not of the highest quality. As sectarians appeared within their parishes, these priests hesitated, not knowing how to react and unable to conduct even the most basic conversations about the Orthodox faith with the apostates. Kologrivov acknowledged that the state had a role to perform in saving Omsk diocese from the clutches of sectarianism; yet, secular authorities had failed to curtail sectarians' illegal activities. The leaders of the sectarian movement, particularly Mazaev, had to be stopped, especially since he acted as if the laws of the empire did not matter – a stance that only served to embolden his followers. If Mazaev continued to engage in illegal practices, Kologrivov argued, he should be expelled from the region.[71] In response to complaints from the clergy that sectarians committed crimes without receiving any sort of reprimand – infractions that ranged from holding unauthorized prayer meetings to blaspheming the Orthodox faith – Kologrivov proposed that the police be better educated to address these issues. They should be supplied with instructions related to sectarianism and encouraged to legally pursue those who attacked the Orthodox Church.[72]

After the 1905 revolution resulted in the possibility of legally leaving the Orthodox Church, official conversion from Orthodoxy to other faiths increased in Omsk diocese, thereby intensifying official fears associated with resettlement and the growth of faiths considered dangerous in the region. In the district of Pavlodar, a village of 259 people petitioned the Semipalatinsk governor for permission to become Baptists. Bishop Vladimir reported that parishioners stubbornly refused to listen to the admonitions of the local priest.[73] This particular village belonged to a parish with a population of over 3,000 settlers, nearly half of whom belonged to faiths considered sectarian by the Orthodox Church.[74]

The province of Akmolinsk experienced a similar exodus from the Orthodox Church. According to the provincial governor, 432 people petitioned to leave the Orthodox faith in 1913; this number represented a decrease from the year before, when 1,218 people petitioned to leave the Orthodox Church, with 1,193 asking to join the Baptist faith.[75] This information raised enough concern within the imperial bureaucracy that after landing on the desks of the Department of Spiritual Affairs, the chief procurator, and the Holy Synod, the bishop of Omsk was invited to provide an explanation.[76] Bishop Vladimir responded defensively to St. Petersburg, insisting that he had kept the Holy Synod well informed of the growth of sectarianism in the diocese.[77] He offered the Holy Synod a litany of explanations for the current situation, including a lack of parishes, an insufficient number of missionaries, poorly trained priests, and interference from Vostorgov. Bishop Vladimir identified the priests trained in Vostorgov's Pastoral Courses in Moscow as one of the main causes of the spread of sectarianism. These men, he argued, possessed such negative personal traits that they pushed Orthodox believers into the arms of sectarian preachers.[78] New converts to the Baptist faith, not surprisingly, disagreed with Bishop Vladimir, instead citing the Baptist interpretation of biblical scripture as an important motivation for their decision to leave the Orthodox Church.[79]

Overlapping Missions

In 1910, the same year that Governor General Shmit raised the alarm in St. Petersburg over the sectarian situation in Omsk diocese, the Russian Orthodox Church held two major congresses focusing on missionary activities: the Kazan congress in June and the Irkutsk congress in July.[80] Three representatives from Omsk diocese joined over two hundred attendees in Kazan to participate in discussions on missionary work among various *inorodtsy* groups, including the translation of religious works into indigenous languages, the opening of schools for the indigenous populations, publications directed at converting Muslims, and other themes related to building missions and Orthodox parishes.[81]

The Kazan congress, which focused primarily on the external mission, provided Omsk representatives with an opportunity to explore proselytizing to Muslims in the broader reaches of the empire, including in such places as Turkestan, Tobol'sk, and the Kazakh steppe. Bishop Gavriil chaired one session focused on missioning to Muslims in these areas. During this session, the deputy head of the Kazakh mission, a monk by the name of Feodorit, gave a presentation on how best to support this enterprise in Omsk, recommending land allotments for the missions and access to loans from the state for establishing farms, which, he proposed, would encourage the Kazakhs to adopt a sedentary way of life. Feodorit also contributed an article to the *Omsk Diocesan News* exploring the lessons learned from the congress. He emphasized the dangers to the empire posed by Islam and reiterated claims that Muslims showed signs of rejecting Russian state authority, especially through the promotion of pan-Islamic thought, whose proponents aspired to create their own state within the empire.[82] Notably, the majority of the article addressed the broader issue of Islam without drawing direct lessons or comparisons to the specific situation in Omsk diocese.

In contrast to the Kazan congress, the event in Irkutsk was smaller, with only ninety-five participants, the majority of whom were from the host diocese of Irkutsk. This did not, however, stop the event from receiving substantial coverage in the *Omsk Diocesan News*. The congress highlighted issues related to the internal and external missions, exploring questions relevant to the church's future work in Siberia, Japan, China, and Korea.[83] Although this congress considered the issue of external missions in Siberia and beyond the boundaries of the Russian Empire, the topic of combatting sectarian and schismatic groups occupied an important place on the agenda.[84] A report given at the conference by Nesmeianov, Omsk's diocesan missionary, provided a detailed explanation of the conditions in Siberian dioceses that contributed to the growth of sectarianism. He ranked the dioceses of Omsk and Blagoveshchensk as sectarian hotspots in the region. Nesmeianov also proposed a more substantial institutional framework to reinforce missionary work, supporting the establishment of a seminary in Omsk and a specialized missionary theological academy in the empire. To address the issue of colonization, he proposed asking the Holy Synod to appoint missionary priests at strategic points along settler migration routes to provide spiritual guidance. Omsk diocese also needed to establish more parish missionary circles to encourage the participation of the laity. Finally, settler parishes in danger of sectarianism should receive priority consideration in the building of new churches and schools.[85]

Omsk clergymen not only participated in these congresses to address missionary work in the diocese, they also proposed its administrative reorganization. In 1910, Bishop Gavriil proposed the appointment of a vicar bishop of Semipalatinsk. He offered the Holy Synod a laundry list of reasons to justify the formation of this position. According to the bishop, the distance and inconvenience of transportation routes between the diocesan capital and Semipalatinsk necessitated such an appointment.[86] Bishop Gavriil also claimed that the absence of religious leadership in the region posed a security risk, as the border between Semipalatinsk and China had served as the historical "window" through which the Mongols entered and conquered Central and Western Asia. Finally, he argued that the local Kazakh population offered a fertile field for missionary work.[87]

The growth of the settler population in the province of Semipalatinsk constituted another reason for creating the position. Bishop Gavriil argued that the multiplying number of Baptists and Old Believers among the settler population required vigilance, which only the presence of a bishop could provide.[88] Governor Troinitskii agreed with Gavriil that his province suffered from pastoral neglect; he complained that parishes existed without any personal oversight from the bishop. In those few instances when the bishop bestowed his attention on the region, Troinitskii lamented the fact that he travelled down the Irtysh in a steamship, thereby bypassing the villagers who needed their faith strengthened; a vicar bishopric based in Semipalatinsk would allow the bishop to travel extensively and inspire Orthodox settlers to remain steadfast in the face of sectarianism.[89]

By the end of 1911, under the leadership of Bishop Vladimir, the Holy Synod created the bishopric of Semipalatinsk and promoted the head of the Kazakh mission, Kiprian (Komarovskii), to the position.[90] From the beginning of his tenure as bishop, Kiprian was expected to not only provide leadership to the Kazakh missionary posts in the diocese, but also support the pastoral care of new settlers dispersed across the province.[91] On one such trip to offer spiritual guidance to settlers, Bishop Kiprian celebrated the liturgy in the village of Lapteva-Loga, established by starving peasants fleeing the 1891–2 famine in European Russia.[92] These villagers had waited seven long years for the honour of hosting a bishop.[93] The prospect of Bishop Kiprian performing a service generated excitement among parishioners, and, according to the local priest, approximately two thousand people arrived at the church, many of whom the priest had not seen for a number of years.

From the start of resettlement, missionaries working with the Kazakh population struggled to balance their duties with Russian settlers' growing demands for religious rites and rituals.[94] As the head of the mission – this was before his appointment as the bishop of Semipalatinsk – Kiprian had complained to the diocesan authorities that the Orthodox settlers establishing villages near missionary posts in the province complicated missionaries' engagement with the Kazakh population. Instead of focusing on the spiritual development of the new converts, these missionaries were forced to dedicate time and effort to supporting the religious life of settlers.[95] For instance, the missionary at the Atbasar post, Father Kyshimov, asked for permission to hold an annual icon procession through the local Orthodox villages. The Omsk diocesan consistory refused on the grounds that the chief purpose of the missionary position was to preach among the indigenous population.[96] This tension intensified throughout the early twentieth century as the number of Orthodox villages grew in size.

After his appointment to the position of vicar bishop of Semipalatinsk, Kiprian continued to emphasize what he perceived as the negative effects on missionary work brought about by the presence of settlers.[97] Three mission stations, in particular, suffered because of the settlement of peasants in their vicinity. Many of the settlers near these stations arrived from Ukrainian-speaking provinces – the "holy" provinces, as Kiprian mockingly referred to them. According to Kiprian, they showed a surprising ignorance of the Orthodox faith, which made it difficult for missionaries to focus their attention on potential Kazakh converts.[98]

The presence of sectarians complicated this issue further. Missionaries were trained to address spiritual issues among the Kazakh people; they were not prepared to defend their converts against other Christian faiths. The spread of non-Orthodox Christian faiths near missionary posts not only affected settlers; missionaries argued that it harmed their mandate as newly baptized Kazakhs struggled to understand how "the Russians" could practise so many different faiths. Sectarians were also potential missionary competitors for the hearts of the Kazakhs. In some cases, Kazakh converts to Orthodoxy decided to leave the faith and join one of the sectarian groups.[99] The prospect of losing new converts to a competing Christian faith, in addition to the demands that Russian settlers placed on Orthodox missionaries, added another layer of complexity to the Kazakh mission and the work of the bishop. Kiprian advocated for the assignment of priests with adequate training to address the issue of sectarianism among Russian peasants.[100]

While promoting the idea of a bishopric in Semipalatinsk, Bishop Vladimir pitched to the Holy Synod the idea of establishing a new bishop position for the province of Akmolinsk. Although the Holy Synod did not agree to this position initially, Bishop Vladimir continued to petition both the Holy Synod and the chief procurator, highlighting his fears of the spread of sectarianism in the diocese and the important role that a new vicar bishop could perform in strengthening Orthodoxy, thereby complementing the role of missionary to the Muslim population previously assigned to the bishop in Semipalatinsk.[101]

This argument must have resonated with the Holy Synod as it agreed to establish a second vicar bishopric in 1913.[102] Assigned with the task of providing leadership and inspiring missionary work in the diocese, the bishop of Akmolinsk focused on the internal mission aimed at sectarians and schismatics.[103] Mefodii (Krasnoperov) travelled from Ufa, where he served as rector of the local seminary, to the chambers of the Holy Synod in St. Petersburg to receive his new assignment. Ten days after Mefodii's consecration at the Alexander Nevsky Lavra, he arrived in Omsk, which initially served as the base of his bishopric. The following year, the position was relocated to the town of Petropavlovsk, which had many mosques, but more importantly for Omsk diocesan officials, it also served as a base for the work of Baptist leader Mazaev.

This strong focus on an anti-sectarian mandate underscored the vision of Akmolinsk as an already Christianized space. Even though nearly half a million Kazakhs still inhabited the province, by 1914 colonization had conferred on Orthodoxy a demographic advantage over other faiths.[104] Bishop Mefodii's anti-sectarian mandate was on full display as he accompanied an icon of St. Nicholas the Miracle Worker on a month-long, five-hundred-kilometre procession. Travelling from Petropavlovsk to Akmolinsk in 1915, the procession sought to provide religious comfort to the province, including to the settler communities that had established homes in the region. Tsar Nicholas II added an element of imperial grandeur to the entire proceeding by gifting the icon to the Alexander Nevsky Church in Akmolinsk.[105] Informed about the procession, Nicholas II sent a telegram asking for prayers for his family.[106]

Descriptions of this trip through the villages of the Kazakh steppe read like a tour of heresy, as the bishop encountered Baptists, Khlysty (a mystical sect), Mormons, and other groups deemed pernicious by the Orthodox Church living among Orthodox believers. Even as the procession moved through districts with a Kazakh population, only obscure references – such as the bishop's entourage stopping to rest from the tyrannical sun in a yurt, a traditional Kazakh home – hinted at that group's presence. As the procession weaved its way through the province, the bishop received an assortment of reactions. In one village, the resident Baptists left for the fields before the arrival of the icon; in another, the Khlysty stayed to chat in the prayer house with the bishop on issues of faith.[107] According to Bishop Mefodii, living among these groups exposed Russian Orthodox settlers to abhorrent practices. As the procession moved through one particular churchless village, isolated on the treeless steppe, the bishop claimed to have witnessed how the presence of the Khlysty had caused the disintegration of moral and religious life in this settler parish.[108]

Religious Wars

This emphasis on sectarianism is not surprising as diocesan officials saw Siberian villages as religious battlegrounds between Orthodoxy and heresy. They feared that Baptists had the sinister goal of destroying

Orthodoxy in Siberia.[109] According to Omsk diocesan missionary Nesmeianov, Mazaev had proudly declared his intent to conquer Siberia like Ermak, who led the first conquest of the region, only this time the victory would be religious. Many Orthodox clergymen repeatedly referenced this remark, illustrating how deeply they perceived the Baptists as usurping a role that the Orthodox Church had claimed for itself.[110] For the Baptists, missionary work among their neighbours constituted an important part of their calling – that is, to spread the good news of the true path to salvation.[111] Even though proselytism among Orthodox believers continued to be illegal, Baptists evangelized their neighbours while itinerant preachers travelled throughout Siberia using any available platform to spread their version of God's word. This activism led the Omsk clergymen to label the Baptist faith as "one of the most serious enemies of Orthodoxy within Omsk diocese."[112]

In addition to proselytizing, after 1905 the Siberian Baptists, with help from their co-religionists in European Russia, moved quickly to develop a local institutional framework for their faith community. In 1906, they opened a branch of the Union of Russian Baptists in Siberia, and the following year they built a large brick church along the banks of the Om River in Omsk, thereby establishing the ultimate symbol of the community's strength and permanency in the administrative centre of western Siberia.[113] As Mazaev himself noted, the prayer house served the Baptist community not only in Omsk, but in all of Siberia.[114] As such, it stood as a physical and spiritual affront to the Orthodox Church by offering Baptists a legitimate space to meet and by drawing curious Orthodox believers through its doors to hear fiery preaching and joyful singing.[115] The Baptists regularly held daytime and evening meetings in this church at which, according to Orthodox clergymen, they zealously preached against Orthodox rites and practices.[116] In the eyes of Orthodox clergymen, blame for the popularity of the Omsk Baptist church resided in the new laws pertaining to religious freedom, which allowed the Baptists to legally purchase the property and hold church services. Even more infuriating must have been the Baptists' dream of opening their own seminary in Omsk; Orthodox writers asserted that the Baptists easily could raise the funds to build such a facility.[117] In contrast, the clergy in Omsk diocese were still unsuccessful in pleading their case to St. Petersburg for financial support to build an Orthodox seminary.

The politicization of religious identity intensified during the First World War. Missionaries in Omsk diocese stridently portrayed Russians who converted to the Baptist faith as having adopted both a political and cultural allegiance to Germany. Nesmeianov encapsulated this view as he described the reactions of Baptists who sent their children off to the front:

> You did not hear the crying typical among simple Orthodox people. On the contrary, they were joyful in a real sense. Why were the Baptists happy? Honoured to fight the enemy? Nothing of the kind – they thirst for the destruction of Russia by Germany and think this hour has come.[118]

This type of portrayal of the Baptists was common in Omsk diocese during the war. The strong anti-German rhetoric linked to the Baptists reflected a fear that their presence in Siberia represented the Germanization of the region.

Although Omsk clergymen had identified the Baptists as a potential source of unrest during the war, it was the Muslim population that actually revolted in Central Asia. In 1916, Nicholas II decided to conscript this population into labour battalions, even though it had been exempted from military service. By June of that year, the governor general of the steppe had informed local Muslims that conscription would begin soon. While unrest and resistance were stronger in Turkestan, Kazakhs in the provinces of Akmolinsk and Semipalatinsk organized and led a brief insurgency against Russian rule. (Russian forces re-established control over these provinces by the end of October.) While ostensibly about conscription, some scholars have argued that the unrest was in fact fuelled by concerns over religious freedom and the disruption brought about by colonization.[119] In fact, during the uprising, the rumour that the tsarist regime had decided to forcibly convert Muslims to Christianity gained traction in the province of Semipalatinsk.[120] This rumour speaks to the hostility that Kazakhs felt was being projected at their faith by the imperial regime, particularly its shift toward less tolerant religious policies.

As waves of settlers arrived in Siberia, state and church officials considered Orthodoxy a necessary stronghold to secure the imperial regime's cultural and political interests in the region against Islam and sectarianism. The establishment of this stronghold, however, was not without its challenges. Even as Orthodox clergymen and secular authorities celebrated the transformation of this land of Islam into a bastion of Orthodoxy, the presence of sectarian groups complicated their self-proclaimed victory. While it could be argued that Baptists helped to draw the attention of secular and religious authorities away from a focus on Islam on the steppe, the rejection of Russian culture and nationality associated with the presence of this Christian sect encouraged the further politicization of religious identity in the region. This emerged as a key issue in the colonizing process, the contours of which mirrored the larger anxieties involved in this daunting imperial enterprise.

Conclusion

After the abdication of Tsar Nicholas II on 2 March 1917 (as per the Old Style calendar), representatives of both church and state continued to pursue the goal of creating settler parishes. Across the empire, the Holy Trinity Day collection took place later that year, contributing money to the Emperor Alexander III Fund for building religious life in Siberia. Although Nicholas II performed a key role in initiating the fund, and he frequently expressed his support for its work, he had little involvement in its operations once it moved into the hands of the Holy Synod and the Resettlement Administration. His abdication, therefore, did not jeopardize the program and plans for the building of churches across Siberia continued to be drawn up under the Provisional Government.

In general, the church quickly reconciled itself to a post-tsarist Russia, which showed that the church's position in the empire was not contingent on the monarchy. Indeed, church officials spent little time mourning the tsar's fall from power and instead focused their attention on the election of the first patriarch since the reign of Peter the Great. The reaction of Omsk Bishop Sil'vestr (Ol'shevskii) illustrates how quickly the bishops adapted to these new circumstances. In a speech after the abdication, Sil'vestr focused mainly on the suffering of the Russian people caused by the current environment of war and displacement. He emphasized that Nicholas's decision freed him from his obligations to the Russian people, just as it freed the Russian people from their oath to him: now everyone had the responsibility of serving the new government.[1] Similar scenes unfolded in dioceses across the country, as bishops informed parishioners of their new allegiances and life continued with only a few tears shed over the end of the Romanovs' three-hundred-year reign.

The absence of tears reflected, in part, the strong relationship that had developed between the church and state ministries during the last years of the tsarist period. The colonization of Siberia, in retrospect, proved to be a fruitful venue for such church-state cooperation. The church and the state both recognized the importance of supporting Orthodox life in settler communities, and they collaborated to help settlers access the building blocks of parish life: churches, schools, and clergy. Through this collaboration, they showed a willingness to use religion as a tool for bringing about the cultural transformation of Siberia, which in turn would allow for the formation of stable agricultural communities and ultimately the region's integration into the empire.

Settlers reaped the benefits of this system. The partnership between church and state provided funds and materials to those who could not afford the added cost of church building as they worked to establish farms in their new homeland. Gratitude, however, does not fully describe the reaction of settlers, many of whom understood this type of financial support as the responsibility of the state. Not only did this expectation demonstrate that peasants assumed that they would have access to the same religious life they had left behind in European Russia, it also indicates that they understood the value of their contribution to the state's work. While the evidence shows that settlers did not adopt a rhetoric of a civilizing mission as part of their migration to Siberia, their petitions reveal that the experience of colonization encouraged them to adopt a "settler" identity, even decades after they had migrated. This seems to indicate some self-awareness of their special status in the region, a status that was only further nurtured through initiatives like the Emperor Alexander III Fund.

The significance of this fund, however, was not confined to settlers. The fundraising efforts undertaken by church and state officials welcomed Orthodox believers to donate their money and send their prayers for the Orthodox settlers fulfilling God's will. By presenting a compelling story about the role of duty and sacrifice in planting Orthodoxy in the region, these officials encouraged Orthodox believers to participate in the building of the empire. While in comparison to other European imperial projects, the formation of a Russian Orthodox imperial identity was still in its infancy, the groundwork had nonetheless been laid for the future growth of this category of belonging.

The colonization of Siberia also offered fertile ground for people like Ioann Vostorgov to nurture their nationalistic vision of Russia's destiny in Siberia. In the western half of the empire, the Russian Orthodox Church encountered constant reminders, in the form of Catholic and Protestant competitors, of its struggle to establish dominance. In Siberia, it was possible for the Russian Orthodox Church to aspire to global significance by completing the work of the apostles in the East.

Recruited into state-church collaboration in Siberia, Vostorgov could do more than simply dream as he worked diligently to help Russia fulfil its destiny, publicizing his exploits along the way.

And yet, despite the strong sense of hope and purpose attached to colonization, it was not a straightforward process. The hardships of the pioneering life often pushed settlers to the brink of their physical, mental, and emotional capacities. Similar to widespread urbanization, which was also unfolding in the empire at this time, colonization caused disruption in the lives of settlers. As they struggled to rebuild their traditional modes of living in this new environment, settlers found themselves engaging in debates over the definition of their religious traditions and the "correct" version of Orthodoxy. Some church officials viewed this as a problem that would be resolved with time; however, the presence of a Ukrainianized version of Orthodoxy in the region surrounding the city of Pavlodar to this day raises questions about that assumption.[2]

Disputes over the correct version of Orthodoxy were not confined to settlers. While Vostorgov, along with Omsk clergymen, framed their dispute as a conflict between Siberian priests and those in European Russia, in reality, the animosity was much more complex. Vostorgov's Pastoral Courses facilitated the further opening of the clerical estate, and Omsk clergymen struggled to find unity in response to the growing diversity of social backgrounds among their ranks. Conflicts among the clergy in Omsk diocese over the inclusion of priests trained under Vostorgov's tutelage offer a window into the ways in which colonization sped up the disruption of Russian social structures, in this case by softening the boundaries of the clerical estate, which arguably encouraged the formation of a regional clerical identity.

Christian pluralism among the Slavic population, which emerged as one of the key issues of colonization, in many respects summarized the anxieties involved in such a daunting enterprise. Russian Baptists, Molokans, Old Believers, and many other religious groups moved with Russian Orthodox settlers to the Kazakh steppe, where they joined approximately a million Muslims. The Russian state dreamed that colonization would be a coordinated and well-organized effort showcasing the power and control of the Russian Empire and contributing to its future strength. As Orthodox clergymen and secular authorities celebrated the transformation of this land of Islam into a bastion of Orthodoxy through colonization, the appearance of sectarian groups complicated this vision. Many secular and religious actors interpreted such a development as a threat to the stability and integration of the imperial periphery. Indeed, even with the presence of a million

Muslims, the issue of sectarianism reduced fears about Islam while encouraging panic over the alleged Germanization of the region through the spread of the Baptist faith.

All of these factors together seem to indicate that at the beginning of the twentieth century, the role of Orthodoxy, often viewed as a pillar of Russian national identity, was less stable than previously imagined. This instability was not derived from the ethnic and religious pluralism engendered by the empire's many minority groups; rather it grew from within the core of the "Russian nation." In Siberia, colonization forced Orthodox settlers and clergy to define the meaning of Orthodoxy, a process that in turn highlighted fractures within the community. Despite the tensions thus illuminated, imperial authorities and Russian Orthodox officials still forged ahead with the task of promoting Orthodoxy as a synonym for Russianness until the collapse of the empire.

Ultimately, it is difficult to determine the legacy of the Russian state's attempts to recreate the religious conditions of European Russia among Orthodox settlers in Siberia. Omsk diocese had just over twenty years to pursue this imperial project in a region continually transformed by the next batch of settlers streaming over the Ural Mountains. With the takeover of power by the Bolsheviks, this version of colonization effectively ended. While under the new regime, Soviet technocrats – some of whom had formerly been employed in the tsarist Resettlement Administration – continued their efforts to integrate Siberia into the larger Russian body politic, Orthodoxy would no longer perform an official role in such work under this self-proclaimed atheist state.[3]

Notes

Introduction

1 Petr A. Stolypin and Aleksandr V. Krivoshein, *Poezdka v Sibir' i povolzh'e: zapiska P.A. Stolypina i A.V. Krivosheina* (St. Petersburg: Tip. A.S. Suvorina, 1911), 7.

2 For more on priests like Ornatskii, see Jennifer Hedda, *His Kingdom Come: Orthodox Pastorship and Social Activism in Revolutionary Russia* (DeKalb: Northern Illinois University Press, 2008).

3 Filosof Ornatskii, "Pouchenie pred sborom na postroenie tservkei i shkol dlia pereselentsev Sibirskikh eparkhii (vo dni Sv.Troitsy i Pokrova Presviatyia Bogoroditsy," *TV* 17 (1915): iii–iv.

4 Yuri Slezkine, "Introduction," in *Between Heaven and Hell: The Myth of Siberia in Russian Culture*, ed. Galya Diment and Yuri Slezkine (New York: Palgrave Macmillan, 1993), 2.

5 Stolypin and Krivoshein, *Poezdka v Sibir'*, 43.

6 A. Kulomzin, *Vsepoddannieishii otchet stats-sekretaria Kulomzina po poezdke v Sibir' dlia oznakomleniia s polozheniem pereselencheskogo dela* (St. Petersburg: Gos. tip., 1896), 122.

7 See, for instance, David Rainbow, "Siberian Patriots: Participatory Autocracy and the Cohesion of the Russian Imperial State, 1858–1920" (PhD diss., New York University, 2013), and Julia Fein, "Cultural Curators and Provincial Publics: Local Museums and Social Change in Siberia, 1887–1941" (PhD diss., University of Chicago, 2012).

8 W. Bruce Lincoln, *The Conquest of a Continent: Siberia and the Russians* (Ithaca, NY: Cornell University Press, 2007); Alan Wood, *Russia's Frozen Frontier: A History of Siberia and the Russian Far East 1581–1991* (New York: Bloomsbury Academic, 2011); James Forsyth, *A History of the Peoples of Siberia: Russia's North Asian Colony, 1581–1990* (Cambridge: Cambridge University Press, 2000); Janet M. Hartley, *Siberia: A History of the People* (New Haven, CT: Yale University Press, 2014).

9   See, for instance, Mark Bassin, "Inventing Siberia: Visions of the Russian
    East in the Early Nineteenth Century," *American Historical Review* 96, no. 3
    (June 1991): 763; Claudia Weiss, "Representing the Empire: The Meaning
    of Siberia for Russian Imperial Identity," *Nationalities Papers* 35, no. 3
    (July 2007): 439–56; Erika Monahan, *The Merchants of Siberia: Trade in Early
    Modern Eurasia* (Ithaca, NY: Cornell University Press, 2016), 359–63.

10 Mark Bassin, *Imperial Visions: Nationalist Imagination and Geographical
    Expansion in the Russian Far East, 1840–1865* (Cambridge: Cambridge
    University Press, 1999), 45–8; Valerie A. Kivelson, *Cartographies of
    Tsardom: The Land and Its Meanings in Seventeenth-Century Russia* (Ithaca,
    NY: Cornell University Press, 2006), 149.

11 On the settler movement as a global process, see Dirk Hoerder, *Cultures
    in Contact: World Migrations in the Second Millennium* (Durham, NC: Duke
    University Press, 2002). For specific case studies showing the significance
    of comparative work, especially between Siberia and North America, see
    Steven Sabol, "Comparing American and Russian Internal Colonization:
    The 'Touch of Civilisation' on the Sioux and Kazakhs," *Western Historical
    Quarterly* 43, no. 1 (Spring 2012): 29–51, and Kate Brown, "Gridded Lives:
    Why Kazakhstan and Montana are Nearly the Same Place," *American
    Historical Review* 106, no.1 (2001): 14–48.

12 Valerie Ann Kivelson and Ronald Grigor Suny, *Russia's Empires* (New
    York: Oxford University Press, 2017), 227–51.

13 James Belich, *Replenishing the Earth: The Settler Revolution and the Rise of
    the Anglo-World, 1783–1939* (Oxford: Oxford University Press, 2009), 292.

14 Lorenzo Veracini, *Settler Colonialism: A Theoretical Overview* (New York:
    Palgrave Macmillan, 2010), 3. Also see Lorenzo Veracini, "Introducing
    Settler Colonial Studies," *Settler Colonial Studies* 1, no. 1 (2011): 1–12;
    Tracey Banivanua-Mar and Penelope Edmonds, eds., *Making Settler
    Colonial Space: Perspectives on Race, Place and Identity* (New York: Palgrave
    Macmillan, 2010), 10.

15 Donald W. Treadgold, *The Great Siberian Migration* (Princeton, NJ:
    Princeton University Press, 1957), 32. This number does not include
    Central Asia, where part of Omsk diocese was located.

16 See, for example, Robert D. Crews, *For Prophet and Tsar: Islam and Empire in
    Russia and Central Asia* (Cambridge, MA: Harvard University Press, 2009);
    Jeff Sahadeo, *Russian Colonial Society in Tashkent: 1865–1923* (Bloomington:
    Indiana University Press, 2007); Andreas Kappeler, *The Russian Empire:
    A Multiethnic History*, trans. Alfred Clayton (Harlow, UK: Longman, 2001).

17 Contemporary literature often assigns Akmolinsk and Semipalatinsk
    to the geographical category of Central Asia. See Richard A. Pierce,
    Russian Central Asia, 1867–1917: A Study in Colonial Rule (Berkeley:
    University of California Press, 1960); S.N. Abashin, D. Iu Arapov, and

N.E. Bekmakhanova, eds., *Tsentral'naia Aziia v sostave rossiiskoi imperii* (Moscow: Novoe literaturnoe obozrenie, 2008); and L. Dameshek and A. Remnev, *Sibir' v sostave rossiiskoi imperii* (Moscow: Novoe literaturnoe obozrenie, 2007). This issue becomes especially important in the discussion of whether Siberia and Central Asia should be considered a frontier or a colony. See "Siberia: Colony and Frontier," *Kritika: Explorations in Russian and Eurasian History* 14, no. 1 (Winter 2013): 1–4; Daniel R. Brower, *Turkestan and the Fate of the Russian Empire* (London: Routledge Curzon, 2003), 126–51.

18 For more on the Kazakhs and the settlement of the Kazakh steppe, see Martha Brill Olcott, *The Kazakhs* (Stanford, CA: Hoover Institution Press, 1987); Virginia Martin, *Law and Custom in the Steppe: The Kazakhs of the Middle Horde and Russian Colonialism in the Nineteenth Century* (Richmond, UK: Routledge Curzon, 2001); George J. Demko, *The Russian Colonization of Kazakhstan, 1896–1916* (Bloomington: Indiana University, 1969); Ian W. Campbell, *Knowledge and the Ends of Empire: Kazak Intermediaries and Russian Rule on the Steppe, 1731–1917* (Ithaca, NY: Cornell University Press, 2017).

19 For more on the right of Kazakhs to rent their land, see Olcott, *The Kazakhs*, 88. For more on the Cossacks in Siberia, see Christoph Witzenrath, *Cossacks and the Russian Empire, 1598–1725: Manipulation, Rebellion and Expansion into Siberia* (New York: Routledge, 2007). For the more on the system of land allocation, see Alberto Masoero, "Layers of Property in the Tsar's Settlement Colony: Projects of Land Privatization in Siberia in the Late Nineteenth Century," *Central Asian Survey* 29, no. 1 (March 2010): 9–32, and Alberto Masoero, "Territorial Colonization in Late Imperial Russia," *Kritika: Explorations in Russian & Eurasian History* 14, no. 1 (Winter 2013): 59–91.

20 *Vsepoddanneishii otchet ober-prokurora sviateishego sinoda za 1896–1897gody* (St. Petersburg, 1899), 14, and *Vsepoddanneishii otchet ober-prokurora sviateishego sinoda za 1914* (St. Petersburg, 1916), 26.

21 Matthew P. Romaniello, *The Elusive Empire: Kazan and the Creation of Russia, 1552–1671* (Madison: University of Wisconsin Press, 2012); Kivelson, *Cartographies of Tsardom*; Isolde Thyrêt, "Creating a Religious Community in Siberia The Cultural Politics of Archbishop Nektarii of Tobol'sk," *Canadian-American Slavic Studies* 51, no. 1 (2017): 87–104; and Michael Khodarkovsky, *Russia's Steppe Frontier: The Making Of a Colonial Empire, 1500–1800* (Bloomington: Indiana University Press, 2005).

22 See, for example, Paul Werth, *At the Margins of Orthodoxy: Mission, Governance, and Confessional Politics in Russia's Volga-Kama Region, 1827–1905* (Ithaca, NY: Cornell University Press, 2002); Nicholas B. Breyfogle, *Heretics and Colonizers: Forging Russia's Empire in the South Caucasus* (Ithaca, NY: Cornell University Press, 2005); Robert P. Geraci

and Michael Khodarkovsky, eds., *Of Religion and Empire: Missions, Conversion, and Tolerance in Tsarist Russia* (Ithaca, NY: Cornell University Press, 2001); M. Dolbilov, *Russkii krai chuzhaia vera: Etnokonfessional'naia politika imperii v Litve i Belorussii pri Aleksandre II* (Moscow: Novoe literaturnoe obozrenie, 2010).

23 Some exceptions include: Robert Geraci, "Going Abroad or Going to Russia? Orthodox Missionaries in the Kazakh Steppe, 1881–1917," in *Of Religion and Empire: Missions, Conversion, and Tolerance in Tsarist Russia*, ed. Robert Geraci and Michael Khordarkovsky (Ithaca, NY: Cornell University Press, 2001), 274–310; Mara Kozelsky, *Christianizing Crimea: Shaping Sacred Space in the Russian Empire and Beyond* (DeKalb: Northern Illinois University Press, 2010); Iu. A. Lysenko, "Tserkovnoe stroitel'stvo v stepnom krae," *Mezhdunarodnyi imidzh Rossii*, 9 June 2008, http://image-of-russia.livejournal.com/19208.html.

24 For a short history of the opening of Yakutsk diocese, see Vladislav Soldatenko, "The Formation of the Yakutsk Eparchy," *Greek Orthodox Theological Review* 44, no. 1 (January 1999): 661–5. I did not include the diocese opened in Alaska in this final count of dioceses in Siberia. For more information on the creation of this diocese, see Ilya Vinkovetsky, "Building a Diocese Overseas: The Orthodox Church in Partnership with the Russian-American Company in Alaska," *Ab Imperio* 3 (July 2010): 152–94.

25 This number was calculated from *Vsepoddanneishii otchet ober-prokurora sviateishego sinoda za 1914 god* (St. Petersburg, 1916), 24–5. It includes the dioceses of Blagoveshchensk, Vladivostok, Ekaterinburg, Enisei, Transbaikal, Irkutsk, Omsk, Orenburg, Tobol'sk, Tomsk, Turkestan, and Yakutsk.

26 See Hilary Carey, *God's Empire: Religion and Colonialism in the British World, c.1801–1908* (New York: Cambridge University Press, 2011).

27 For treatment of the state structures that supported colonization, see Willard Sunderland, "The Ministry of Asiatic Russia: The Colonial Office That Never Was but Might Have Been," *Slavic Review* 69, no. 1 (April 2010): 120–50; Robert Geraci, "On 'Colonial' Forms and Functions," *Slavic Review* 69, no. 1 (Spring 2010): 180–4; Willard Sunderland, *Taming the Wild Field: Colonization and Empire on the Russian Steppe* (Ithaca, NY: Cornell University Press, 2004).

28 Howard Le Couteur, "Anglican High Churchmen and the Expansion of Empire," *Journal of Religious History* 32, no. 2 (June 2008): 213. In some cases, this could also produce a distinct identity among settlers; see Pamela Welch, *Church and Settler in Colonial Zimbabwe: A Study in the History of the Anglican Diocese of Mashonaland/Southern Rhodesia, 1890–1925* (Boston: Brill, 2008), 232.

29 For more on the British case, see Carey, *God's Empire*, xiv.

30 This speaks to the question of how religious diversity influenced definitions of Russianness, asked by Geraci and Khordarkovsky. See Robert P. Geraci and Michael Khodarkovsky, "Introduction," in *Of Religion and Empire: Missions, Conversion, and Tolerance in Tsarist Russia*, ed. Robert P. Geraci and Michael Khordarkovsky (Ithaca, NY: Cornell University Press, 2001), 3.

31 Lewis H. Siegelbaum and Leslie Page Moch, *Broad Is My Native Land: Repertoires and Regimes of Migration in Russia's Twentieth Century* (Ithaca, NY: Cornell University Press, 2014), 39.

32 Michael Pasquier, *Fathers on the Frontier: French Missionaries and the Roman Catholic Priesthood in the United States, 1789–1870* (Oxford: Oxford University Press, 2010), 7.

33 Frances Swyripa, *Storied Landscapes: Ethno-Religious Identity and the Canadian Prairies* (Winnipeg: University of Manitoba Press, 2010).

34 Willard Sunderland and David Moon have explored this issue in most detail. See David Moon, "Peasant Migration and the Settlement of Russia's Frontiers, 1550–1897," *The Historical Journal* 40, no. 4 (December 1997): 859; Willard Sunderland, "Peasants on the Move: State Peasant Resettlement in Imperial Russia, 1805–1830s," *Russian Review* 52, no. 4 (October 1993): 472; Willard Sunderland, "Peasant Pioneering: Russian Peasant Settlers Describe Colonization and the Eastern Frontier, 1880s–1910s," *Journal of Social History* 34, no. 4 (Summer 2001): 895. A recent article by Lewis Siegelbaum explores the role of scouts on the frontier; see "Those Elusive Scouts: Pioneering Peasants and the Russian State, 1870–1950," *Kritika: Explorations in Russian and Eurasian History* 14, no.1 (Winter 2013): 31–58.

35 See Sunderland, "Peasant Pioneering," 909. In general, collections of letters written by peasants describing Siberian life are difficult to find. A few document collections exist that shed light on the lives of peasants in the region as they described it to each other; see Olga Yokoyama, *Russian Peasant Letters: Life and Times of a 19th-Century Family* (Wiesbaden, DE: Harrassowitz, 2010). For a general treatment of biases in letters from peasants, see Sunderland, "Peasant Pioneers," 902–3.

36 The agency shown by settlers during this process is one of the main reasons I have not incorporated the notion of internal colonization. For more on this approach, see Aleksandr Etkind, *Internal Colonization: Russia's Imperial Experience* (Cambridge: Polity Press, 2011).

37 Patrick L. Michelson and Judith Deutsch Kornblatt, eds., *Thinking Orthodox in Modern Russia: Culture, History, Context* (Madison: University of Wisconsin Press, 2014), 3; Mark D. Steinberg and Heather J. Coleman, eds., *Sacred Stories: Religion and Spirituality in Modern Russia* (Bloomington: Indiana University Press, 2007), 12–15.

38 Robert H. Greene, "Bodies in Motion: Steam-Powered Pilgrimages in Late Imperial Russia," *Russian History* 39, no. 1/2 (January 2012): 247–68; Vera Shevzov, "Scripting the Gaze: Liturgy, Homilies and the Kazan Icon of the Mother of God in Late Imperial Russia," in *Sacred Stories: Religion and Spirituality in Modern Russia*, ed. Mark D. Steinberg and Heather J. Coleman (Bloomington: Indiana University Press, 2007), 61–92.

39 Alla Litiagina has argued that while participation in formal displays of worship declined over the second half of the nineteenth century – especially among urban populations – many other forms of personal and informal religiosity remained in Siberia. See "Uroven' religioznosti naseleniia zapadnoi Sibiri (1861–1917)," *Voprosy istorii* 9 (2006): 124.

1. A Settler Diocese

1 Allen J. Frank and M.G. Gosmanov, eds., *Materials for the Islamic History of Semipalatinsk: Two Manuscripts by Aḥmad-Walī al-Qazānī and Qurbān'alī Khālidī* (Berlin: Das Arabische Buch, 2001), 1.

2 George Kennan, *Siberia and the Exile System*, vol. 1 (New York: Century Co., 1891), 140.

3 Virginia Martin, *Law and Custom in the Steppe: The Kazakhs of the Middle Horde and Russian Colonialism in the Nineteenth Century* (Richmond, UK: Routledge Curzon, 2001), 61.

4 Allen J. Frank, *Muslim Religious Institutions in Imperial Russia: The Islamic World of Novouzensk District and the Kazakh Inner Horde, 1780–1910* (Leiden, NL: Brill, 2001), 87.

5 The state would revisit these allotments to the Cossacks during the nineteenth century. See George J. Demko, *The Russian Colonization of Kazakhstan, 1896–1916* (Bloomington: Indiana University Press, 1969), 44.

6 For more on colonization and Siberia, see Eva-Maria Stolberg, *Sibirien: Russlands "Wilder Osten": Mythos und soziale Realität im 19. und 20. Jahrhundert* (Stuttgart, DE: Steiner, 2009); Eva-Maria Stolberg, "The Siberian Frontier and Russia's Position in World History: A Reply to Aust and Nolte," *Review (Fernand Braudel Center)* 27, no. 3 (January 2004): 243–67; Martin Aust, "Rossia Siberica: Russian-Siberian History Compared to Medieval Conquest and Modern Colonialism," *Review (Fernand Braudel Center)* 27, no. 3 (January 2004): 181–205; Eva-Maria Stolberg, "The Siberian Frontier Between 'White Mission' and 'Yellow Peril,' 1890s–1920s," *Nationalities Papers* 32, no. 1 (March 2004): 165–81; Alan Wood, *The History of Siberia: From Russian Conquest to Revolution* (New York: Routledge, 1991); and W. Bruce Lincoln, *The Conquest of a Continent: Siberia and the Russians* (Ithaca, NY: Cornell University Press, 2007).

7 James Forsyth, *A History of the Peoples of Siberia: Russia's North Asian Colony, 1581–1990* (Cambridge: Cambridge University Press, 2000), 193.

8 Ibid., 195.

9 Ibid., 44. Some, however, settled in the northern part of the region, as illustrated by their involvement in the 1722 Tara revolt, an event in which they rebelled against the Petrine reforms. See N.N. Pokrovskii, "The Book Registers from the 1722 Tara Revolt," *Russian Studies in History* 49, no. 3 (Winter 2010): 8–41.

10 The quotation is from Anatolii Remnev, "Colonization and 'Russification' in the Imperial Geography of Asiatic Russia: From the Nineteenth to the Early Twentieth Centuries," in *Asiatic Russia: Imperial Power in Regional and International Contexts*, ed. Tomohiko Uyama (New York: Routledge, 2012), 106–7. Nicholas Breyfogle has analysed how the state's perspective on sectarianism and colonization changed over the course of the nineteenth century in the Caucasus. See Nicholas B. Breyfogle, *Heretics and Colonizers: Forging Russia's Empire in the South Caucasus* (Ithaca, NY: Cornell University Press, 2005), 128–72.

11 Steven Sabol, "Comparing American and Russian Internal Colonization: The 'Touch of Civilisation' on the Sioux and Kazakhs," *Western Historical Quarterly* 43, no. 1 (Spring 2012): 44.

12 Marie Antoinette Czaplicka, *The Collected Works of M.A. Czaplicka*, trans. David Norman Collins, vol. 3 (Richmond, UK: Curzon Press, 1999), 253–4. In some rare cases, this term could even include settlers who had moved to Siberia in the 1890s. For instance, a priest reporting to the Omsk consistory about the possibility of transferring a village to another parish called a group of settlers *Sibiriaki* since they had lived in Siberia for more than twenty years. See Istoricheskii arkhiv Omskoi oblasti (henceforth IAOO), f. 16, op.1, d.164, l.153 (Report to consistory, 1916). Even more interesting, the priest, Mikhail Inozemtsev, was raised in Siberia. See Ioann Goloshubin, *Spravochnaia kniga Omskoi eparkhii* (Omsk: Tipografiia "Irtysh," 1914), 1124.

13 Elena Kovalaschina and Alia A. Chaptykova, "The Historical and Cultural Ideals of the Siberian Oblastnichestvo," *Sibirica* 6, no. 2 (October 2007): 87–119.

14 For more on the role of race in the development of this identity, see David Rainbow, "Racial 'Degeneration' and Siberian Regionalism in the Late Imperial Period," in *Ideologies of Race: Imperial Russia and the Soviet Union in Global Context*, ed. David Rainbow (Montreal: McGill-Queen's University Press, 2019).

15 Igor Volgine, "Entrepreneurship and the Siberian Peasant Commune," in *Rural Reform in Post-Soviet Russia*, ed. Stephen K. Wegren and David J. O'Brien (Washington, DC: Woodrow Wilson Center Press, 2002), 36.

16 A. Kulomzin, *Vsepoddannieishii otchet stats-sekretaria Kulomzina po poezdke v Sibir' dlia oznakomleniia s polozheniem pereselencheskogo dela* (St. Petersburg: Gos. tip., 1896), 123. See also *Vsepoddanneishii otchet ober-prokurora sviateishego sinoda po vedomstvu pravoslavnogo ispovedaniia za 1902 god* (St. Petersburg, 1905), 148.

17 Pantleimon Papshev, "Usloviia, blagopriiatstvuiushchie sektantskoi propagande," *OEV* (chast' neoffitsial'naia) 29 (1916): 18.

18 Kulomzin, *Vsepoddannieishii otchet stats-sekretaria*, 123. Ioann Vostorgov also identified this separation from Russia and the church as an influence on the state of their religious faith. See RGIA, f.796, op.440, d.1274, l.5 (Vostorgov's report on the missionary work in dioceses beyond the Urals, 1911).

19 M. Philips Price, *Siberia* (London: Methuen and Co., 1912), 167–8.

20 See S. Abashin, *Tsentral'naia Aziia v sostave Rossiiskoi imperii* (Moscow: Novoe literaturnoe obozrenie, 2008), 384. In the northern territory of Omsk diocese, Tatars lives around the town of Tara. See M.G. Levin and L.P. Potapov, eds., *The Peoples of Siberia*, trans. Stephen P. Dunn (Chicago: University of Chicago Press, 1964), 423.

21 Martha Brill Olcott, *The Kazakhs* (Stanford, CA: Hoover Institution Press, Stanford University, 1987), 16.

22 John W. Slocum, "Who, and When, Were the Inorodtsy? The Evolution of the Category of 'Aliens' in Imperial Russia," *Russian Review* 57, no. 2 (April 1998): 173–90.

23 Matthew Payne, "Do You Want Me to Exterminate All of Them or Just the Ones Who Oppose Us?," in *Empire and Belonging in the European Borderlands*, ed., Krista A. Goff and Lewis H. Siegelbaum (Ithaca, NY: Cornell University Press, 2019), 69.

24 For the localized culture, see Isolde Thyrêt, "Creating a Religious Community in Siberia: The Cultural Politics of Archbishop Nektarii of Tobol'sk," *Canadian-American Slavic Studies* 51, no. 1 (2017): 89. For the Christianizing of space through church building, see Valerie A. Kivelson, *Cartographies of Tsardom: The Land and Its Meanings in Seventeenth-Century Russia* (Ithaca, NY: Cornell University Press, 2006), 159.

25 For examples of both these approaches in the nineteenth century, see Mara Kozelsky, *Christianizing Crimea: Shaping Sacred Space in the Russian Empire and Beyond* (DeKalb: Northern Illinois University Press, 2010).

26 Yuri Slezkine, *Arctic Mirrors: Russia and the Small Peoples of the North* (Ithaca, NY: Cornell University Press, 1994), 48–50.

27 Sergei Kan, "Russian Orthodox Missionaries at Home and Abroad: The Case of Siberian and Alaskan Indigenous Peoples," in *Of Religion and Empire: Missions, Conversion, and Tolerance in Tsarist Russia*, ed. Robert Geraci and Michael Khordarkovsky (Ithaca, NY: Cornell University Press, 2001), 177.

28 Ibid., 178.

29 Robert P. Geraci, *Window on the East: National and Imperial Identities in Late Tsarist Russia* (Ithaca, NY: Cornell University Press, 2001), 199; Allen J. Frank, "Islamic Transformation on the Kazakh Steppe, 1742–1917: Toward an Islamic History of Kazakhstan under Russian Rule," in *The Construction and Deconstruction of National Histories in Slavic Eurasia*, ed. Hayashi Tadayuki (Sapporo, JP: Hokkaido University Press, 2003), 270.

30 Robert D. Crews, *For Prophet and Tsar: Islam and Empire in Russia and Central Asia* (Cambridge, MA: Harvard University Press, 2009), 200.

31 Iu. A. Lysenko, *Missionerstvo Russkoi pravoslavnoi tserkvi v Kazakhstane: (vtoraia polovina XIX–nachalo XX v.)* (Barnaul: Izd-vo Altaiskogo gos. universiteta, 2010), 37; Tomohiko Uyama, "A Particularist Empire: The Russian Policies of Christianization and Military Conscription in Central Asia," in *Empire, Islam, and Politics in Central Eurasia*, ed. Tomohiko Uyama (Sapporo, JP: Slavic Research Center, 2007), 43.

32 Iu. A. Lysenko, "Pravoslavie i Islam: praktiki etnokonfessional'noi kommunikatsii na primere Russkikh i Kazakhov verkhnego priirtysh'ia (XIX–nachalo XXv)," *Vestnik arkhelogii, antropologii i etnografii* 15, no. 2 (2011): 196. Larger towns like Semipalatinsk and Akmolinsk had mosques. See Kennan, *Siberia and the Exile System*, 158. As the Kazakhs were a nomadic people, the absence of mosques in the rural areas is not surprising. Many Tatar mullahs also criticized the faith of Muslim Kazakhs, especially their lax attitude toward sharia. See Geraci, *Window on the East*, 196.

33 Martin, *Law and Custom in the Steppe*, 58.

34 O.V. Ignatenko, "Kirgiz dukhovnaia missiia," *Sovremennoe obshchestvo*, vyp.1 (Omsk, 1999), 118. For more on the mission and its role in the region, see Robert Geraci, "Going Abroad or Going to Russia? Orthodox Missionaries in the Kazakh Steppe, 1881–1917," in *Of Religion and Empire: Missions, Conversion, and Tolerance in Tsarist Russia*, ed. Robert Geraci and Michael Khordarkovsky (Ithaca, NY: Cornell University Press, 2001), 274–310.

35 Aleksandr Kravetskii, *Tserkovnaia missiia v epokhu peremen* (Moscow: Krugly i stol po religioznomu obrazovaniiu i diakonii, 2012), 39.

36 Anna Peck, "The Image of Heathens: Archbishop Veniamin Blagonravov's Perception of Religion and Nationality in the Transbaikal," *Sibirica* 10, no. 2 (2011): 50–72. For the church's attempts to convert the Buriats in the Baikal region, see Jesse D. Murray, "Building Empire among the Buryats: Conversion Encounters in Russia's Baikal Region, 1860s–1917" (PhD diss., University of Illinois at Urbana-Champaign, 2012).

37 Rossiiskii gosudarstvennyi istoricheskii arkhiv (henceforth RGIA), f.796, op.174, d.1047, l.35ob (Proposal to open two new dioceses, 1893–97). Dittmar Schorkowitz also demonstrates the importance of the church's mission to the Buriats in the agenda of this meeting. See "The Orthodox

Church, Lamaism, and Shamanism among the Buriats and Kalmyks 1825–1925," in *Of Religion and Empire: Missions, Conversion, and Tolerance in Tsarist Russia*, ed. Robert Geraci and Michael Khodarkovsky (Ithaca, NY: Cornell University Press, 2001), 213.

38   RGIA, f.796, op.166, d.1553, ll.47–49ob (Report of the Irkutsk Council, 1885).

39   RGIA, f.796, op.166, d.1553, l.48.

40   S.V. Golubtsov, *Istoriia Omskoi eparkhii: obrazovanie Omskoi eparkhii, predstoiatel'stvo preosviashchennogo Grigoriia na Omskoi kafedre, 1895–1900 gg* (Omsk: Poligraf, 2008), 27.

41   *Vsepoddanneishii otchet ober-prokurora sviateishego sinoda po vedomstvu pravoslavnogo ispovedaniia za 1885 god* (St. Petersburg, 1887), 27.

42   Konstantin Pobedonostsev, *Pis'ma Pobedonostseva k Aleksandru III*, vol. 1 (Moscow: Novaia Moskva, 1925), 82–3. Schorkowitz claims that the meeting was Pobedonostsev's idea; see Schorkowitz, "The Orthodox Church, Lamaism, and Shamanism," 213.

43   N. Gorodkov, "Obrazovanie novoi Omskoi eparkhii," *Tobol'skie eparkhial'nye vedomosti* (chast' neoffitsial'naia) 19 (1895): 321–2.

44   Stolberg, "The Siberian Frontier and Russia's Position in World History," 247.

45   William Husband, "Happy Birthday, Siberia! Reform and Public Opinion in Russia's 'Colony,' 1881–1882," in *The Human Tradition in Imperial Russia*, ed. Christine Worobec (Lanham, MD: Rowman and Littlefield Publishers, 2009), 96.

46   Quoted in Steven G. Marks, *Road to Power: The Trans-Siberian Railroad and the Colonization of Asian Russia, 1850–1917* (Ithaca, NY: Cornell University Press, 1991), 143.

47   This impulse to give advice to the tsarevich was hardly surprising: throughout his career Pobedonostsev showed an intense "desire to instruct everyone, not to leave anything to chance." A. Iu. Polunov, "Konstantin Petrovich Pobedonostsev – Man and Politician," *Russian Studies in History* 39, no. 4 (Spring 2001): 21. For an insightful portrait of Pobedonostsev, see A. Iu. Polunov, *K.P. Pobedonostsev v obshchestvenno-politicheskoii i dukhovnoii zhizni Rossii* (Moscow: Rosspen, 2010).

48   Konstantin Petrovich Pobedonostsev, *Pis'ma Pobedonostseva k Aleksandru III*, tom 2 (Moscow: Novaia Moskva, 1925), 297–8.

49   Ibid., 295.

50   William Durban, "The Trans-Siberian Railway," *Contemporary Review*, August 1899, 262.

51   United States Government, *The Russian Empire and the Trans-Siberian Railway* (Washington, DC, 1899), 2504.

52   Durban, "The Trans-Siberian Railway," 269.

53   Price, *Siberia*, 8.

54 John Foster Fraser, *The Real Siberia: Together with an Account of a Dash Through Manchuria* (London: Cassell, 1907), 45.
55 Ian W. Campbell, *Knowledge and the Ends of Empire: Kazak Intermediaries and Russian Rule on the Steppe, 1731–1917* (Ithaca, NY: Cornell University Press, 2017), 100–1; Olcott, *The Kazakhs*, 87.
56 For more on the gathering of data to divide the land, see Ian W. Campbell, "Settlement Promoted, Settlement Contested: The Shcherbina Expedition of 1896–1903," *Central Asian Survey* 30, no. 3–4 (2011): 423–36.
57 Demko, *The Russian Colonization of Kazakhstan*, 53.
58 Donald W. Treadgold, *The Great Siberian Migration: Government and Peasant in Resettlement from Emancipation to the First World War* (Princeton, NJ: Princeton University Press, 1957), 33. Treadgold estimates the number of illegal migrants at approximately 700,000. See also, Forsyth, *A History of the Peoples of Siberia*, 191.
59 Unfortunately, no figures exist based on the borders of the dioceses.
60 Treadgold, *The Great Siberian Migration*, 174.
61 L. Dameshek and A. Remnev, *Sibir' v sostave Rossiiskoi imperii* (Moscow: Novoe literaturnoe obozrenie, 2007), 258. Wheat became a staple crop on the steppe, with approximately 70 per cent of cultivated land in this territory planted with the grain. Treadgold, *The Great Siberian Migration*, 172.
62 Treadgold, *The Great Siberian Migration*, 89.
63 For a case of tsarist officials experimenting with the category of nationality and settlement, see Charles Steinwedel, "Resettling People, Upsetting the Empire: Migration and the Challenges of Governance 1861–1917," in *Peopling the Russian Periphery: Borderland Colonization in Eurasian History*, ed. Nicholas B. Breyfogle, Abby M. Schrader, and Willard Sunderland (New York: Routledge, 2007), 132–3.
64 Ihor Stebelsky, "Ukraine Settlement Patterns in the Kirgiz Steppe Before 1917: Ukrainian Colonies or Russian Integration?," in *Transforming Peasants: Society, State and the Peasantry, 1861–1930*, ed. Judith Pallot (New York: Palgrave Macmillan, 1998), 141–2. The concrete numbers are: 65,062 Russians in Semipalatinsk and 174,292 in Akmolinsk. For Ukrainians, the census records 3,257 in Semipalatinsk and 51,103 in Akmolinsk. See S. Abashin et al., *Tsentral'naia Aziia v sostave Rossiiskoi imperii* (Moscow: Novoe literaturnoe obozrenie, 2008), 384.
65 Ibid., 384.
66 Stebelsky, "Ukraine Settlement Patterns," 141–2.
67 Demko, *The Russian Colonization of Kazakhstan*, 91.
68 Yuriy Anatolyevich Malikov, "Formation of a Borderland Culture: Myths and Realities of Cossack-Kazakh Relations in Northern Kazakhstan in the Eighteenth and Nineteenth Centuries" (PhD diss., University of California, Santa Barbara, 2006), 108–9. For more on state concerns in

relations to such intermixing, see Willard Sunderland, "Russians into Iakuts? 'Going Native' and Problems of Russian National Identity in the Siberian North, 1870s–1914," *Slavic Review* 55, no. 4 (1996): 806–25.

69 Martin, *Law and Custom in the Steppe*, 66.

70 This does not mean that all Cossacks were accepting of Kazakhs. During a trip through the province of Semipalatinsk, Bishop Sergii chastised a group of Cossacks for referring to local Kazakhs as "dogs." See "Poseshchenie Sergiem," *OEV* 20 (1901): 11. Willard Sunderland has shown that settler writings also refer to Kazakhs in the same way. See Sunderland, "Peasant Pioneering: Russian Peasant Settlers Describe Colonization and the Eastern Frontier, 1880s–1910s," *Journal of Social History* 34, no. 4 (Summer 2001): 909.

71 Corinne Gaudin, *Ruling Peasants: Village and State in Late Imperial Russia* (DeKalb: Northern Illinois University Press, 2007), 132.

72 Treadgold, *The Great Siberian Migration*, 213–14.

73 Peter Gatrell, *A Whole Empire Walking: Refugees in Russia During World War I* (Bloomington: Indiana University Press, 2005), 66.

74 RGIA, f.796, op.442, d.2287, l.25ob (Annual report to the Holy Synod by Bishop Gavriil, 1908).

75 RGIA, f.bib-ka, op.1, d.91, l.82 (Annual report of the governor general of the steppe, 1897); Stolypin and Krivoshein, *Poezdka v Sibir'*, 40–2.

76 RGIA, f.bib-ka, op.1, d.91, l.82 (Annual report of the governor general of the steppe, 1897).

77 Serapion Shulgin, "O pereselenii," *Sel'skii vestnik* 17 (1896): 217.

78 Ibid.

79 Zemlemer, "Kak zhivut novosely," *Sel'skii vestnik* 40 (1913): 3.

80 *Materialy po pereselencheskomu khoziaistvu v stepnoi i Turganskoi oblasti tom.1* (St. Petersburg, 1907), 93. For more on how settlement transformed the Kazakh way of life, see Sarah I. Cameron, *The Hungry Steppe: Famine, Violence, and the Making of Soviet Kazakhstan* (Ithaca, NY: Cornell University Press, 2018), 34–44.

81 *Materialy po pereselencheskomu khoziaistvu v stepnoi i Turganskoi*, 37.

82 P.P. Liubimov, "Religii i veroispovednyi sostav naseleniia Aziatskoi Rossii," in *Aziatskaia Rossiia: liudi i poriadki za Uralom*, ed. G.V. Glinka, vol. 1 (St. Petersburg: Izd. pereselencheskogo upravleniia glavnogo upravleniia zemleustroistva i zemledieliia, 1914), 241–2. Another source offers the breakdown of the population of Akmolinsk in 1910: 1,324,000 in total, with 505,000 Kazakhs, 131,000 Cossacks, and 544,000 Russian peasants. See *Spravochnaia knizhka po Akmolinskomu pereselencheskomu raionu na 1912* (1912), 22. One source lists the Russian population at 58 per cent in the province of Akmolinsk. See Richard A. Pierce, *Russian Central Asia, 1867–1917*, 137.

83 Willard Sunderland, "The 'Colonization Question': Visions of Colonization in Late Imperial Russia," *Jahrbücher für Geschichte Osteuropas* 48, no. 2 (May 2000): 222; and Lewis H. Siegelbaum and Leslie Page Moch, *Broad Is My Native Land: Repertoires and Regimes of Migration in Russia's Twentieth Century* (Ithaca, NY: Cornell University Press, 2014), 31.

84 For more on negative views about settlers, see Anatoli Remnev and Natal'ia Suvorova, "'Russkoe delo' na aziatskikh okrainakh: 'Russkost' pod ugrozoi ili 'somnitel'nye kul'turtregery'," *Ab Imperio* 2 (April 2008): 157–222; Jeff Sahadeo, *Russian Colonial Society in Tashkent: 1865–1923* (Bloomington: Indiana University Press, 2007), 135; and Alexander Morrison, "Peasant Settlers and the 'Civilising Mission' in Russian Turkestan, 1865–1917," *Journal of Imperial and Commonwealth History* 43, no. 3 (2015): 387–400.

85 Alberto Masoero, "Layers of Property in the Tsar's Settlement Colony: Projects of Land Privatization in Siberia in the Late Nineteenth Century," *Central Asian Survey* 29, no. 1 (March 2010): 21.

86 "Gospodi blagoslovi," *OEV*, no. 1 (1898): 1.

87 Mikhail Mefod'ev, "Blagochestivye zhiteli Bogospasaemyia vesi seia!," *OEV* (chast' neoffitsial'naia) 24 (1908): 34.

88 RGIA, f.391, op.3, d.1797, ll.6–7ob (Fr. Mikhail Sukhanov to Ioann Vostorgov, 1910). Sukhanov was a graduate of the Pastoral Courses in Moscow. See, Goloshubin, *Spravochnaia kniga*, 1202.

89 Gregory Freeze, *The Parish Clergy in Nineteenth-Century Russia: Crisis, Reform, Counter-Reform* (Princeton, NJ: Princeton University Press, 1983), 28–9.

90 Jan Plamper, "The Russian Orthodox Episcopate, 1721–1917: A Prosopography," *Journal of Social History* 34, no. 1 (Fall 2000): 17–18.

91 Thanks to Victor Taki for drawing my attention to the similarities between bishops and governors. For more information on the role of provincial governors, see Richard G. Robbins, *The Tsar's Viceroys: Russian Provincial Governors in the Last Years of the Empire* (Ithaca, NY: Cornell University Press, 1987), 27–37.

92 Plamper, "The Russian Orthodox Episcopate," 18.

93 For more on the characteristics of the western Siberian bishops as a social group, see O.V. Ushakova, "Zapadnosibirskii episkopat v 1907–1914 gg: k kharakteristike episkopov Russkoi pravoslavnoi tserkvi kak sotsial'noi gruppy," in *Slavianskoe edinstvo: mezhunarodnaia nauchnaia konferentsiia* (Omsk, 2000), 126–9.

94 Akmolinsk and Semipalatinsk were initially military governorships that became governorships.

95 The following men served as governor general of the steppe: G.A. Kolpakovskii (1882–9), M.A. Taube (1890–1900), N.N. Sukhotin

(1900–6), I.P. Nadarov (1906–8), E.O. Shmit (1908–15), and
N.A. Suhkomlinov (1915–17). See Sergei Abashin et al., *Tsentral'naia Aziia v sostave Rossiiskoi imperii* (Moscow: Novoe literaturnoe obozrenie, 2008), 424.

96 RGIA, f.1284, op.194, d.56, ll.24–26ob (Annual report of the Tobol'sk governor, 1912); RGIA, f.391, op.5, d.690, l.5ob (Report on assignment in Siberian dioceses by Vostorgov, 1912).

97 RGIA, f.796, op.442, d.1965, l.16 (Annual report to Holy Synod by Bishop Mikhail, 1904).

98 RGIA, f.796, op.442, d.2593, l.8ob (Annual report to the Holy Synod by Bishop Andronik, 1913).

99 *Vsepoddanneishii otchet ober-prokurora Sviateishego Sinoda po vedomstvu pravoslavnogo ispovedaniia za 1896 i 1897 gody, prilozheniia za 1895–96 gg* (St. Petersburg, 1899), 10–11; population figures on page 4.

100 *Vsepoddanneishii otchet ober-prokurora Sviateishego Sinoda sinoda po vedomstvu pravoslavnogo ispovedaniia za 1914 god* (St. Petersburg, 1916), 26–9; ibid., 24–5. This data shows a significant increase in the number of cantors in Omsk – a trend also taking place in other parts of the empire at the beginning of the twentieth century.

101 *Vsepoddanneishii otchet ober-prokurora Sviateishego Sinod a za 1914 god* (1916), 6–7.

102 The Omsk ratio was calculated from numbers obtained in the chief procurator's report from 1914. The ratio for European Russian was provided by Freeze, *The Parish Clergy in Nineteenth-Century Russia*, 178.

103 RGIA, f.799, op.15, d.1220, l.63ob (Petition of peasant village to Maria Feodorovna, 1911).

104 See entries for Kiev, Poltava, and Riazan provinces in *Entsiklopedicheskii Slovar'* (St. Petersburg: Brockhaus-Efron, 1890–1907), available at http://www.vehi.net/brokgauz/index.html (accessed 23 March 2011).

105 *Spravochnaia knizhka po Akmolinskomu pereselencheskomu raionu na 1912* (1912), 3.

106 Gregory Freeze, "Russian Orthodoxy on the Periphery: Decoding the Raporty Blagochinnykh in Lithuania Diocese," in *Problemy vsemirnoi istorii*, ed. B.V. Anan'ich (St. Petersburg: Vilanin, 2000), 129. The problem of distance plagued clergy working in other underdeveloped regions – for example, in Australia.

107 RGIA, f.796, op.442, d.1965, l.4ob (Annual report to Holy Synod by Bishop Sergii, 1901–1902).

108 K.F. Skal'skii, *Omskaia eparkhiia* (Omsk: Tipografiia A.K. Demidova, 1900), 41–52; Ioann Goloshubin, *Spravochnaia kniga Omskoi eparkhii* (Omsk: Tipografiia "Irtysh," 1914), 35–88.

109 IAOO, f.16, op.1, d.151, l.2 ("To the Omsk Settler Committee from the Bishop of Omsk, 7 September 1913").

2. Churches as a National Project

1 I.I. Vostorgov, "Narod tserkovnyi," *Pribavleniia k tserkovnym vedomostiam* (henceforth *PTsV*) 15 (1912): 606–7.
2 For more on how the British Empire fostered an imperial identity, see Jim English, "Empire Day in Britain, 1904–1958," *Historical Journal* 49, no. 1 (2006): 247–76; Robert S.M. Withycombe, "Australian Anglicans and Imperial Identity, 1900–1914," *Journal of Religious History* 25, no. 3 (October 2001): 286.
3 Anatolii Remnev, "Colonization and 'Russification' in Asiatic Russia," in *Asiatic Russia: Imperial Power in Regional and International Contexts*, ed. Uyama Tomohiko (New York: Routledge, 2012), 103.
4 For more on this topic, see Aileen Friesen, "Building an Orthodox Empire: Archpriest Ioann Vostorgov and Russian Missionary Aspirations in Asia," *Canadian Slavonic Papers* 57, no. 1–2 (2015): 56–75.
5 For more on Russia's messianic interpretation of Siberia and the Far East, see Mark Bassin, *Imperial Visions: Nationalist Imagination and Geographical Expansion in the Russian Far East, 1840–1865* (Cambridge: Cambridge University Press, 1999).
6 Vera Shevzov, *Russian Orthodoxy on the Eve of Revolution* (Oxford: Oxford University Press, 2004), 59.
7 Ibid., 60.
8 For the development of the parish system in western Siberia, see A. Adamenko, *Prikhody Russkoi pravoslavnoi tserkvi na iuge zapadnoi Sibiri v XVII–nachale XX veka* (Kemerovo: Kuzbassvuzizdat, 2004), 11–29.
9 *Polozhenie tserkovnogo i shkol'nogo stroitel'stva v raione Sibirskoi zheleznoi dorogi na sredstva fonda imeni imperatora Aleksandra III* (St. Petersburg: Gos. tip., 1898), 3.
10 M.F. Lebedev, *Puteshestvie naslednika tsesarevicha po Tobol'skoi eparkhii v 1891 godu* (Tobol'sk, 1892), 8–10.
11 Richard Wortman, *Scenarios of Power: Myth and Ceremony in Russian Monarchy from Peter the Great to the Abdication of Nicholas II* (Princeton, NJ: Princeton University Press, 2006), 347.
12 Lebedev, *Puteshestvie naslednika tsesarevicha*, 13.
13 *Polozhenie tserkovnogo* (1898), 3.
14 Nicholas II, "Dnevnik Nikolaia II," *Russkoe Nebo*, http://www.rus-sky.com/history/library/diaris/1896.htm (accessed 14 March 2016).
15 For pictures of the inside and outside of the church wagons, see *Aziatskaia Rossiia*, vol. 2: *Zemlia i khoziaistvo*, edited by G.V. Glinka. (St. Petersburg, 1914), 518–19.
16 Kulomzin was an important government figure throughout the second half of the nineteenth century. For more on his background, see

D.C.B. Lieven, "Bureaucratic Liberalism in Late Imperial Russia: The Personality, Career and Opinions of A.N. Kulomzin," *Slavonic and East European Review* 60, no. 3 (July 1982): 413–32.

17 Steven G. Marks, "Conquering the Great East: Kulomzin, Peasant Resettlement, and the Creation of Modern Siberia," in *Rediscovering Russia in Asia: Siberia and the Russian Far East*, ed. Stephen Kotkin and David Wolff (Armonk, NY: M.E. Sharpe, 1995), 24–5.

18 Howard Le Couteur, "Anglican High Churchmen and the Expansion of Empire," *Journal of Religious History* 32, no. 2 (June 2008): 212.

19 Pamela Welch, *Church and Settler in Colonial Zimbabwe: A Study in the History of the Anglican Diocese of Mashonaland/Southern Rhodesia, 1890–1925* (Leiden, NL: Brill, 2008), 119.

20 For another perspective on diocese building in the context of empire, see Ilya Vinkovetsky, "Building a Diocese Overseas: The Orthodox Church in Partnership with the Russian-American Company in Alaska," *Ab Imperio* 3 (July 2010): 152–94.

21 A.N. Kulomzin, *Nuzhdy tserkovnogo dela na Sibirskoi doroge i v Zabaikal'e* (St. Petersburg: God. Tip., 1897), 2.

22 Ibid., 3.

23 Rossiiskii gosudarstvennyi istoricheskii arkhiv (henceforth, RGIA), f.1273, op.1, d.459, l.20; *Sibirskie tserkvi i shkoly* (St. Petersburg: Gos. tip, 1904), 8. Kulomzin, however, showed flexibility in his approach to the indigenous population, particularly in the realm of education. See A.V. Remnev, "Anatolii Nikolaevich Kulomzin," *Voprosy istorii*, no. 8 (2009): 39–40.

24 *Sibirskie tserkvi i shkoly*, 9. Kulomzin expressed great happiness at attending the liturgy at the new church in Tatarsk. See Kulomzin, *Nuzhdy tserkovnogo*, 2.

25 *Sibirskie tserkvi i shkoly*, 10.

26 Ibid.

27 *Pribavleniia k tserkovnym vedomostiam* 14 (1897): 545.

28 "Pozhertvovaniia na postroenie tserkvei i shkol v Sibiri," *PTsV* 50 (1898): 1935. This is not to say that donations to churches constituted the only way in which individuals could support Siberian settlers. For instance, the Russian Red Cross created a collection to assist the efforts of doctors in the region to help settlers, particularly in the struggle against epidemics. Church building, however, received special emphasis by the state.

29 See, Alena Eskridge-Kosmach, "The Russian-Turkish War of 1877–1878 and the Attitude of Russian Society (Based on Memoirs, Diaries, and the Epistolary Heritage of Contemporaries)," *Journal of Slavic Military Studies* 29, no. 3 (2016): 423–72.

30 Theofanis George Stavrou, *Russian Interests in Palestine, 1882–1914: A Study of Religious and Educational Enterprise* (Thessaloniki, GR: Inst. for Balkan Studies, 1963), 91.

31 Adele Lindenmeyr, "Voluntary Associations and the Russian Autocracy: The Case of Private Charity," *Carl Beck Papers in Russian and East European Studies* 807 (June 1990): 13.
32 Adele Lindenmeyr, "The Ethos of Charity in Imperial Russia," *Journal of Social History* 23, no. 4 (1990): 679.
33 Nadieszda Kizenko, *A Prodigal Saint: Father John of Kronstadt and the Russian People* (University Park: Pennsylvania State University Press, 2000), 137.
34 "Raznaia izvestiia," *Sel'skii vestnik* 9 (1904): 155.
35 RGIA, f.1273, op.1, d.451, l.34ob (Preparatory Committee of the Siberian Railway Commission, 1897); *Polozhenie tserkovnogo i shkol'nogo stroi-tel'stva v raione Sibirskoi zheleznoi dorogi na sredstva fonda imeni imperatora Aleksandra III* (St. Petersburg: Gos. tip., 1900), 4; In 1899, the Trinity Lavra of St. Sergius in Moscow contributed 10,000 rubles to church building in Siberia through the Siberian Railway Committee; see "Znamenatel'nyia sobytiia v zhizni monastyrei," *Tserkovnye vedomosti (TV)* 4 (1903): 27.
36 "Vysochaishee povelenie," *TV* 39 (1904): 417.
37 RGIA, f.1273, op.1, d.517, l.120 (To Kulomzin from a dean of Petersburg and Novgorod).
38 *Polozhenie tserkovnogo* (1898), 5.
39 N.I. Lebedeva, *Khramy i molitvennye doma Omskogo priirtysh'ia* (Omsk: Izd-vo OmGPU, 2003), 27.
40 *Sibirskie tserkvi i shkoly* (1904), 5.
41 For more on the royal family's involvement with the fund in Siberia, see Sviatoslav Vladimirovich Sabler, Ivan Vasil'evich Sosnovskii, and A.N. Kulomzin, *Sibirskaia zhelieznaia doroga v ee proshlom i nastoiashchem: istoricheskii ocherk* (St. Petersburg: Gos. tip., 1903), 345–6.
42 For more on the *Village Herald*, see James H. Krukones, "To the People: The Russian Government and the Newspaper Sel'skii Vestnik ('Village herald'), 1881–1917" (PhD diss., University of Wisconsin-Madison, 1983).
43 "Tserkvi i shkoly v Sibiri," *Sel'skii vestnik* 6 (1904): 97. For another list of donors, see *Sel'skii vestnik* 4 (1898): 43; "Sibirskoe tserkovnoe i shkol'noe stroitel'stvo," *Sel'skii vestnik* 21 (1902): 373.
44 *Sibirskie tserkvi i shkoly fonda imeni imperatora Aleksandra III* (St. Petersburg: Gos. tip., 1902), 6. Ivan A. Kolesnikov, a hereditary honoured citizen, also donated 10,000 rubles to the fund to build a church in a village that had been recently overwhelmed by settlers. See *PTsV* 8 (1898): 328.
45 People left money in last testaments to help settlers in Siberia until the end of the empire. For example, the daughter of a deacon left 17,502 rubles to build a church called "All Saints" with an alms house for elderly settlers along the Trans-Siberian Railway in 1916. The chief procurator consulted with the bishop of Omsk to find a suitable location. They decided to build the church in Novo-Omsk. See RGIA, f.391, op.6, d.542, l.81.

46 RGIA, f.796, op.194, d.2037, 1.44 (To the Holy Synod from Chief Procurator Sabler, 1912).

47 RGIA, f.1273, op.1, d.517, 1.29 (Peasant letter to the Siberian Railway Committee, 1894).

48 Adele Lindenmeyr, "Public Life, Private Virtues: Women in Russian Charity, 1762–1914," *Signs* 18, no. 3 (Spring 1993): 563.

49 RGIA, f.796, op.204 (2ot, 2st), d.235, 1.2 (Report on aid for church and school building in settler villages, 1917). Churches, of course, could not be named after their benefactors; nonetheless, benefactors could choose a traditional church name, which also meant the local community had no input in the naming of their own church. Anatolii Kulomzin informed an official with the Ministry of Internal Affairs that churches built in three different villages must be consecrated in honour of the Resurrection of Christ, as that was the wish of the donor. See RGIA, f.1273, op.1, d.465, 1.1. For more examples of donors choosing names for churches, see RGIA, f.1273, op.1, d.517, 1.108, 110.

50 F.I. Parvitskii, "Tserkovno-prikhodskiia shkoly Akmolinskoi oblasti, voznikshiia na sredstva ili pri posobii iz fonda Imeni Imperatora Aleksandra III," *Omskie eparkhial'nye vedomosti* (henceforth *OEV*) (chast' neoffitsial'naia) 24 (1905): 18–19.

51 Ioann Goloshubin, *Spravochnaia kniga Omskoi eparkhii* (Omsk: Tipografiia "Irtysh," 1914), 98–9.

52 *Pouchenie po sluchaiu sbora pozhertvovanii na postroenie khrama v sele Mogil'no-Posel'skom Tarskogo uezda, Omskoi eparkhii* (Moscow, 1899).

53 "Ot khoziaistvennogo upravleniia pri sviateishem sinode," *TV* 1 (1907): 5.

54 P.P. Liubimov, "Religii i veroispovednyi sostav naseleniia Aziatskoi Rossii," in *Aziatskaia Rossiia: liudi i poriadki za uralom*, vol. 1, ed. G.V. Glinka (St. Petersburg: Izd. Pereselencheskogo upravleniia glavnogo upravleniia zemleustroistva i zemledieliia, 1914), 238.

55 RGIA, f.1273, op.1, d.554, l. 175, 203, 208, 226, 241, 255 (Requests from various individuals for a medallion).

56 *Sibirskie tserkvi i shkoly* (1904), 19–20.

57 Ibid., 20–3. The list included the following: the metropolitan of Moscow and Kolomensk, the metropolitan of St. Petersburg and Ladoga, two archbishops, five bishops, Father John of Kronstadt, Konstantin Pobedonostsev, Sergei Witte, as well as a number of governors.

58 "Ot khoziaistvennogo upravleniia pri sviateishem sinode," 6.

59 Peter Holquist, "'In Accord with State Interests and the People's Wishes': The Technocratic Ideology of Imperial Russia's Resettlement Administration," *Slavic Review* 69, no. 1 (Spring 2010): 157.

60 V. Vvedenskii, "Tserkovnoe delo sredi pereselentsev Sibiri," *PTsV* 12 (1913): 536.

61 Ibid.

62 Istoricheskii arkhiv Omskoi oblasti, f.16, op.1, d.10, l.174 (Decree of the Omsk diocesan consistory, 1913).

63 See "Pis'mo Semipalatinskogo gubernatora na imia Andronika," *OEV* 13 (1914): 2.

64 V. Vvedenskii, "Tserkovnoe delo sredi pereselentsev Sibiri," *PTsV* 13, (1913): 606–7.

65 Ibid., 606. The title for the committee was Osoboe Soveshchanie pri Sviateishem Sinode o religioznykh nuzhdakh pereselentsev.

66 Ibid.

67 Paul W. Werth, *The Tsar's Foreign Faiths: Toleration and the Fate of Religious Freedom in Imperial Russia* (Oxford: Oxford University Press, 2014), especially chs. 8 and 9.

68 For an example of a request from Catholic settlers in Tomsk diocese, see *Gosudarvennyi arkhiv Tomskoi oblasti*, f.3, op.77, d.100, l.8a.

69 RGIA, f.391, op.4, d.573, ll.19–20 (To MVD from A. Krivoshein).

70 RGIA, f.391, op.4, d.573, l.19 (To Krivoshein from Stolypin).

71 Liubimov, "Religii i veroispovednyi sostav naseleniia Aziatskoi Rossii," 240–1. The Resettlement Administration also provided loans and support to Old Believers for believing prayer houses.

72 Ibid., 240.

73 Farid Shafiyev, *Resettling the Borderlands: State Relocations and Ethnic Conflict in the South Caucasus* (Montreal: McGill-Queen's University Press, 2018), 109.

74 For a discussion of the Duma's involvement in resettlement, see Donald W. Treadgold, *The Great Siberian Migration: Government and Peasant in Resettlement from Emancipation to the First World War* (Princeton, NJ: Princeton University Press, 1957), 192–204.

75 *Gosudarstvennaia duma: stenograficheskie otchety, chetvertyi sozyv, sessiia II, chast' 5* (St. Petersburg: Gos. tip., 1914), 1156.

76 Ibid., 1158.

77 Glinka's heartfelt plea did not appeal to everyone. In response to Glinka's appeal that Duma officials search their hearts to find the favourable answer, a voice on the left responded, "We find nothing." Ibid., 1159.

78 Ibid.

79 For more on the rules, regulations, and structures for building churches with financing through the Resettlement Administration, see V.P. Voshchinin, *Pereselenie i zemleustroistvo v Aziatskoi Rossii. Sbornik zakonov i rasporiazhenii* (St. Petersburg, 1915), 8–10.

80 The citation for the article is as follows: "Kak poluchit' pereselentsam den'gi na postroiku tserkvei i shkol," *Sel'skii vestnik* 42 (1912): 1–2. A copy of the article can be found in the Resettlement Administration fond; see RGIA, f.391, op.5, d.23, l.31ob.

81 RGIA, f.391, op.5, d.23, l.33.
82 Liubimov, "Religii i veroispovednyi sostav naseleniia Aziatskoi Rossii," 239.
83 Ibid.
84 I.I. Vostorgov, "Zabota o russkikh pereselentsakh," in *Polnoe sobranie sochinenii*, v.1 (Moscow: s.n., 1914), 315–16.
85 Gosudarstvennyi arkhiv Rossiiskoi federatsii (henceforth, GARF), f.9452, op.1, d.14, ll.1–110.
86 RGIA, f.796, op.197, 6ot., 3st., d.30, l.8ob (Service record of Ioann Vostorgov, 1913).
87 RGIA, f.796, op.197, 6ot., 3st., d.30, l.10ob.
88 See, for example, RGIA, f.796, op.445, d.301, ll.239–54 (Report on the Pastoral Missionary Courses in Siberia by Vostorgov, 1912); RGIA, f.391, op.4, d.1354, ll.1–60 (Report on the Spiritual Needs of Settlers, 1910).
89 I.I. Vostorgov, "Rossiia i Vostok," *Pribavleniia k tserkovnym vedomostiam* 25 (1909): 1145. This article was also published locally in I.I. Vostorgov, "Rossiia i Vostok," *Vladivostokskie eparkhial'nye vedomosti* 11 (1909): 327–37.
90 Vostorgov, "Rossiia i Vostok," 1148.
91 Ibid; Ioann Vostorgov, *Dobroe slovo pereselentsy* (Moscow, 1909), 9.
92 Ibid., 8.
93 Ibid., 10. Bishop Ioann (Smirnov), the vicar bishop of Kirensk, agreed with Vostorgov of the danger of leaving the Russian borderlands – especially with China – unoccupied. He believed war to be on the horizon, although he accepted whatever might happen as God's will. See Episkop Ioann, "Drakon prosnulsia," *Irkutskie eparkhial'nye vedomosti*, (chast' neoffitsial'naia) no. 8 (1910): 218–23.
94 Vostorgov, *Dobroe slovo pereselentsy*, 11–12.
95 Vostorgov, "Rossiia i Vostok," 1150. See also Vostorgov, *Dobroe slovo pereselentsy*, 11–12.
96 For more on the conservative movement in late imperial Russia, see Laura Engelstein, *Slavophile Empire: Imperial Russia's Illiberal Path* (Ithaca, NY: Cornell University Press, 2009).
97 John Strickland, *The Making of Holy Russia: The Orthodox Church and Russian Nationalism Before the Revolution* (Jordanville, NY: Holy Trinity Publications, 2013), xv.
98 *PTsV* 44 (1902): 44.
99 "Opredeleniia Sviateishego Sinoda," *TV* 37 (1910): 445.
100 See *TV* 17 (1915): I–II; "Ukaz," *OEV* 23 (1916): 1–4.
101 RGIA, f.391, op.4, d.2047, ll.1–2ob (To A. Krivoshein from the chair of the Holy Synod Special Council); "Ot Vysochaishe uchrezhdennogo pri Sviateishem Sinode Osobogo Soveshchaniia po udovletvoreniiu religioznykh nuzhd pereselentsev v zaural'skikh eparkhiiakh," *TV* 22 (1910): I–II.

102 RGIA, f.391, op.4, d.2047, ll. 13–16 (Certifications for commissioners).
103 RGIA, f.391, op.4, d.2047, l. 47.
104 Included on the list: *Novoe Vremia, Rech', Moskovskii Vedomosti, Sel'skii Vestnik, Russkii Vedomosti,* and a number of regional papers. See RGIA, f.391, op.4, d.2047, l.37.
105 RGIA, f.391, op.4, d. 2047, l.41 (Resettlement Administration, undated).
106 "V pomoshch' russkim pereselentsam," *TV* 22 (1910): III. For another example of a sermon, see "Pouchenie," *TV* 37(1910): III–IV.
107 This language of "faith and blood" was also common during the Russo-Turkish War; see Eskridge-Kosmach, "The Russian-Turkish War of 1877–1878," 432.
108 Pouchenie," *TV* 37(1910): IV.
109 *TV* 18–19 (1917): 1–4. Over the course of the first three years, Russian Orthodox believers donated approximately 300,000 rubles. See Liubimov, "Religii i veroispovednyi sostav naseleniia Aziatskoi Rossii," 239. Somewhat humorously, parishioners in Siberia also contributed to this collection. For instance, Omsk diocese raised 903 rubles and 56 kopeks during the Holy Trinity Collection. Istoricheskii arkhiv Omskoi oblasti (henceforth IAOO), f.16, op.1, d.148a, l.149. Local tsarist officials even reminded priests in Omsk diocese that they should participate. See IAOO, f.16, op.1, d.66, l.218 (Resettlement official to priest).
110 RGIA, f.391, op.6, d.827, l.9 (Telegram, 1916). For more on the Pastoral Courses in Moscow, see chapter 5 in this book.
111 RGIA, f.796, op.204, d.149, ll.1–2 (To Holy Synod from the chief procurator, 1917); RGIA, f.796, op.204, 2ot., 2st., d.235, ll.1–4 (To the Holy Synod from the chief procurator, 1917).

3. Parishes under Construction

1 RGIA, f.391, op.6, d.542, ll. 60ob–61 (Kirichenko's petition to Grigorii Glinka, 1916).
2 Ioann Goloshubin, *Spravochnaia kniga Omskoi eparkhii* (Omsk: Tipografiia "Irtysh," 1914), 232.
3 RGIA, f.391, op.6, d.542, l.60.
4 RGIA, f.796, op.198, 2ot., 2st., d.21, l.5ob (Kirichenko petition to Boris Stürmer, 1916).
5 For an example of this argument, see RGIA, f.796, op.191, 2ot., 2st., d.338, l.6 (Resolution from village assembly, 1908).
6 The Provisional Government, in 1917, introduced the zemstvo into Siberia (and the provinces of Akmolinsk and Semipalatinsk). See Robert Paul Browder and Aleksandr Kerensky, eds., *The Russian Provisional Government, 1917: Documents* (Stanford, CA: Stanford University Press, 1961), 303–4.

7   Gregory Freeze, "All Power to the Parish? The Problems and Politics of Church Reform in Late Imperial Russia," in *Social Identities in Revolutionary Russia*, ed. Madhavan Palat (Houndmills, UK: Palgrave, 2001), 175.

8   For more on the desire to reform the parish, see ibid., 174–96.

9   For more on "colonial paternalism" see Willard Sunderland, *Taming the Wild Field: Colonization and Empire on the Russian Steppe* (Ithaca, NY: Cornell University Press, 2004), 4.

10   As in European Russia, members of the community petitioned for permission from the consistory to solicit money for their building projects. See Istoricheskii arkhiv Omskoi oblasti (henceforth IAOO), f.16, op.1, d.74, l.25 (Parish priest to bishop of Omsk, 1904).

11   RGIA, f.391, op.4, d.210, l.61 (Annual report of the governor general of the steppe, 1909).

12   A.S. Ermolov, *Vsepoddannieishii doklad ministra zemledieliia i gosudarstvennykh' imushchestv' po poiezdkie v Sibir' oseniu 1895 goda* (St. Petersburg: Tip. "V. Kirshbauma," 1896), 26.

13   Petr A. Stolypin and Aleksandr V. Krivoshein, *Poezdka v Sibir' i povolzh'e: zapiska P. A. Stolypina i A. V. Krivosheina* (St. Petersburg: Tip. A.S. Suvorina, 1911), 78.

14   George J. Demko, *The Russian Colonization of Kazakhstan, 1896–1916* (Bloomington: Indiana University Press, 1969), 101.

15   Stolypin and Krivoshein, *Poezdka v Sibir' i povolzh'e*, 78.

16   *Pamiatnyia knizhki g. Omska i Akmolinskoi oblasti na 1913 god* (Omsk: Akmolinskaia Oblastnaia Tipografiia, 1913), 8–9.

17   A.L. Tregubov, *Pereselencheskoe delo v Semipalatinskoi i Semirechenskoi oblastiakh* (St. Petersburg, 1910), 6–7.

18   Ibid., 8.

19   M. Shilovskii, *Sibirskie Pereseleniia: dokumenty i materialy v.1* (Novosibirsk: Novosibirskii gos. universitet, 2003), 108.

20   RGIA, f.799, op.15, d.1220, l.211ob (Resolution, village assembly of Novo-Georgievskoe, 1913).

21   S.S.L., "Moia poezdka s treboiu k pereselentsam," *Pravoslavnyi blagovestnik (PB)* 4 (1912): 173.

22   *Vsepoddanneishii otchet ober-prokurora sviateishego sinoda po vedomstvu pravoslavnogo ispovedaniia za 1902 god* (St. Petersburg, 1905), 148. For more examples of church official expressing this view, see IAOO, f.16, op.1, d.74, l.4 (Prigovor of village assembly, 1902); "Tserkvi i shkoly dlia pereselentsev," *Pribavleniia k tserkovnym vedomostiam* 49 (1910): 2156–7.

23   RGIA, f.796, op.192, d.1935, ll.3ob–4 (Petition from a village to the Holy Synod).

24   IAOO, f.16, op.1, d.106, l.14 (Petition to priest from village, 1907).

25   IAOO, f.16, op.1, d.106, l.34 (Petition from village, 1907).

26 IAOO, f.16, op.1, d.92, l.80 (Journal of the Omsk diocesan consistory, 1904).
27 Cemeteries should be over five hundred metres away from the village; see IAOO, f.16, op.1, d.88, l.95 (Journal of Omsk diocesan consistory, 1903).
28 IAOO, f.16, op.1, d.88, ll.47–48 (Journal of the Omsk diocesan consistory, 1903).
29 Ioann Goloshubin, "Iz vpechatlenii sel'skogo sviashchennika," OEV (chast' neoffitsial'naia) 14 (1911): 21–2. For confirmation that this petition was submitted, see IAOO f.16, op.1, d.106, l.9; IAOO, f.16, op.1, d.133, l.309.
30 IAOO, f.16, op.1, d.133, ll.309–309ob (Journal of the Omsk diocesan consistory, 1908).
31 Goloshubin, "Iz vpechatlenii sel'skogo sviashchennika," 27.
32 Ibid., 21.
33 RGIA, f.796, op.191, 2ot., 2st., d.638, l.3 (Petition to the Holy Synod).
34 IAOO, f.16, op.1, d.126, l.3ob (petition to Bishop Gavriil, 1908).
35 Pereseleniia iz Poltavskoi gubernii s 1861 goda po 1900 g. (Poltava, 1900), 397–8. State and church officials also used the term "comfort" (uteshenie) to characterize the role that faith performed in these communities. See RGIA, f.802, op.10, d.912, l.12 (To Holy Synod from Bishop Gavriil, undated); Mefod'ev, "Blagochestivye zhiteli," 34; RGIA, f.821, op.133, d.289, l.2ob; RGIA, f.799, op.15, d.1197, l.1.
36 RGIA, f.796, op.194, d.2037, ll.162–162ob (Bishop Vladimir reproduced the statement from villager in correspondence with the Holy Synod, 1912).
37 RGIA, f.797, op.86, 2ot., 3st., d.166, l.1 (Petition from peasant village to chief procurator). For another example, see RGIA, f.799, op.15, d.1220, l.199 (Petition to Mariia Feodorovna from a peasant village).
38 See Jeffrey Burds, Peasant Dreams and Market Politics: Labor Migration and the Russian Village, 1861–1905 (Pittsburgh: University of Pittsburgh Press, 1998), 45.
39 IAOO, f.16, op.1, d.61, l.3 (petition to Bishop Grigorii).
40 IAOO, f.16, op.1, d.61, l.19 (Resolution of village society to Bishop Grigorii).
41 In 1902, this parish, relying on its own resources, began to build a church. In the meantime, parishioners from twenty-three different provinces in the Russian Empire, the majority of whom were from Poltava and Kharkov, worshipped in a prayer house. See Goloshubin, Spravochnaia kniga, 251–2.
42 Zhurnaly 3-go obshcheeparkhial'nogo s"ezda o.o. deputatov ot dukhovenstva Omskoi eparkhii, proizvodivshegosia v 1902 v g. Omske Akmolinskoi oblasti (Omsk, 1902), 26.
43 The diversity of acts labelled hooliganism – everything from mischief to murder – contributed to its almost indefinable character. Yet the attitude accompanying the act – a disregard for authority – appeared to be a common thread. See Neil B. Weissman, "Rural Crime in Tsarist Russia: The Question of Hooliganism, 1905–1914," Slavic Review 37, no. 2 (June 1978): 230.

While the Lykoshin commission described hooliganism as absent from Siberia and Central Asia, local secular and religious leaders in Omsk diocese clearly did not agree with this assessment. For an analysis of hooliganism in the city, see Joan Neuberger, *Hooliganism: Crime, Culture, and Power in St. Petersburg, 1900–1914* (Berkeley: University of California Press, 1993).

44 IAOO, f.16, op.1, d.10, l.178 (Deanery congress in Tara district, 1912).
45 Mefod'ev, "Blagochestivye zhiteli," 34–5.
46 "Eparkhial'naia khronika," *OEV* (chast' neoffitsial'naia) 4 (1914): 41. Bishop Andronik responded to Lebedev's article by reminding local clergymen that they must create a spiritual foundation for young parishioners: only through singing, teaching about prayer, processions, organizing study groups, and instilling the values of the Orthodox faith could the youth be reclaimed by the church; ibid., 43.
47 Panteleimon Papshev, "Usloviia, blagopriiatstvuiushchie sektantskoi propagande," *OEV* (chast' neoffitsial'naia) 29 (1916): 19.
48 "Ot khoziaistvennogo upravleniia pri Sviateishim Sinode," *OEV* 7 (1907): 1.
49 RGIA, f.1284, op.194, d.45, l.16 (Annual report of the governor of Akmolinsk, 1912).
50 RGIA, f. bib-ka, op.1, d.91, l.169ob (Annual report of the governor general of the steppe, 1912).
51 IAOO, f.16, op.1, d.92, l.8 (Journal of the Omsk diocesan consistory, 1904).
52 Goloshubin, *Spravochnaia kniga*, 85.
53 IAOO, f.16, op.1, d.92, l.47ob (Journal of the Omsk diocesan consistory, 1904).
54 Evgenii Krylov, "Raport ego preosviashchenstvy preosviashchenneishemu Sil'vestru, episkopu Omskomu i Pavlodarskomu, sviashchennika sela Kupina, Kainskogo uezda, Evgeniia Krylova," *OEV* (chast' neoffitsial'naia) 13 (1917): 5.
55 O.N. Ust'iantseva, *Tomskaia eparkhiia v kontse XIX–nachale XX veka* (Candidate diss., Kemerovskii gosudarstvennyi universitet, 2003), 84. The Ministry of War also had portable church tents; Nikolai Nekrasov borrowed one for his wedding in 1877. See Walter G. Moss, *Russia in the Age of Alexander II, Tolstoy and Dostoevsky* (London: Anthem Press, 2002), 191.
56 IAOO, f.16, op.1, d.122, ll.25–25ob (To Bishop Gavriil from the Resettlement Administration in Tomsk province, 1907).
57 During the war, these types of churches were still being ordered for settler parishes; see RGIA, f.391, op.6, d.827, l.1 and RGIA, f.391, op.6, d.539, l.34 (Holy Synod Economic Administration, 1915).
58 N. Venetskii, "Po prikhodu," *OEV* (chast' neoffitsial'naia) 3 (1904): 23.
59 For the case of Australian settlers, see Rowan Strong, "The Reverend John Wollaston and Colonial Christianity in Western Australia, 1840–1863," *Journal of Religious History* 25, no. 3 (October 2001): 278.

60 RGIA, f.796, op.442, d.1965, l.16 (Annual report to the Holy Synod by Bishop Sergii, 1901–1902).

61 Paul Yuzyk, "Religious Life," in *A Heritage in Transition: Essays in the History of Ukrainians in Canada*, ed. Manoly R. Lupul (Toronto: McClelland and Stewart, 1982), 147.

62 N.A. Minenko, *Russkaia krest'ianskaia sem'ia v zapadnoi Sibiri: XVIII–pervoi polovine XIX v.* (Novosibirsk: Nauka, Sibirskoe otd-nie, 1979), 262–3.

63 Goloshubin, "Iz vpechatlenii sel'skogo sviashchennika," 28–9.

64 IAOO, f.16, op.1, d.66, l.145 (Circular Omsk diocesan consistory, 1908).

65 Minenko, *Russkaia krest'ianskaia sem'ia v zapadnoi Sibiri*, 262–3.

66 RGIA, f.391, op.4, d.210, l.68 (Report of the governor general of the steppe on the needs of colonization work in the steppe region, 1910).

67 IAOO, f.16, op.1, d.122, l.1 (Decree of the Holy Synod, 1907).

68 Mark George McGowan, *Michael Power: The Struggle to Build the Catholic Church on the Canadian Frontier* (Montreal: McGill-Queen's University Press, 2005), 66.

69 RGIA, f.796, op. 191, 2ot, 2st, d.338, l.3 (Resolution from village assembly, 1909). For other examples, see IAOO, f.16, op.1, d.118, l.7ob; IAOO, f.16, op.1, d.118, l.7ob; RGIA, f.796, op.191, d.338, l.6; RGIA, f.797, op.86, 2ot., 3st., d.166, l.2.

70 RGIA, f.799, op.15, d.1679, l.220ob (Report by parish cantor, 1910); RGIA, f.799, op.15, d.1197, l.141ob (Resolution of village assembly, 1909); IAOO, f.16, op.1, d.142, l.368; RGIA, f.796, op.194, d.2037, l.162 (To the Holy Synod from Bishop Vladimir, 1912).

71 RGIA, f.bib-ka, op.1, d.85, l.119ob (Annual report of the governor of Semipalatinsk, 1908).

72 Christine Worobec, "Death Rituals among Russian and Ukrainian Peasants: Linkages between the Living and the Dead," in *Letters from Heaven: Popular Religion in Russia and Ukraine*, ed. John-Paul Himka and Andriy Zayarnyuk (Toronto: University of Toronto Press, 2006), 17–18.

73 Ibid., 25.

74 For more on the official meaning of baptism, see Timothy Ware, *The Orthodox Church*, 2nd ed. (New York: Penguin Books, 1997), 278. These rites not only held religious meaning, they were also essential for the Russian state. Orthodox priests recorded births, marriages, and deaths in metrical books that served as the only record of these events for both church and state officials.

75 Shilkin, *Otchet inzhenera Shilkina ob osmotre v 1900 gody tserkvei i shkol, sooruzhennykh i sooruzhaemykh na sredstva fonda imeni Imperatora Aleksandra III v Akmolinskoi oblasti i Eniseiskoi gubernii* (St. Petersburg, 1900), 2.

76 Based on parish descriptions in Tiukalinsk district from Goloshubin, *Spravochnaia kniga*, 536–706.

77 Willard Sunderland, "The 'Colonization Question': Visions of Colonization in Late Imperial Russia," *Jahrbücher für Geschichte Osteuropas* 48 (2000): 218.

78 RGIA, f.391, op.4, d.210, l.68 (Annual report of the governor general, 1910). Some examples of petitions from villages within Omsk diocese include: RGIA, f.796, op.191, d.338, l.6; RGIA, f.796, op.198, d.6, l.1ob; RGIA, f.799, op.15, d.1197, l.135. In a description of several settlements in the districts of Zaisan and Ust-kamenogorsk (the furthest south-eastern reaches of the diocese), the author reported that many of the villagers requested support for a local school. These villages primarily consisted of settlers. See *Opisanie nekotorykh pereselencheskikh poselkov Ust'kamenogorskogo i Zaisanskogo uezdov Semipalatinskoi oblasti v sel'skokho-ziaistvennom otnoshenie* (St. Petersburg, 1913).

79 RGIA, f.796, op.192, d.1935, ll.4–4ob (Petition of a village to the Holy Synod). Even though parents wanted their children to have a basic education, not all children shared that aspiration. One peasant indicated that young boys studying in his settler village did not enjoy studying and therefore learned very little. Fedor Korban, "Iz Makinskogo, Kokchetovskogo uezda, Akmolinsk oblasti," *Sel'skii vestnik* 39 (1904): 780.

80 For more information on how the zemstvo system operated, see Terence Emmons and Wayne S. Vucinich, eds., *The Zemstvo in Russia: An Experiment in Local Self-government* (New York: Cambridge University Press, 1982).

81 Nicole Young, "The Arduous Road to Enlightenment: The Development of Primary Education in Tobol'sk Guberniia, 1816–1914" (PhD diss., University of Toronto, 1996), 9.

82 Ibid., 301.

83 "Otchet Omskogo eparkhial'nogo nabliudatelia o sostoianii shkol tserkovno-prikhodskikh i gramoty Omskoi eparkhii v uchebno-vospitatel'nom otnoshenii za 1910–11 uch. god," *OEV* 4 (1912): 9. The author mentions that peasants were tempted to open ministry schools because of funding. This was a trend across the empire.

84 Feodor Abelfin, "Otkrytie odnoklassnoi tserkovno-prikhodskoi shkoly v sele Novorozhdestvennskom, Tarskogo uezda," *OEV* (chast' neoffitsi-al'naia) 9 (1902): 11.

85 Local clergy raised this issue countless times in the *Omsk Diocesan News*. For example, P.A.D., "Nastavlenie zakonouchitelia uchashchimsia ostav-liaiushchim shkolu," *OEV* (chast' neoffitsial'naia) 11 (1913): 28–30.

86 Nikolai Venetskii, "Po prokhodu," *OEV* (chast' neoffitsial'naia) 17 (1903): 31. Booksellers constituted one means by which parishioners in Siberia could purchase their own copy of the Gospel in Church Slavonic, Russian, or Ukrainian languages. See G. Peeddoobny, "Ukraintsy v

Sibiri," *Ukrainskaia zhizn'* 12 (1913): 11. This estimation seems high considering the low rate of literacy in the empire, especially in rural areas. For more on the literacy rates in the empire, see Jeffrey Brooks, *When Russia Learned to Read: Literacy and Popular Literature, 1861–1917* (Evanston, IL: Northwestern University Press, 1985).

87 *Materialy po pereselencheskomu khoziaistvu, Omskii uezd* (St. Petersburg, 1907), 18–19.

88 "Obozrenie Ego preosviashchenstvom, preosiashchenneishim Grigoriem, episkopom Omskim i Semipalatinskim tserkvei i prikhodov v 1897 godu," *OEV* 10 (1898): 6.

89 One of these stations was located at Petukhovo; T.I. Tarasov, *Tserkvi, shkoly i prichtovye doma, sooruzhennye na sredstva fonda imeni imperatora Aleksandra III. Otchet po komandirovke 1903 chinovnika kantseliarii kom. ministrov T.I. Tarasova ch.2* (1904), 8–9. For more on the conditions for building, see RGIA, f.1273, op.1, d.451, ll.33–33ob (Preparatory Committee of the Siberian Railway Commission, 1897).

90 RGIA, f.1273, op.1, d.451, l.33.

91 K. Skal'skii, "Doklad," *OEV* (chast' neoffitsial'naia) 17 (1898): 8.

92 S. Shilkin, *Otchet ob osmotre v 1900 gody tserkvei i shkol, sooruzhennykh i sooruzhaemykh na sredstva fonda imeni Imperatora Aleksandra III v Tobol'skoi i Tomskoi guberniiakh na sredstva fonda imeni Imperatora Aleksandra III* (St. Petersburg, 1900), 12.

93 Shevzov, *Russian Orthodoxy on the Eve of Revolution*, 61.

94 Shilkin, *Otchet ob osmotre*, 8.

95 RGIA, f. bib-ka, op.1, d.85, l.137 (Annual report of the governor of Semipalatinsk, 1912).

96 S. Shilkin, *Otchet inzhenera*, 1.

97 S. Shilkin, *Otchet ob osmotre*, 1–28.

98 *Zhurnaly 4-go obshcheeparkhial'nogo s"ezda o.o. deputatov ot dukhovenstva, Omskoi eparkhii byvshego v 1905 godu v g. Omske Akmolinskoi oblasti* (Omsk, 1905), 66–7.

99 *Omskii eparkhial'nyi s"ezd dukhovenstva, zhurnal obshcheeparkhial'nogo s" ezda v 1909* (1910), 34.

100 "Nuzhen li nam arkhitektor?," *OEV* (chast' neoffitsial'naia) 6 (1916): 27.

101 "Osviashchenie tserkvi v sele Poltavskom Omskogo uezda," *OEV* (chast' neoffitsial'naia) 13–14 (1901): 4–6; Tarasov, *Tserkvi i shkoly ch.2* (1904), 38–40.

102 "Osviashchenie tserkvi v sele Poltavskom," 6.

103 RGIA, f.796, op.442, d.2041, l.18ob (Annual report to the Holy Synod by Bishop Mikhail, 1904).

104 RGIA, f.796, op.442, d.2593, l.15 (Annual report to the Holy Synod by Bishop Andronik, 1914).

105 T.I. Tarasov, *Tserkvi, shkoly i prichtovye doma, sooruzhennye na sredstva fonda imeni imperatora Aleksandra III. Otchet po komandirovke 1903 chinovnika kantseliarii kom. ministrov T.I. Tarasova ch.1* (St. Petersburg, 1904), 126.

106 RGIA, f.391, op.6, d.542, l.60ob.

107 Based on Goloshubin, *Spravochnaia kniga*, 98–167.

108 Ibid., 404.

4. The Politics of Pastoring

1 Pamela Welch, *Church and Settler in Colonial Zimbabwe: A Study in the History of the Anglican Diocese of Mashonaland/Southern Rhodesia, 1890–1925* (Leiden, NL: Brill, 2008), 156–7.

2 Hilary M. Carey, *God's Empire: Religion and Colonialism in the British World, c.1801–1908* (Cambridge: Cambridge University Press, 2011), 258.

3 Tobol'sk seminary opened in 1743, Tomsk in 1858, Irkutsk in 1788, Yakutsk in 1858 (which was transferred to Blagoveshchensk in 1871), Orenburg in 1889, and Enisei in 1894. A seminary in Ekaterinburg was also opened in 1916, but such a late opening made little difference to the supply of priests. The reasons given for the opening of the seminary in Krasnoyarsk included providing an opportunity for priests' sons in Enisei diocese to be educated and raising the educational level of the local clergy. Before receiving its own seminary, Enisei diocese had relied on the seminaries of Tomsk, located 555 kilometres away from Krasnoyarsk, and of Irkutsk, which was 1,000 kilometres away. See *Vsepoddanneishii otchet ober-prokurora sviateishego sinoda za 1894 i 1895 gody* (St. Petersburg, 1898), 318. To improve the level of education in Siberia, some proposed opening a theological academy in Tomsk. See Alla V. Litiagina, "Deiatel'nost' Russkoi pravoslavnoi tserkvi v gorodakh zapadnoi Sibiri vo vtoroi polovine XIX – nachale XX v.," *Voprosy istorii* 9 (2008): 94; V.A. Tarasova, *Vysshaia dukhovnaia shkola v Rossii v kontse XIX – nachale XX veka: istoriia imperatorskikh pravoslavnykh dukhovnykh akademii* (Moscow: Novyi khronograf, 2005), 401; L. Lavrent'ev, *Sibirskaia dukhovnaia akademiia* (Tomsk: Pechatnia S.P. Iakovleva, 1914).

4 Jennifer Hedda, *His Kingdom Come: Orthodox Pastorship and Social Activism in Revolutionary Russia* (DeKalb: Northern Illinois University Press, 2008), 65. For more on the pastoral movement, see Laurie Manchester, *Holy Fathers, Secular Sons: Clergy, Intelligentsia, and the Modern Self in Revolutionary Russia* (DeKalb: Northern Illinois University Press, 2008), 70.

5 The wives of Orthodox clergymen performed an important role in parish life. Unfortunately, the sources in Omsk diocese shed little light on this topic. For a general treatment of this issue, see Laurie Manchester,

"Gender and Social Estate as National Identity: The Wives and Daughters of Orthodox Clergymen as Civilizing Agents in Imperial Russia," *Journal of Modern History* 83 (March 2011): 48–77.

6 Nicholas Atkin, *Priests, Prelates and People: A History of European Catholicism since 1750* (New York: I.B. Tauris, 2003), 29–30. For more on the development of the clergy as a profession in Europe, see W.M. Jacob, *The Clerical Profession in the Long Eighteenth Century, 1680–1840* (Oxford: Oxford University Press, 2007).

7 Gregory L. Freeze, *The Parish Clergy in Nineteenth-Century Russia: Crisis, Reform, Counter-Reform* (Princeton, NJ: Princeton University Press, 1983), 159.

8 Laurie Manchester, *Holy Fathers, Secular Sons: Clergy, Intelligentsia, and the Modern Self in Revolutionary Russia* (DeKalb: Northern Illinois University Press, 2008), 7.

9 For figures on the social origins of seminarians for 1913–14, see A.V. Sushko, "Religious Seminaries in Russia (to 1917)," *Russian Studies in History* 44, no.4 (Spring 2006): 55.

10 The number of students enrolled in seminary increased from 13,834 in 1855 to 19,845 in 1904; Freeze, *The Parish Clergy in Nineteenth-Century Russia*, 452. Bishops in European Russia expressed their unhappiness with the number of seminary graduates pursuing other careers. See ibid., 454.

11 Ibid., 455.

12 The share of priests with a seminary education was 82.6 per cent in 1860 and increased to a high point of 88.1 per cent in 1890. Only fourteen years later, it was 63.8 per cent; ibid.

13 For example, in Tver diocese, there were 321 unplaced seminary graduates in 1850. While other dioceses did not reach such high numbers, Kostroma, Novgorod, Tula, and Vladimir dioceses all had over a hundred seminary graduates without positions; see ibid., 152.

14 N. Aleksandov, "Sviashchennik A.N. Shestakov," *Omskie eparkhial'nye vedomosti (OEV)* (chast' neoffitsial'naia) 22 (1902): 11–12. Obituaries of other priests confirm that professional development was a strong motivation for relocating to Siberia. See Ioann Savel'ev, "Nekrolog," *OEV* (chast' neoffitsial'naia) 12 (1914): 43–6, and "Nekrolog," *OEV* (chast' neof-fitsial'naia) 22 (1898): 7.

15 For a similar trend in the British Empire, see Hilary M. Carey, *God's Empire: Religion and Colonialism in the British World, c.1801–1908* (Cambridge: Cambridge University Press, 2011), 247.

16 Gosudarstvennyi arkhiv Rossiiskoi Federatsii (henceforth GARF), f.9452, op.1, d.44, l.27ob (Report to the chief procurator by Vostorgov, 1909).

17 Tarasova, *Vysshaia dukhovnaia shkola*, 253–4. Tarasova also notes that dioceses in Siberia and Central Asia also had very few men with a degree from one of the four theological academies working in their consistories.

18 Viacheslav Sofronov, *Missionerskaia i dukhovno-prosvetitel'skaia deiatel'nost' Russkoi pravoslavnoi tserkvi v zapadnoi Sibiri: konets XVII – nachalo XX vv.* (Tobol'sk: GOU VPO "Tobol'skii gosudarstvennyi pedagogicheskii institut imeni D.I. Mendeleeva," 2005), 82.

19 A.L., "Iz zhizni dukhovnoi shkoly," *Vestnik vospitaniia* 20, no. 3 (1909): 119.

20 Such an advertisement appeared in the *Samara Diocesan News*. See *Tobol'skie eparkhial'nye vedomosti* 13 (1896): 311. A short article in an 1896 issue of *Tobol'sk Diocesan News* referred to the advertisement.

21 Rossiiskii gosudarstvennyi istoricheskii arkhiv (henceforth RGIA), f.796, op.442, d.1965, l.18ob (Annual report to the Holy Synod by Bishop Sergii, 1901–02).

22 RGIA, f.796, op.442, d.1965, l.17ob. Although Omsk priests (and Siberian priests in general) were undereducated, the reality is that they still composed the bulk of the educated population in Siberia. For a discussion of the large role performed by Siberian priests in this regard, see "Ocherki sibirskoi zhizni," *Sibirskie voprosy* 3–4 (1912): 43–52.

23 RGIA, f.796, op.442, d.2287, l.27 (Annual report to the Holy Synod by Bishop Gavriil, 1908).

24 This number is below the Russian average. According to Freeze, in 1904 only 63.8 per cent of priests had a seminary degree. See Freeze, *The Parish Clergy in Nineteenth-Century Russia*, 455.

25 RGIA, f.796, op.442, d.2287, l.21.

26 This information is based on a spreadsheet created from figures contained in Ioann Goloshubin, *Spravochnaia kniga Omskoi eparkhii* (Omsk: Tipografiia Irtysh, 1914), 1081–223. The number of priests listed in this reference book was 711. In many cases, information was missing from the entries; instead of disregarding these, I include a category of "unknown" in my statistical analysis. While Goloshubin provides information on the entire (male) clerical population, priests are my focus. Merchants, townspeople, Cossacks, and bureaucrats constituted 14.2 per cent; 0.6 per cent came from the nobility; 10.4 per cent from peasant background; and 22.2 per cent of Omsk priests had an unknown social background.

27 Goloshubin, *Spravochnaia kniga*, 1081–223.

28 Ibid.

29 RGIA, f.796, op.442, d.2225, l.8ob (Annual report to the Holy Synod by Bishop Graviil, 1907). Perhaps more significant than the distance was the associated cost for the diocese: 15,000 rubles a year. This source does not reveal how many students this payment supported.

30 For those young men who left the clerical estate, clerical culture nonetheless remained a significant influence on their values and outlooks. See Manchester, *Holy Fathers, Secular Sons*, 4–7.

31 *Omskii eparkhial'nyi s"ezd dukhovenstva, zhurnaly s"ezda o.o. deputatov ot dukhovenstva Omskoi eparkhii, proiskhodivshego v 1899 godu v Omske Akmolinskoi oblasti* (1899), 42.

32 Istoricheskii arkhiv Omskoi oblasti (henceforth IAOO), f.16, op.1, d.140, ll.11–11ob (Commission on the opening of an ecclesiastical seminary in the city of Omsk, 1909–16).

33 IAOO, f.16, op.1, d.140, l.12.

34 O.V. Ushakova, "K voprosu ob otkrytii dukhovnoi seminarii v Omskoi eparkhii," *Stepnoi krai zona vzaimodeistviia russkogo i kazakhskogo narodov* (Omsk, 1998), 149.

35 Ibid.

36 IAOO, f.16, op.1, d.140, l.19.

37 *Omskii eparkhial'nyi s"ezd dukhovenstva, zhurnal obshcheeparkhial'nogo s"ezda v 1909* (1910), 46. For more on clergymen's support for educating their daughters, see Scarborough, "The White Priest at Work," 160–6.

38 *Omskii eparkhial'nyi s"ezd dukhovenstva, zhurnal obshcheeparkhial'nogo s"ezda v 1909* (1910), 46.

39 IAOO, f.16, op.1, d.140, l.66–66ob (Journal of the deanery council of Omsk, 1909).

40 IAOO, f.16, op.1, d.140, l.62, l.74, l.79. According to the deanery council of Tiukalinsk district, Omsk diocese was young and burdened with other financial obligations. See IAOO, f.16, op.1, d.140, l.31.

41 IAOO, f.16, op.1, d.140, ll.235–240 (To Bishop Sil'vestr from the economic administration of the Holy Synod, 1915).

42 "O poriadke opredeleniia sviashchennotserkovnosluzhitlei v prichty pereselencheskikh prikhodov Zaural'skikh eparkhii i ob usloviiakh obezpecheniia sikh prichtov," *TV* 27 (1908): 228–30.

43 For a positive response to the ad from a priest in Kishinev, see RGIA, f.391, op.3, d.671, l.231 (To Resettlement Administration from Fr. Gavriil Miriliubov, 1908).

44 RGIA, f.391, op.3, d.1819, l.1–1ob (Correspondence to GUZiZ from chief procurator, 1909).

45 RGIA, f.391, op.3, d.1819, l.11 (Correspondence to Vostorgov from Glinka, 1909).

46 RGIA, f.391, op.3, d.1819, l.16 (Plan to the Council of Ministers from GUZiZ, undated).

47 GARF, f.9452, op.1, d.18, l.19 (Report on the Pastoral Courses by Vostorgov).

48 For an interpretation of a similar process taking place within state structures, see Willard Sunderland, "The Ministry of Asiatic Russia: The Colonial Office That Never Was but Might Have Been," *Slavic Review* 69, no. 1 (April 2010): 120–50.

49 "Pastyrskie kursy," *OEV* 17 (1909): 39.

50 RGIA, f.821, op.133, d.90, l.21ob (Report on Pastoral Courses in Moscow by Semen Bondar, 1911). Also see Ioann Vostorgov, "Pastyrskie kursy v Moskve," *Pribavleniia k tserkovnym vedomostiam* (henceforth PTsV) 10 (1910): 450. The courses received coverage in the periodical *Voprosy kolonizatsii* (Questions of Colonization). See "Moskovskie pastyrskie kursy dlia podgotovki sviashchennosluzhitelei komandiruemykh v pereselencheskie raiony," *Voprosy kolonizatsii* 9 (1911): 420–8.

51 Vostorgov also started a course for cantors. See I.I. Vostorgov, "Sluzhenie psalomshchika," *PTsV* 48 (1911): 2046–50.

52 RGIA, f.821, op.133, d.90, l.21ob.

53 RGIA, f.821, op.133, d.90, l.28. While Vostorgov himself never made this connection, it is clear that Orthodox clergymen watched and learned from the Baptist techniques of engaging with ordinary people. See Heather J. Coleman, "Defining Heresy: The Fourth Missionary Congress and the Problem of Cultural Power after 1905 in Russia," *Jahrbücher Für Geschichte Osteuropas* 52, no. 1 (2004): 81. The governor general of the steppe identified the Baptists' clear and convincing sermons as one key to their success in the region. See RGIA, f.1276, op.17, d.165, l.232ob.

54 RGIA, f.821, op.133, d.90, l.28ob.

55 RGIA, f.821, op.133, d.90, l.29. For more on debates about preaching in the Orthodox Church, see Hedda, *His Kingdom Come*, 58–63.

56 RGIA, f.821, op.133, d.90, l.27.

57 RGIA, f.821, op.133, d.90, l.21ob (Report on Pastoral Courses in Moscow by Semen Bondar, 1911).

58 RGIA, f.391, op.5, d.680, l.83. This file has five other letters from priests making similar enquiries.

59 RGIA, f.391, op.5, d.680, l.84. (Telegram to St. Petersburg from Semipalatinsk, 1914).

60 RGIA, f.391, op.5, d.680, l.85 (Correspondence to Mel'nichenko from Chirkin, 1914). Representatives of the Resettlement Administration regularly found themselves acting as intermediaries between clergy in European Russia and Siberian dioceses. See RGIA, f.391, op.6, d.539, ll.92–94.

61 Omsk diocese held such an event in 1908. See "Pastyrskoe missionerskoe sobranie Omskogo gorodskogo dukhovenstva," *OEV* (chast' neoffitsial'naia) 4 (1908): 29; "Vtoroe missionersko–pastyrskoe sobranie Omskogo gorodskogo duzhovenstva," *OEV* (chast' neoffitsial'naia) 5 (1908): 44. The idea that pastoral courses were necessary to prepare clergy for settler parishes continued to the end of the empire. At the beginning of 1917, plans were in the works for a pastoral course to be held in the city of Krasnoyarsk. See "Ob otkrytii pastyrskikh kursov pri Krasnoyarskoi," *OEV* (chast' neoffitsial'naia) 1 (1917): 6–7.

62 RGIA, f.1284, op.194, d.56, l.26 (Annual report of the Tobol'sk governor, 1912).

63 RGIA, f.796, op.445, d.301, l.218. Vostorgov gives credit to the Missionary Council of the Holy Synod for the idea of establishing pastoral missionary courses in the empire.

64 Aleksii, episkop Tobol'skii i Sibirskii, "Rech, skazannaia protoiereiu Ioannu Vostorgovu 2-go avgustva 1912 goda v den' zakrytiia Tobol'skikh missionerskikh kursov," *Tobol'skie eparkhial'nye vedomosti* 16 (1912): 355–6. Bishop Aleksii was not fawning over the archpriest; he inserted some choice critiques, including that the first set of courses had been too short, thereby implying that training had been inadequate.

65 RGIA, f.797, op.82, 2ot., 3st., d.477, l.3 (To the chief procurator of the Holy Synod from Bishop Vladimir, 1912).

66 RGIA, f.797, op.82, 2ot., 3st., d.477, l.4.

67 In reality, Bishop Vladimir had ultimate authority over whether to accept graduates from the courses into his diocese. For example, no priests from the courses received a position in Omsk from 1912 to 1913. Ninety graduates were assigned to nine other dioceses. See *Gosudarstvennaia duma: stenograficheskie otchety, chetvertyi sozyv, sessiia I, chast' 3* (St. Petersburg: Gos. tip., 1914), no.337.

68 Metropolitan Manuil (Lemesevskij), *Die Russischen Orthodoxen Bischöfe von 1893 bis 1965*, Teil II (Erlangen, DE: Erlangen Lehrstuhl für Geschichte u. Theologie d. Christl. Ostens, 1981), 234.

69 D. Pospielovsky, "The Renovationist Movement in the Orthodox Church in the Light of Archival Documents," *Journal of Church and State* 39, no. 1 (1997): 95.

70 For more on Renovationism, see Edward Roslof, *Red Priests: Renovationism, Russian Orthodoxy, and Revolution, 1905–1946* (Bloomington: Indiana University Press, 2002).

71 GARF, f.9452, op.1, d.39, l.2ob (Report by Vostorgov to the Metropolitan of Moscow, 1911). For more specific complaints from Bishop Vladimir against graduates of the Moscow courses, see RGIA, f.796, op.194, d.2037, l.56 (Report to Sabler by Bishop Vladimir, 1912); RGIA, f.797, op.82, d.83, l.3 (Report to the chief procurator from Bishop Vladimir, 1912).

72 GARF, f.9452, op.1, d.39, ll.2–3ob.

73 Ioann Vostorgov, "Kogo posliu," *PTsV* 11 (1912): 462. Vostorgov is referencing Siberian regionalism, a political movement that started in the mid-nineteenth century and which stressed the cultural differences between Siberia and European Russia and opposed the colonization of Siberia by settlers from Russia. See N.M. Iadrintsev, *Sibir' kak koloniia: sovremennoe polozhenie Sibiri, ee nuzhdy i potrebnosti, ee proshloe i budushchee* (St. Petersburg: Tip. M.M. Stasiulevicha, 1882). For a recent

academic treatment of this topic, see David Rainbow, "Siberian Patriots: Participatory Autocracy and the Cohesion of the Russian Imperial State, 1858–1920" (PhD diss., New York University, 2013).

74 Vostorgov, "Kogo posliu," 462–4.

75 Ibid.

76 Ibid., 463.

77 *Zhurnaly 7-go obshcheeparkhial'nogo s"ezda o. o. deputatov ot dukhovenstva Omskoi eparkhii byvshego v 1912 godu v g. Omske, Akmolinskoi oblasti* (Omsk, 1912), 120, 125.

78 Ibid., 132.

79 Ibid., 128.

80 Ibid., 150.

81 Sibirskii sviashchennik, "Sibirskie skorpiony i ovtsy prot. Ioanna Vostorgova," *OEV* (chast' neoffitsial'naia) 14 (1912): 40.

82 *Zhurnaly 7-go obshcheeparkhial'nogo s"ezda*, 152.

83 Ibid., 151.

84 Ibid., 122.

85 Sibirskii sviashchennik, "Sibirskie skorpiony i ovtsy," 35.

86 *Zhurnaly 7-go obshcheeparkhial'nogo s"ezda*, 128.

87 Sibirskii sviashchennik, "Sibirskie skorpiony i ovtsy," 36.

88 *Zhurnaly 7-go obshcheeparkhial'nogo s"ezda*, 125.

89 Sibirskii sviashchennik, "Sibirskie skorpiony i ovtsy," 36.

90 *Zhurnaly 7-go obshcheeparkhial'nogo s"ezda*, 126.

91 Ibid., 150.

92 Ibid., 152. This issue – opening more local seminaries versus importing priests from Russia through the Pastoral Courses in Moscow – also appeared in Tomsk. See Litiagina, "Deiatel'nost' Russkoi pravoslavnoi tserkvi v gorodakh zapadnoi Sibiri vo vtoroi polovine XIX – nachale XX v.," 94.

93 Sibirskii sviashchennik, "Sibirskie skorpiony i ovtsy," 40.

94 Ibid., 40.

95 Despite this conviction that priests trained by Vostorgov would choose not to stay in Siberia beyond their five-year term, in reality, not enough time had passed to confirm such a trend.

96 While the fate of Father Dmitrii cannot be confirmed, he was noticeably absent from the list of clergy in the Omsk diocesan reference book published two years after this event.

97 GARF, f.9452, op.1, d.39, l.95ob (Unpublished article by Karveev, 1912). Less than 10 per cent of priests were from these courses.

98 GARF, f.9452, op.1, d.39, l.96.

99 Ibid.

100 I.I. Vostorgov, "Smirennomudrie sviashchennika," *PkTV* 18–19 (1913): 789–90.

101 RGIA, f.797, op.82, 2ot., 3st., d.75, l.47. For more on the planning of the
     courses, see GARF, f.9452, op.1, d.55, ll.6–9.
102 "Missionerskie kursy v g. Omske," *OEV* 16 (1913): 49. For more coverage,
     see Khronika: Deiatel'nost' pravoslavnoi missii," *MO* 9 (1913): 154.
103 "Missionerskie kursy v g. Omske," *OEV* (chast' neoffitsial'naia)
     16 (1913): 51–2.
104 Stolypin and Krivoshein, *Poezdka v Sibir' i povolzh'e*, 54–5.
105 *Vsepoddanneishii otchet ober-prokurora sviateishego sinoda za 1908 i 1909 gody*
     (St. Petersburg, 1911), 163–4.
106 RGIA, f.821, op.133, d.289, ll.26–26ob (Report by A. Kologrivov to MVD).
107 GARF, f.9452, op.1, d.55, l.1 (Report on the Pastoral Courses, undated).
     The vicar bishop, Modest (Nikitin), replaced Vostorgov as the head of the
     Pastoral Courses in Moscow. See RGIA, f.796, op.198, d.167, l.43 (To the
     Holy Synod from the Holy Synod Economic Administration, 1914). It
     should be noted that the Fourth Duma was actually quite conservative in
     its outlook.
108 A.L. Tregubov, *Po novym mestam* (St. Petersburg: Tip. Iu. H. Erlikh, 1913), 48.
109 RGIA, f.391, op.5, d.680, l.151 (Report by GUZiZ, 1915).
110 RGIA, f.391, op.5, d.680, l.169 (A. Naumov, 1916).
111 RGIA, f.1276, op.12, d.1767, l.3. They were sent to Blagoveshchensk,
     Vladivostok, Enisei, Irkutsk, Omsk, Orenburg, Samara, Tobol'sk, Tomsk,
     Turkestan, and Transbaikal.
112 RGIA, f.391, op.6, d.539, l.87 (Correspondence to the minister of agri-
     culture from the chief procurator, 1916); RGIA, f.796, op.198, d.167, l.1
     (Proposal on the spiritual needs of settlers to the Holy Synod from the
     chief procurator, 1914).

5. Living and Dying among Strangers

1 This was a slight exaggeration as a description of this parish in the Omsk
   diocese reference book lists the number of parishioners at 4,193 and
   the furthest village from the parish church as twenty-two kilometres
   away. See Ioann Goloshubin, *Spravochnaia kniga Omskoi eparkhii* (Omsk:
   Tipografiia "Irtysh," 1914), 265.
2 Ioann Savel'ev, "Sviashchennik Andrei Soltanovskii (nekrolog),"
   Omskie eparkhial'nye vedomosti (henceforth *OEV*) (chast' neoffitsial'naia)
   20 (1914): 42.
3 Ibid., 43. For the composition of the parish, see Goloshubin, *Spravochnaia
   kniga*, 265.
4 A petition from the village of Okoneshinkovskii in Tiukalinsk district
   requested that an Estonian-speaking Orthodox priest be assigned to the
   neighbouring village of Zalotinivskii, which was filled with Estonian

settlers: half the village was Orthodox while the other half was Lutheran. See Rossiiskii gosudarstvennyi istoricheskii arkhiv (henceforth, RGIA), f.796, op.198, 2ot., 2st., d.764, l.1 (Petition from parishioners of a peasant village to the chief procurator, 1914).

5 For more on the traditional clothing of Ukrainian settlers in Siberia, see E.F. Fursova and L.I. Vasekha, *Ocherki traditsionnoi kul'tury Ukrainskikh pereselentsev Sibiri XIX–pervoi treti XX veka: po materialam Novosibirskoi oblasti* (Novosibirsk: Agro-Sibir', 2004), 15–25. For more on changes to peasant clothing in late imperial Russia, see Christine Ruane, *The Empire's New Clothes: A History of the Russian Fashion Industry 1700–1917* (New Haven, CT: Yale University Press, 2009), 156–7.

6 For more on this "Great Russian" identity, see Anatolyi Remnev, "Siberia and the Russian Far East in the Imperial Geography of Power," in *Russian Empire: Space, People, Power: 1700–1930*, ed. Jane Burbank and Mark Von Hagen (Bloomington: Indiana University Press, 2007), 441–2. Eva-Maria Stolberg also emphasizes the homogeneity of settlers to Siberia in contrast to the North American case; see Stolberg, "The Siberian Frontier and Russia's Position in World History: A Reply to Aust and Nolte," *Review (Fernand Braudel Center)* 27, no. 3 (January 2004): 255. While the depth of diversity was more intensely felt in North America, differences still existed in Siberia between settlers, which influenced the development of villages.

7 See V.A. Berdinskikh, "The Parish Clergy and the Development of Local History in Nineteenth-Century Russia," *Russian Studies in History* 44, no. 4 (Spring 2006): 9–18.

8 I. Korovkin, "Pop Rasstriga," *Znamia il'icha* 117 (1959): 2.

9 Heather J. Coleman, "Introduction," in *Orthodox Christianity in Imperial Russia: A Source Book on Lived Religion* (Bloomington: Indiana University Press, 2014), 13.

10 David D. Hall, ed., *Lived Religion in America: Toward a History of Practice* (Princeton, NJ: Princeton University Press, 1997), ix.

11 In her discussion of the celebration of local feasts, Vera Shevzov notes that these events acquired a local flavour, even though commonality existed across parishes. See Shevzov, *Orthodoxy on the Eve of Revolution* (Oxford: Oxford University Press, 2004), 144.

12 For more on the history of the commune, see David Moon, *The Russian Peasantry, 1600–1930: The World the Peasants Made* (New York: Longman, 1999), 199–236.

13 Caroline Ford, "Religion and Popular Culture in Modern Europe," *Journal of Modern History* 65, no. 1 (1993): 175.

14 Gregory Freeze, "Institutionalizing Piety: The Church and Popular Religion, 1750–1850," in *Imperial Russia: New Histories for the Empire*, ed.

Jane Burbank and David L. Ransel (Bloomington: Indiana University Press, 1998), 215.

15 Fedor Korban, "Iz Makinskogo, Kokchetovskogo uezda, Akmolinskoi oblasti," *Sel'skii vestnik* 39 (1904): 780.

16 Gerasim Tsybenko, "Iz Kiminskoi volost'," *Sel'skii vestnik* 47 (1900): 843–4.

17 Tikhon Bobylev, "Iz Kulundinskoi volosti," *Sel'skii vestnik* 7 (1900): 118. For more on a "clash of attitudes between settlers and *Sibiriaki,* see Peter Holquist, "The Shifting Boundary: Regional and Religious Identity among Old Believers and Orthodox Peasants in Western Siberia, 1880s–1914" (MA thesis, Columbia University, 1990), 140–2.

18 Istoricheskii arkhiv Omskoi oblasti (henceforth IAOO), f.16, op.1, d.72, l.233 (Journal of the Omsk diocesan consistory, 1901–02).

19 Goloshubin, *Spravochnaia kniga,* 653.

20 IAOO, f.16, op.1, d.121, l.128 (Journal of the Omsk diocesan consistory, 1907).

21 "Pervaia poezdka ego preosviashchenstva, preosviashchenneishogo Mikhaila, episkopa Omskogo i Semipalatinskogo, dlia obozreniia tserkvei eparkhii," *OEV* (chast' neoffitsial'naia), 3 (1905): 44.

22 Ibid., 44–5.

23 Shevzov, *Russian Orthodoxy on the Eve of Revolution,* 145–7.

24 Goloshubin, "Iz vpechatlenii sel'skogo sviashchennika," 31.

25 See Chris J. Chulos, *Converging Worlds: Religion and Community in Peasant Russia, 1861–1917* (DeKalb: Northern Illinois University Press, 2003). See also Vera Shevzov, *Russian Orthodoxy on the Eve of Revolution* (Oxford: Oxford University Press, 2004).

26 Shevzov, *Russian Orthodoxy on the Eve of Revolution,* 88–9.

27 Chulos, *Converging Worlds,* 6.

28 For more on the difference between old resident and settler performance of rituals, such as marriage, see V.A. Lipinskaia, *Starozhily i pereselentsy: Russkie na Altae: XVIII–nachalo XX veka* (Moscow: Nauka, 1996), 198–225.

29 Ioann Goloshubin, "Iz vpechatlenii sel'skogo sviashchennika," *OEV* (chast' neoffitsial'naia), no.14 (1911): 32.

30 IAOO, f.16, op.1, d.159, l.122 (Journal of the Omsk diocesan consistory, 1915).

31 Goloshubin, "Iz vpechatlenii sel'skogo sviashchennika," 27.

32 Ibid., 32–3. For more on the calendar of customs of Ukrainian settlers to Siberia, see E.F. Fursova and L.I. Vasekha, *Ocherki traditsionnoi kul'tury Ukrainskikh pereselentsev Sibiri XIX–pervoi treti XX veka: po materialam Novosibirskoi oblasti* (Novosibirsk: Agro-Sibir', 2004), 26–66. They do not mention the celebration of the Theophany.

33 Goloshubin, "Iz vpechatlenii sel'skogo sviashchennika," 33.

34 Ibid., 36. For more on this ritual, see Natalie Kononenko, "Folk Orthodoxy: Popular Religion in Contemporary Ukraine," in *Letters from Heaven: Popular Religion in Russia and Ukraine*, ed. John-Paul Himka and Andriy Zayarnyuk (Toronto: University of Toronto, 2006), 57–61.

35 *Ukraintsy* (Moscow: Nauka, 2000), 325. Christine Worobec, "Death Ritual among Russian and Ukrainian Peasants: Linkages between the Living and the Dead," in *Letters from Heaven: Popular Religion in Russia and Ukraine*, ed. John-Paul Himka and Andriy Zayarnyuk (Toronto: University of Toronto Press, 2006), 28.

36 *Zhurnaly 3-go obshcheeparkhialnogo s"ezda o.o. deputatov ot dukhovenstva Omskoi eparkhii, proizvodivshegosia v 1902 godu v g.Omske Akmolinskoi oblasti* (Omsk, 1902), 59.

37 RGIA, bib-ka op.1, d.1, l.155ob (Annual report of the governor of Akmolinsk, 1897).

38 Ioann Vostorgov, *Dobroe slovo pereselentsy* (Moscow, 1909), 19. Vostorgov also referred to this problem in another new settler village. See RGIA, f.796, op.440, d.1274, ll.6–7.

39 Nikolai Venetskii, "Po prikhodu," *OEV* (chast' neoffitsial'naia), 17 (1903): 25.

40 Nikolai Venetskii, "Po prikhodu," *OEV* (chast' neoffitsial'naia), 16 (1903): 22.

41 For a religious history of the western borderlands, see Barbara Skinner, *The Western Front of the Eastern Church: Uniate and Orthodox Conflict in 18th-century Poland, Ukraine, Belarus, and Russia* (DeKalb: Northern Illinois University Press, 2009). For a discussion on the concern within the Orthodox Church with the Uniate issue in the late nineteenth century, see A. Iu. Polunov, "The Religious Department and the Uniate Question, 1881–1894," *Russian Studies in History* 39, no. 4 (Spring 2001): 77–85.

42 Nikolai Venetskii, "Po prikhodu," *OEV* (chast' neoffitsial'naia) 16 (1903): 19.

43 Goloshubin, "Iz vpechatlenii sel'skogo sviashchennika," 29.

44 Timothy Ware, *The Orthodox Church* (New York: Penguin, 1993), 278.

45 Chulos, *Converging Worlds*, 39.

46 *Omskii eparkhial'nyi s"ezd dukhovenstva, zhurnal obshcheeparkhial'nogo s"ezda v 1909* (1910), 141.

47 Goloshubin, "Iz vpechatlenii sel'skogo sviashchennika," 30.

48 Nikolai Kudriavtsev, "K voprosu o religioznom sostoianii i nekotorykh tserkovno-obriadovykh osobennostiakh pereselentsev, poselivshikhsia v predelakh Omskoi eparkhii," *OEV* (chast' neoffitsial'naia), 6 (1911): 54–5.

49 Ibid.

50 Ibid. Archimandrite Kiprian sarcastically referred to the "holy" provinces Kiev and Chernigov in his denigration of Ukrainian settlers. He criticized

these settlers as being undeveloped in their faith, not knowing the most important prayers, not understanding the blessing of the priest and how to receive it, and taking communion like it was "honey" without first confessing. See "O deiatel'nosti i sostoianii Kirgizskoi missii za 1908 g," *OEV* 10 (1909): 40.

51 Afanasii Liasetskii, "V zashchitu pereselentsev-malorossov," *OEV* (chast' neoffitsial'naia) 10 (1911): 41.

52 Ibid., 42.

53 For a brief description of Liasetskii's background, see Goloshubin, *Spravochnaia kniga*, 1150.

54 Ibid., 1140.

55 RGIA, f.391, op.3, d.671, l.460 (Local tsarist officials to the Resettlement Administration).

56 Frances Swyripa, *Storied Landscapes: Ethno-Religious Identity and the Canadian Prairies* (Winnipeg: University of Manitoba Press, 2010), 43–74.

57 Aleksandr Krivoshchekov, "Na novom meste," *OEV* (chast' neoffitsial'naia) 13 (1903): 35. In European Russia, Orthodox believers also relied on Orthodox religious rituals to "reaffirm their ancestral bonds." See Shevzov, *Russian Orthodoxy on the Eve of Revolution*, 75.

58 A.L. Tregubov, *Pereselencheskoe delo v Semipalatinskoi i Semirechenskoi oblastiakh* (St. Petersburg, 1910), 12.

59 Ibid., 13.

60 Papshev, "Usloviia, blagopriiatstvuiushchie sektantskoi propagande," 19.

61 RGIA, f.bib-ka, op.1, d.1, l.155ob (Annual report of the governor general of the steppe, 1897).

62 Vostorgov, *Dobroe*, 20.

63 Papshev, "Usloviia, blagopriiatstvuiushchie sektantskoi propagande," 19.

64 Goloshubin, *Spravochnaia kniga*, 430.

65 "Osviashchenie khrama v pereselencheskom poselke Pokrovskom Ust'kamenogorskogo uezda," *OEV* (chast' neoffitsial'naia) 1 (1909): 29.

66 RGIA, f.391, op.3, d.671, l.121 (Letter from Governor Troiinitskii to Grigorii Glinka, 1910). These priests even felt entitled to ask the Resettlement Administration for financial support. Father Peshekhonov explained to Glinka that for the past nine years he had dedicated his efforts to building churches in the parish of Georgievskii. Peshekhonov travelled throughout the region, and even made the 1,013-kilometre journey to Omsk, collecting money, materials, and religious clothing and objects for the parish. See RGIA, f.391 op.3, d.671, l.124.

67 N. Venetskii, "Po prikhodu," *OEV* (chast' neoffitsial'naia) 3 (1904): 23.

68 S.N.M, "Osviashenie khrama v der. Paletskoi," *OEV* (chast' neoffitsial'naia) 10 (1917): 25. For more examples of old resident and settlers

building churches together, see I.V. Matros, "Pereselencheskaia zhizn' v stepnom krae," *Sel'skii vestnik* 77 (1909): 2–3; IAOO, f.16, op.1, d.159, l.18.

69 P. Kuznetsov, "Osviashchenie khrama v poselke Potaninskom, Tiukalinskogo uezda," *OEV* (chast' neoffitsial'naia) 10 (1901): 2–3. For another story about a *Sibiriki* parish receiving a church after the arrival of settlers, see *OEV* 47 (1916): 21–5.

70 Kuznetsov, "Osviashchenie khrama," 3.

71 "Sviatoe delo dlia Sibiri," *Pravoslavnyi blagovestnik* 12 (1916): 170–4.

72 Robert H. Greene, *Bodies Like Bright Stars: Saints and Relics in Orthodox Russia* (DeKalb: Northern Illinois University Press, 2010), 89–99.

6. An Anthill of Baptists in a Land of Muslims

1 Andronik (Nikol'skii), *Pishu ot izbytka skorbiashchego serdtsa* (Moscow: Sretenskii monastyr', 2007), 221. Other clergy mentioned Omsk's notoriety as a centre of sectarianism. See Gerasim Shorets, "Sektantstvo v Tiukalinskom uezde, Tobol'skoi gubernii," *OEV* (chast' neoffitsial'naia) 16 (1916): 12.

2 "O deiatel'nosti protivosektantskikh missionerov i prikhodskikh sviash-chennikov," *OEV* (chast' neoffitsial'naia) 15 (1905): 22. Some predicted that Omsk would have the same notoriety in the history of sectarianism as Kiev and Kiev diocese. See "Sektantstvo priblizhaetsia," *OEV* (chast' neoffitsial'naia) 17 (1906): 34.

3 Nicholas B. Breyfogle, *Heretics and Colonizers: Forging Russia's Empire in the South Caucasus* (Ithaca, NY: Cornell University Press, 2005), 305.

4 Heather Coleman, *Russian Baptists and Spiritual Revolution, 1905–1929* (Bloomington: Indiana University Press, 2005), 92–108.

5 Robert D. Crews, *For Prophet and Tsar: Islam and Empire in Russia and Central Asia* (Cambridge, MA: Harvard University Press, 2009), 195.

6 Paul W. Werth, *The Tsar's Foreign Faiths: Toleration and the Fate of Religious Freedom in Imperial Russia* (Oxford: Oxford University Press, 2014), 252–3. As Elena Campbell notes, not everyone assigned a political slant to Pan-Islamism; see Elena I. Campbell, "The Muslim Question in Late Imperial Russia," in *Russian Empire: Space, People, Power, 1700–1930*, ed. Jane Burbank, Mark Von Hagen, and A.V. Remnev (Bloomington: Indiana University Press, 2007), 334–5.

7 For more on this interpretation of Muslims in Turkestan, see Alexander Morrison, *Russian Rule in Samarkand 1868–1910: A Comparison with British India* (New York: Oxford University Press, 2008), 51; for the Volga region see Gulmira Sultangalieva, "The Intermediary Role of Tatars in

Kazakhstan," in *Asiatic Russia: Imperial Power in Regional and International Contexts*, ed. Tomohiko Uyama (New York: Routledge, 2012), 65.

8 Ian W. Campbell, *Knowledge and the Ends of Empire: Kazak Intermediaries and Russian Rule on the Steppe, 1731–1917* (Ithaca, NY: Cornell University Press, 2017), 168–9.

9 Rossiiskii gosudarstvennyi istoricheskii arkhiv (henceforth, RGIA), f.bib-ka, op.1, d.85, l.111ob (Annual report of the Semipalatinsk governor, 1907). Two years later, in 1909, the governor general expressed the same point; see RGIA, f.391, op.4, d.210, l.60ob. Also see, "Poezdka Preosviashchennogo Kipriana v selo Alekseevskoe," *OEV* 17 (1912): 43. For opinions on Akmolinsk province, see RGIA, f.1273, op.1, d.459, l.29 (Kulomzin to V. Sabler, 1898).

10 S.D.B., "Poezdka Ego Preosviashchenstva, Preosviashchenneishogo Gavriila, Episkopa Omskogo i Semipalatinskogo v g. Pavlodar dlia soversheniia zakladki khrama," *OEV* 18 (1910): 22.

11 RGIA, f.796, op.440, d.1274, l.13 (Report by Vostorgov surveying missionary work in dioceses beyond the Urals in 1911). Other secular and religious leaders expressed a similar concern that Omsk diocese would become a sectarian stronghold because of the settler movement. See RGIA, f.1284, op.194, d.56, l.24ob (Annual report of the governor general of Tobol'sk, 1913).

12 RGIA, f.796, op.440, d.1274, l.14 (Report on missionary activities in Siberian diocese by Vostorgov, 1911). This is similar to the argument he made about the Caucasus. See Breyfogle, *Heretics and Colonizers*, 168. He also raised this point in his opening speech to the Missionary Pastoral Courses in Khabarovsk. See Vostorgov, "O missionerstve," 337–8.

13 Coleman, *Russian Baptists and Spiritual Revolution, 1905–1929*, 25. For more on debates over the meaning of this concept, see Werth, *The Tsar's Foreign Faiths*, 207–39.

14 O.V. Ignatenko, "Kirgiz dukhovnaia missiia," *Sovremennoe obshchestvo*, vyp.1 (Omsk, 1999), 118; RGIA, f.796, op.442, d.2287, l.24ob. For more on the mission and its role in the region, see Robert Geraci, "Going Abroad or Going to Russia? Orthodox Missionaries in the Kazakh Steppe, 1881–1917," in *Of Religion and Empire: Missions, Conversion, and Tolerance in Tsarist Russia*, ed. Robert Geraci and Michael Khordarkovsky (Ithaca, NY: Cornell University Press, 2001), 274–310.

15 Kiprian, "Otchet: O sostoianii Kirgizskoi missii Omskoi eparkhii za 1909 god,"*OEV* 19 (1910): 18.

16 Robert Geraci, "Going Abroad or Going to Russia? Orthodox Missionaries in the Kazakh Steppe, 1881–1917," in *Of Religion and Empire: Missions, Conversion, and Tolerance in Tsarist Russia*, ed. Robert

Geraci and Michael Khordarkovsky (Ithaca, NY: Cornell University Press, 2001), 295.

17 RGIA, f.bib-ka, op.1, d.1, l. 75. Konstantin Pobedonostsev's copy of the report is preserved at the archives. In the margin next to this statement he wrote the word "correct." For an academic treatment of Russians "going native," see Willard Sunderland, "Russians into Iakuts? 'Going Native' and Problems of Russian National Identity in the Siberian North, 1870s–1914," *Slavic Review* 55, no.4 (1996): 806–25.

18 "O Kirgizskoi missii," *OEV* 20 (1900): 12; Lysenko, "Stepen' islamizatsii kazakhskogo obshchestva," 153.

19 Lysenko, *Ocherki istorii Russkoi pravoslavnoi tserkvi*, 71; Efrem Eliseev, "K voprosu o perekhode prirodnykh pravoslavnykh Russkikh liudei v islam," *Pravoslavnyi blagovestnik* 23–4 (1913): 688–703.

20 RGIA, f.799, op.15, d.1197, l.135 (Peasant petition to I. Vostorgov, 1908). This village of Sretenskii would end up with a secular school. See Ioann Goloshubin, *Spravochnaia kniga Omskoi eparkhii* (Omsk: Tipografiia "Irtysh," 1914), 163.

21 For populations, see Ihor Stebelsky, "Ukraine Settlement Patterns in the Kirgiz Steppe Before 1917: Ukrainian Colonies or Russian Integration?" in *Transforming Peasants: Society, State and the Peasantry, 1861–1930*, ed. Judith Pallot (New York: Palgrave Macmillan, 1998), 141–2.

22 Iu. A. Lysenko, *Ocherki istorii Russkoi pravoslavnoi tserkvi v Kazakhstane (XVIII–nachalo XX v.)* (Barnaul: Azbuka, 2011), 147.

23 Iu. A. Lysenko, "Stepen' islamizatsii kazakhskogo obshchestva na rubezhe XIX–XX vv. v otsenke missionerov kirgizskoi dukhovnoi missii," *Izvestiia altaiskogo gosudarstvennogo universiteta* 4–3 (2008): 150–3.

24 RGIA, f.bib-ka, op.1, d.1, l.249 (Annual report of the governor of Akmolinsk, 1902).

25 RGIA, bib-ka, op.1, d.85, l.111ob (Semipalatinsk governor's annual report, 1907)

26 RGIA, f.391, op.5, d.231, l.5ob (Annual report of the Semipalatinsk governor, 1910). For the governor general of the steppe, Orthodox settlers were a bulwark of Russian nationality, helping to culturally Russify the territory and secure the region for Russia's future political aspirations. See RGIA, f.1276, op.4, d.853, l.28 (To Stolypin from Shmit, 1910).

27 RGIA, f.797, op.2, 2ot., 3st., d.242, l.1. For a photograph of the members of the commission, including Tregubov, see G.V. Glinka, ed., *Aziatskaia Rossiia: liudi i poriadki za Uralom*, vol. 1 (St. Petersburg: Izd. Pereselencheskogo upravleniia glavnogo upravleniia zemleustroistva i zemledieliia, 1914), 467.

28 RGIA, f.797, op.193, d.1763, ll.1ob–3ob (Proposal from the Office of Economic Management of the Orthodox Confession to Holy Synod, 1911)

29 RGIA, f.796, op.193, d.1763, l.7 (Directive from the Holy Synod, 1911).
30 RGIA, f.797, op.2, 2ot., 3st., d.242, l.2 (Correspondence from GUZiZ to the Holy Synod, 1912); RGIA, f.796, op.440, d.1274, 21ob (Report by Vostorgov, 1911).
31 RGIA, f.391, op.4, d.1663, l.3 (Correspondence from GUZiZ to the governor general of the steppe, 1912).
32 RGIA, f.391, op.4, d.1663, l.8 (Petition from the Kazakh representative of the Kipchak tribe in Turgai province to the Council of Ministers, 1912).
33 Campbell, *Knowledge and the Ends of Empire*, 173–9.
34 Werth, *The Tsar's Foreign Faiths*, 254.
35 Campbell, *Knowledge and the Ends of Empire*, 170–1.
36 Istoricheskii arkhiv Omskoi oblasti (henceforward IAOO), 9(c)176(c18) B-84 3869, l.21–22 (Annual report of the governor general of the steppe, 1911).
37 Lysenko, "Stepen' islamizatsii kazakhskogo obshchestva," 153.
38 A.T. "Kreshchenie magometanina," *OEV* 3 (1916): 22.
39 RGIA, f.bib-ka, op.1, d.1, ll.75, 55ob (Annual report of the Akmolinsk governor, 1894); RGIA, f.bib-ka, op.1, d.91, l.97 (Annual report of the governor general of the steppe, 1899).
40 Vasilii Vinogradov, *Poezdka ego preosviashchenstva, preosviashchenneishogo Andronika* (Omsk: Tip. K.I. Demidovoi, 1913), 51.
41 Ibid., 29.
42 Ibid., 33. For another example of a church presented as a marker of Russianness in a land presented as belonging to the Kazakhs, see U.A.P., "Osviashchenie khrama v pereselencheskom poselke Pokrovskom, Ust'-Kamenogorskogo uezda," *OEV* (chast' neoffitsial'naia) 1 (1909): 27. For a similar description, see I. Oksiiuk, "Novyi khram," *OEV* 20 (1908): 19.
43 The accuracy of this number is difficult to assess. In 1902, Father F. Troitskii reported that the dissenter population was at least twenty-four thousand. F. Troitskii, "Raskol v Omskoi eparkhii," *MO* 11 (1902): 694.
44 "Otchet Omskogo eparkhial'nogo bratstva za 1911 god," *OEV* 16 (1912): 5.
45 RGIA, f.796, op.440, d.1274, ll.5–6.
46 Goloshubin, "Iz vpechatlenii sel'skogo sviashchennika," 35.
47 "Korrespondentsiia," *OEV* (chast' neoffitsial'naia) 1 (1905): 47. Although 444 kilometres away from Omsk, the Orthodox clergymen of Pavlodar had a reputation as being very active and they took the appearance of sectarians seriously. "Mery k podniatiiu religiozno-nravstvennoi zhizni v prikhodakh s sektantskim naseleniem," *OEV* (chast' neoffitsial'naia) 15 (1905): 21.
48 RGIA, f.796, op.442, d.2225, l.7ob (Annual report to the Holy Synod by Bishop Graviil, 1907).
49 Panteleimon Papshev, "Usloviia, blagopriiatstvuiushchie sektantskoi propagande," *OEV* (chast' neoffitsial'naia) 29 (1916): 20.

50 RGIA, f.796, op.194, d.2037, l.164ob (Directive of the Holy Synod, 1912); RGIA, f.bib-ka, op.1, d.1, l.297 (Annual report of the Akmolinsk governor, 1913); RGIA, f.796, op.440, d.1274, l.16. (Report by Vostorgov, 1911)

51 RGIA, f.391, op.4, d.1655, ll.6–6ob (To GUZiZ from MVD, 1912).

52 RGIA, f.391, op.4, d.286, l.49 (To Resettlement Administration from GUZiZ, head of Resettlement activity in Akmolinsk). For Shmit's recommendation that Orthodox and sectarian colonists be settled in different areas, see P.P. Vibe, *Nemetskie kolonii v Sibiri: sotsial'no-ekonomicheskii aspect* (Omsk: Omskii gos. pedagogicheskii universitet, 2007), 35.

53 Vostorgov, "Znachenie i zadachi," 39. Vostorgov also presents the railway as facilitating the spread of the Baptist faith; see RGIA, f.796, op.445, d.301, l.241 (Report by Vostorgov, 1912), and RGIA, f.796, op.440, d.1274, l.15 (Report by Vostorgov, 1911).

54 RGIA, f.796, op.201, 6ot., 3st., d.233, l.7 (To the Holy Synod from the chief procurator, 1915).

55 "Sektantstvo priblizhaetsia," *OEV* 17 (1906): 33. The towns were Petropavlovsk, Omsk, and Marianovka.

56 "Otchetnye svedeniia o sostoianii sektantva v Omskoi eparkhii za vtoryi polovinu 1899 goda i pervuiu polovinu 1900 goda," *OEV* 22 (1900): 10.

57 Gavriel I. Mazaev, *Obrashchenie na istinnyi put' i vospominaniia baptista G.I.M.* (Omsk: Board of the Siberian Department of the Baptist Union, 1919), 52.

58 Ibid., 59.

59 For an analysis of the politics behind statistics relating to dissent, see Irina Paert, "'Two or Twenty Million?' The Languages of Official Statistics and Religious Dissent in Imperial Russia," *Ab Imperio* 3 (July 2006): 75–98.

60 The figure breaks down as follows: 6,120 Shtundo-Baptists, 2,116 Molokans, 12 Adventists, 64 Subbotniks, 125 Ioannity, and 37 Khlysty. See "Postanovleniia Irkutskogo missioerskogo s"ezda po voprosam missii protivoraskol'nicheskoi i protivosektantskoi (6-ia sektsiia)," *OEV* 20 (1910): 30. The exact number of sectarians is difficult to ascertain. In his annual report to the Holy Synod, Bishop Andronik placed the number at 10,000 in 1914. See RGIA, f.796, op.442, d.2654, l.13 (Annual report by Bishop Andronik, 1914).

61 RGIA, f.bib-ka, op.1, d.1, l.297. The report provides the following statistic for the province of Akmolinsk: Orthodox population 866,183 (57 per cent); Edinoverie 3,640 (0.23 per cent); Old Believers 3,976 (0.26 per cent); Catholics 15,183 (0.99 per cent); Evangelical Lutheran 30,375 (1.9 per cent); Jews 4,495 (0.22 per cent); Muslims 580,467 (38.04 per cent); other confessions 350 (0.001 per cent); Baptists 10,226 (0.67 per cent); Molokans 9,126 (0.59 per cent); Adventists 782 (0.05 per cent); and Mennonites 740

(0.04 per cent). For more on the difference between rational and mystical sects according to the Russian Orthodox Church, see Coleman, *Russian Baptists and Spiritual Revolution*, 101.

62 P.P. Liubimov, "Religii i veroispovednyi sostav naseleniia Aziatskoi Rossii," in *Aziatskaia Rossiia: liudi i poriadki za Uralom*, vol. 1, ed. G.V. Glinka (St. Petersburg: Izd. Pereselencheskogo upravleniia glavnogo upravleniia zemleustroistva i zemledieliia, 1914), 241–2.

63 *Omskii eparkhial'nyi s"ezd dukhovenstva, zhurnaly s"ezda o.o. deputatov ot dukhovenstva Omskoi eparkhii, proiskhodivshego v 1899 godu v Omske Akmolinskoi oblasti* (1899), 23.

64 RGIA, f.796, op.191–2, 3st., 6ot., d.69, l.2 (Report to the Holy Synod from Gavriil, 1910).

65 For more on Shmit's claim that Bishop Gavriil had lost his moral leadership in the diocese, see RGIA, f.1276, op.4, d.853, l.32. Prime Minister Stolypin found this critique convincing, and he wrote to the chief procurator informing him of the situation. The chief procurator began his own investigation and in 1911 Bishop Gavriil retired to a monastery. See RGIA, f.1276, op.4, d.853, l.34ob (To the chief procurator from Stolpyin, 1910).

66 RGIA, f.821, op.133, d.289, ll.2ob–3ob (Excerpt of the 1910 report by Shmit).

67 RGIA, f.821, op.133, d.289, l.5 (Excerpt of the 1910 report by Shmit). For more on Shmit's fears of the political implications of Orthodox apostasy for Russia, see RGIA, 1276, op.17, d.165, ll.233–233ob.

68 RGIA, f.821, op.133, d.289, l.3ob.

69 RGIA, f.821, op.133, d.289, l.8 (Ministry of Internal Affairs to the Department of Spiritual Affairs, 1911).

70 RGIA, f.821, op.133, d.289, ll.38ob–46 (Report by Kologrivov, addressed to the minister of the MVD).

71 RGIA, f.821, op.133, d.289, l.63 (Report by Kologrivov).

72 RGIA, f.821, op.133, d.289, l.54ob.

73 RGIA, f.796, op.194, d.2037, ll.70–70ob (Correspondence Bishop Vladimir to V. Sabler, 1912).

74 Goloshubin, *Spravochnaia kniga Omskoi eparkhii*, 388.

75 RGIA, f.bib-ka, op.1, d.1, l.297ob (Annual report of the Akmolinsk governor, 1913). In 1911, Vostorgov claimed that 900 families had recently left the Orthodox Church to become dissenters in Omsk diocese. See RGIA, f.796, op.440, d.1274, l.8; Vostorgov, "Znachenie i zadachi," 40. In 1912, 1,068 people petitioned to leave the Orthodox Church and join "sectarian" faiths in Tomsk province, with 914 from three villages asking to be recognized as Molokans. In 1913, 457 people from Tomsk province petitioned to leave the Orthodox Church. See L.M. Goriushkin,

Krest'ianskoe dvizhenie v Sibiri 1907–1914 gg. Khronika i istoriografiia (Novosibirsk: Nauka, 1986), 172.

76 RGIA, f.797, op.82, 2ot., 3st., d.477, ll.2–2ob (chief procurator's office to Bishop Vladimir, 1912).

77 Bishop Vladimir was accurate in his assertion that he had warned Vladimir Sabler about the widespread apostasy of Orthodox believers in his diocese. See RGIA, f.796, op.194, d.2037, ll.70–70ob.

78 RGIA, f.797, op.82, 2ot., 3st., d.477, ll.3–4ob (Assistant chief procurator to Bishop Vladimir, 1912). For another example of Bishop Vladimir blaming Vostorgov for sectarianism in Omsk diocese, see RGIA, f.796, op.194, d.2037, ll.68–69.

79 RGIA, f.796, op.193, d.1763, l.3 (Petition to Bishop of Omsk, 1911). For a comprehensive analysis of Orthodox believers' reasons for conversion to the Baptist faith, see Heather Coleman, *Russian Baptists and Spiritual Revolution*, 47–64.

80 For more on the congress in Kazan, see Robert P. Geraci, *Window on the East: National and Imperial Identities in Late Tsarist Russia* (Ithaca, NY: Cornell University Press, 2001), 395–400, 421–30, and Frank T. McCarthy, "The Kazan Missionary Congress," *Cahiers du monde russe et sovietque* 13 (1973): 308–22. On the Kiev Congress, which was the first missionary congress held, see Heather J. Coleman, "Definitions of Heresy: The Fourth Missionary Congress and the Problem of Cultural Power in Russia after 1905," *Jahrbücher für Geschichte Osteuropas* 52, no.1 (2004): 70–91. The Kiev Congress helped those in Siberia to consider their own missionary efforts; see P. Golovachev, "Sibirskie Missii," *SV* 17 (1908): 1–7.

81 "Missionerskii s"ezd v Kazani," *OEV* (chast' neoffitsial'naia) 13 (1910): 39–40.

82 Ieromonakh Feodorit, "Mery bor'by s islamom, priniatye Kazanskim missionerskim s"ezdom," *OEV* (chast' neoffitsial'naia) 20 (1910): 27–33. For another example of the church's concerns about the Kazakh steppe, see "O Musul'manstve v kirgizskoi stepi i ob upravelenii dukhovnymi delami Kirgizov," *Pravoslavnyi blagovestnik* 11 (1912): 475–86. For more on the congress's interpretation of the "Muslim question," see Campbell, "The Muslim Question in Late Imperial Russia," 337–8.

83 Skortsov, "Deiatel'nost' pravoslavnoi missii," 174.

84 See, I. Vostorgov, "Znachenie i zadachi obshchesibirskogo missionerskogo s"ezda," *OEV* (chast' neoffitsial'naia) 17 (1910): 30–42.

85 See Dimitrii Nesmeianov, "Doklad Irkutskomu missionerskomu s"ezdu Omskogo eparkhial'nogo missionera Dimitriia Nesmeianova," *OEV* (chast' neoffitsial'naia) 18 (1910): 42–51; Dimitrii Nesmeianov,"Doklad Irkutskomu missionerskomu s"ezdu Omskogo eparkhial'nogo

missionera Dimitriia Nesmeianova," *OEV* (chast' neoffitsial'naia) 19
(1910): 20–39; "Postanovleniia Irkutskogo missionerskogo s"ezda po
voprosam missii protivoraskol'nicheskoi i protivosektantskoi," *OEV*
(chast' neoffitsial'naia) 20 (1910): 37–46.

86   RGIA, f.796, op.191, 2ot., 2st., d.841, l.16. By 1917, seventy vicar bishop
positions existed in the empire. Although vicar bishoprics were clearly a
widespread practice, the Holy Synod, for the most part, did not regulate
the duties of a vicar bishop. Only a few dioceses had documented the
responsibilities of the vicar bishop; in most cases, the duties were left to
the personal discretion of the bishop. See Igor Smolich, *Istoriia Russkoi
tserkvi*, vol. 1 (Moscow: Izd-vo Spaso-Preobrazhenskogo Valaamskogo
monastyria, 1996), 269–70.

87   RGIA, f.796, op.191, 2ot., 2st., d.841, l.2 (Proposal to the Holy Synod from
the Holy Synod Economic Administration, 1910).

88   RGIA, f.796, op.191, 2ot., 2st., d.841, l.2 (Proposal to the Holy Synod from
the Holy Synod Economic Administration, 1910).

89   RGIA, f.bib-ka, op.1, d.85, l.130 (Semipalatinsk governor annual report,
1910). Vostorgov also called for a vicar bishopric to be opened in
Semipalatinsk, claiming that the distance from Omsk, along with the
missionary significance of the region, necessitated the creation of this
position. Ioann Vostorgov, *Polnoe sobranie sochinenii*, tom. 4 (Moscow: s.n.,
1914), 492.

90   Kiprian, born in 1876, had studied at the Kazan Ecclesiastical Academy.
He joined the Kazakh mission in 1899, becoming its head in 1906.
See S.V.P., "Narechenie i khirotoniia Nachal'nika Kirgizskoi missii
Arkhimandrita Kipriana vo Episkopa Semipalatinskogo," *OEV* 24
(1911): 25.

91   "Sluzhenie preosviashchennogo Kipriana v Semipalatinske," *OEV* (chast'
neoffitsial'naia) 5 (1912): 44. For the trip near the border with China,
see "Poezdka preosviashchennogo Kipriana v selo Alekseevskoe," *OEV*
(chast' neoffitsial'naia) 17 (1912): 45. Issues arose at this post connected to
Ukrainian settlers; see IAOO, f.16, op.1, d.164, ll.368–368ob (Journal of
the Omsk diocesan consistory, 1916)

92   "Iz Belagachskoi stepi," *OEV* (chast' neoffitsial'naia) 1 (1901): 10–11.

93   I. Nikiforov, "Pervoe poseshchenie sela Lapteva-Loga, Zmeinogorskogo
i, preosviashchennym Kiprianom, episkopom Semipalatinskim," *OEV*
(chast' neoffitsial'naia) 5 (1912): 44.

94   As Robert Geraci's research shows, this was an issue that affected
missionary work in the pre-1905 period. See Geraci, "Going Abroad
or Going to Russia? Orthodox Missionaries in the Kazakh Steppe,
1881–1917," in *Of Religion and Empire: Missions, Conversion, and Tolerance*

in Tsarist Russia, ed. Robert Geraci and Michael Khordarkovsky (Ithaca, NY: Cornell University Press, 2001), 296. For a request by a missionary to be allowed to perform marriages for settlers, see IAOO, f.16, op.1, d.133, l.389.

95 IAOO, f.16, op.1, d.136, l.18 (Report by Kiprian to Omsk diocesan consistory).

96 IAOO, f.16, op.1, d.88, l.2 (Journal of Omsk diocesan consistory, 1902).

97 Kiprian, "Kratkii obzor polozheniia i deiatel'nosti kirgizskoi missii Omskoi eparkhii za 1913," *OEV* 11 (1914): 7. Bishop Kiprian (vicar bishop of Semipalatinsk) raised his concerns about the distraction of settlers to diocesan authorities; see IAOO, f.16, op.1, d.136, l.18 (Report to the Omsk diocesan consistory by Kiprian, 1911).

98 Arkhimandrit Kiprian, "O deiatel'nosti i sostoianii kirgizskoi missii za 1908," *OEV* 10 (1909): 40–1.

99 RGIA, f.796, op.442, d.2287, ll.25–25ob (Annual report of the Omsk bishop, 1908).

100 IAOO, f.16, op.1, d.127, l.12 (Report to Omsk consistory by Kiprian, 1908).

101 RGIA, f.796, op.191, 2ot., 2st., d.841, l.36ob (Submission to the Holy Synod from Bishop Vladimir, 1912).

102 RGIA, f. 796, op.191, 2ot., 2st., d.841, l.82 (Submission to the Holy Synod from Bishop Andronik, 1913). In 1914, the position was renamed the "Petropavlovsk bishop," although Mefodii (Krasnoperov) continued to be the bishop.

103 "Novoe vikariatstvo v Omskoi eparkhii i perviy vikarnyi episkop Akmolinskii," *OEV* 5 (1913): 36–7.

104 N.V. Turchaninov, "Naselenie Aziatskoi Rossii: Statisticheskii ocherk," in *Aziatskaia Rossiia: liudi i poriadki za Uralom*, vol. 1, ed. G.V. Glinka (St. Petersburg, 1914), 82. For population percentages, see Ihor Stebelsky, "Ukraine Settlement Patterns in the Kirgiz Steppe Before 1917: Ukrainian Colonies or Russian Integration?" in *Transforming Peasants: Society, State and the Peasantry, 1861–1930*, ed. Judith Pallot (New York: Palgrave Macmillan, 1998), 142.

105 "Krestnyi khod," *OEV* (chast' neoffitsial'naia) 18 (1915): 27.

106 "Krestnyi khod," *OEV* (chast' neoffitsial'naia) 21 (1915): 7.

107 "Krestnyi khod," *OEV* (chast' neoffitsial'naia) 19 (1915): 34.

108 Ibid., 27.

109 I. Fokin, "Okolo Baptistov," *OEV* (chast' neoffitsial'naia) 13 (1910): 29.

110 D. Nesmeianov, "Pervye vpechatleniia i shagi missionera," *OEV* (chast' neoffitsial'naia) 3 (1908): 23. Bishop Gavriil made the same comment that the Baptists sought to conquer Siberia like Ermak. See "Pastyrskoe missionerskoe sobranie Omskogo gorodskogo dukhovenstva," *OEV*

(chast' neoffitsial'naia) 4 (1908): 26, and RGIA, f.796, op.422, d.2225, l.8 (Annual report to the Holy Synod by Bishop Graviil, 1907). This idea was also expressed in *MO*; see V. Skortsov, "Deiatel'nost' pravoslavnoi missii," *MO* 1 (1911): 176, and V. Skvortsov, "Nedavnee-proshloe i nas-toiashchee pravoslavnoi missii: skazano na otkrytii pervogo Sibirskogo obshche-missionerskogo s"ezda," *MO* 10 (1910): 1739.

111 For more on the importance of missionary work to the faith of Russian Baptists, see Coleman, *Russian Baptists and Spiritual Revolution*, 41.

112 D. Nesmeianov, "Pervye vpechatleniia shagi missionera," *OEV* (chast' neoffitsial'naia) 3 (1908): 23. Secular and religious officials identified sec-tarians like the Molokans to be less pernicious in comparison to Baptists. The governor of Akmolinsk called the Molokans simpler, modest, and less organized in their propaganda than the Baptists. RGIA, f.bib-ka, op.1, d.1, l.43.

113 Petr Epp, *100 let pod krovom Vsevyshnego: istoriia Omskikh obshchin EKhB i ikh ob"edineniia, 1907–2007* (Omsk: Samenkorn, 2007), 172. Accessing public space through the building of churches by sectarian groups caused problems in other parts of the empire as well. See Nicholas Breyfogle, "Prayer and the Politics of Place: Molokan Church Building, Tsarist Law and the Quest for a Public Sphere in Late Imperial Russia" in *Sacred Stories: Religion and Spirituality in Modern Russia*, 222–52. To provide a sense of comparison, by 1910, ten Orthodox churches existed in the city of Omsk; see Z.N. Berkovskaia, "Omskaia eparkhiia v kul'turnoi zhizni stepnogo kraia v kontse XIX–nachale XX veka," *Nauchnye soobshchestva istorikov i arkhivistov: intellektual'nye dialogi so vremenem i mirom* (Omsk, 2006), 202.

114 RGIA, f.796, op.201, 6ot., 3st., d.233, l.3ob (Copy of a letter sent by Mazaev, 1915).

115 RGIA, f.796, op.442, d.2225, l.7ob (Annual report to the Holy Synod by Bishop Graviil, 1907).

116 I. Fokin, "Okolo Baptistov," *OEV* (chast' neoffitsial'naia) 13 (1910): 31.

117 Dimitrii Nesmeianov, "Sektantstvo i ego propaganda v Sibiri," *MO* no. 2 (1911): 339.

118 D.A. Nesmeianov, "Sviatost' i patriotizm baptistov," *OEV* (chast' neof-fitsial'naia) 46 (1916): 9–18. Particularly after 1910, missionary writings emphasized the connection between Baptists and Germans. Also see Gerasim Shorets, "Sektanty i voina," *OEV* 14 (1915): 34–6.

119 Martha Brill Olcott, *The Kazakhs* (Stanford, CA: Hoover Institution Press, Stanford University, 1987), 120–4.

120 Richard A. Pierce, *Russian Central Asia, 1867–1917: A Study in Colonial Rule* (Berkeley: University of California Press, 1960), 290.

Conclusion

1   Sil'vestr (Ol'shevskii), "Rech' Preosviashchenneishego Sil'vestra na mitinge, posviashchennomu prazdnovaniiu 'grazhdanskikh svobod' v g. Omske 10 marta 1917 g.," in *V vere li vy? Zhitie i trudy sviashchennomuchenika Sil'vestra, archiepiskopa Omskogo*, ed. Mitropolit Feodosii (Protsiuk) (Moscow: Voskresen'e, 2006), 582.

2   Natalie Kononenko, "Ukrainian Folklore in Kazakhstan," *Folklorica* 16 (2011): 163–83. Audio interviews with Ukrainians in Pavlodar are available at http://www.artsrn.ualberta.ca/KazakhstanAudio/index.php.

3   See Peter Holquist, "'In Accord with State Interests and the People's Wishes': The Technocratic Ideology of Imperial Russia's Resettlement Administration," *Slavic Review* 69, no. 1 (Spring 2010): 151–79. For more on resettlement during the Soviet period, see Lewis H. Siegelbaum and Leslie Page Moch, *Broad Is My Native Land: Repertoires and Regimes of Migration in Russia's Twentieth Century* (Ithaca, NY: Cornell University Press, 2014).

Bibliography

Archival Sources

Moscow, Russia

GARF, Gosudarstvennyi arkhiv Rossiiskoi Federatsii, State Archive of the
    Russian Federation
        fond 9452 – Personal Papers of I.I. Vostorgov

Omsk, Russia

IAOO, Istoricheskii arkhiv Omskoi oblasti, Historical Archives of Omsk
    Province
        fond 16 – Omsk Diocesan Consistory

St. Petersburg, Russia

RGIA, Rossiiskii gosudarstvennyi istoricheskii arkhiv, Russian State Historical
    Archive
        fond biblioteka – Annual Reports of the Governors
        fond 391 – Resettlement Administration
        fond 796 – Chancellery of the Holy Synod
        fond 797 – Chancellery of the Chief Procurator of the Holy Synod
        fond 799 – Economic Administration of the Holy Synod
        fond 821 – Department of Spiritual Affairs, Ministry of Internal Affairs
        fond 1273 – Siberian Railway Committee
        fond 1276 – Council of Ministers
        fond 1284 – Ministry of Internal Affairs

Newspapers and Journals

Missionerskoe obozrenie
Omskie eparkhial'nye vedomosti
Pravoslavnyi blagovestnik
Tobol'skie eparkhial'nye vedomosti
Tserkovnyie vedomosti
Sel'skii vestnik
Sibirskie vosprosy
Voprosy kolonizatsii
Vsepoddanneishii otchet ober-prokurora sviateishego sinoda

Primary Sources

Aziatskaia Rossiia, vol. 1: *Liudi i poriadki za Uralom*. Edited by G.V. Glinka. St. Petersburg, 1914.
Aziatskaia Rossiia, vol. 2: *Zemlia i khoziaistvo*. Edited by G.V. Glinka. St. Petersburg, 1914.
Browder Robert Paul and Aleksandr Kerensky, eds., *The Russian Provisional Government, 1917: Documents*. Stanford, CA: Stanford University Press, 1961.
Czaplicka, Marie Antoinette. *The Collected Works of M.A. Czaplicka*. Vol. 3. Translated by David Norman Collins. Richmond, UK: Curzon Press, 1999.
Durban, William. "The Trans-Siberian Railway." *Contemporary Review*, August 1899.
Fraser, John Foster. *The Real Siberia: Together With an Account of a Dash Through Manchuria*. London: Cassell, 1912.
Goloshubin, Ioann. *Spravochnaia kniga Omskoi eparkhii*. Omsk: Tipografiia "Irtysh," 1914.
Kennan, George. *Siberia and the Exile System*. Vol. 1. New York: Century Co., 1891.
Kulomzin, A.N. *Nuzhdy tserkovnogo dela na sibirskoi doroge i v Zabaikal'e*. St. Petersburg: Gos. tip., 1897.
– *Vsepoddanneishii otchet stats-sekretaria Kulomzina po poezdke v Sibir' dlia oznakomleniia s polozheniem pereselencheskogo dela*. St. Petersburg: Gos. tip., 1896.
Lavrent'ev, L.I. *Sibirskaia dukhovnaia akademiia*. Tomsk: Pech. S.P. Iakovleva, 1914.
Lebedev, M.F. *Puteshestvie naslednika tsesarevicha po Tobol'skoi eparkhii v 1891godu*. Tobol'sk, 1892.
Liubimov, P.P. "Religii i veroispovednyi sostav naseleniia Aziatskoi Rossii." In *Aziatskaia Rossiia: Liudi i poriadki za Uralom*, edited by G.V. Glinka, Vol. 1. St. Petersburg: Izd. Pereselencheskogo upravleniia glavnogo upravleniia zemleustroistva i zemledieliia, 1914.

Neverov, A.N. *Vsepoddanneishii otchet Akmolinskogo gubernatora za 1910 i 1911 gody*. Omsk, 1912.

Omskii eparkhial'nyi s"ezd dukhovenstva, zhurnal obshcheeparkhial'nogo s"ezda v 1909 (1910).

Opisanie nekotorykh pereselencheskikh poselkov Ust'kamenogorskogo i Zaisanskogo uezdov Semipalatinskoi oblasti v sel'skokhoziaistvennom otnoshenie. St. Petersburg, 1913.

Pamiatnaia knizhka Akmolinskoi oblasti na 1913 g. Omsk: Akmolinskaia Oblastnaia tip., 1913.

Pamiatnaia knizhka Semipalatinskoi oblasti na 1901 g. Semipalatinsk: Tip., Semipalatinskogo oblastnogo pravleniia, 1901.

Peeddoobny, G. "Ukraintsy v Sibiri." *Ukrainskaia zhizn'* 12 (1913): 11–19.

Pobedonostsev, Konstantin. *Pis'ma Pobedonostseva k Aleksandru III*. Vol. 1. Moscow: Novaia Moskva, 1925.

– *Pis'ma Pobedonostseva k Aleksandru III*. Vol. 2. Moscow: Novaia Moskva, 1926.

Polozhenie tserkovnogo i shkol'nogo stroitel'stva v raione sibirskoi zheleznoi dorogi na sredstva fonda imeni imperatora Aleksandra III. St. Petersburg: Gos tip., 1898.

Polozhenie tserkovnogo i shkol'nogo stroitel'stva v raione sibirskoi zheleznoi dorogi na sredstva fonda imeni imperatora Aleksandra III. St. Petersburg: Gos. tip., 1900.

Pouchenie po sluchaiu sbora pozhertvovanii na postroenie khrama v sele Mogil'no-Posel'skom Tarskogo uezda, Omskoi eparkhii. Moscow: Pech. A.I. Snegirevoi, 1899.

Price, M. Philips. *Siberia*. London: Methuen and Co., 1912.

Sabler, Sviatoslav Vladimirovich, Ivan Vasil'evich Sosnovskii, and A.N. Kulomzin. *Sibirskaia zhelieznaia doroga v ee proshlom i nastoiashchem: istoricheskii ocherk*. St. Petersburg: Gos. tip., 1903.

Shilkin, Sergei. *Otchet inzhenera Shilkina ob osmotre v 1900 gody tserkvei i shkol, sooruzhennykh i sooruzhaemykh na sredstva fonda imeni Imperatora Aleksandra III v Akmolinskoi oblasti i Eniseiskoi gubernii*. St. Petersburg, 1900.

– *Otchet ob osmotre v 1900 gody tserkvei i shkol, sooruzhennykh i sooruzhaemykh na sredstva fonda imeni Imperatora Aleksandra III v Tobol'skoi i Tomskoi guberniiakh*. St. Petersburg, 1900.

Shilovskii, M. *Sibirskie Pereseleniia: dokumenty i materialy*. Vol. 1. Novosibirsk: Novosibirskii gos. universitet, 2003.

Sibirskie tserkvi i shkoly fonda imeni imperatora Aleksandra III. St. Petersburg: Gos. tip., 1902.

Sibirskie tserkvi i shkoly. St. Petersburg: Gos. tip., 1904.

Spravochnaia knizhka po Akmolinskomu pereselencheskomu raionu na 1912 (1912).

Stolypin, Petr A., and Aleksandr V. Krivoshein. *Poezdka v Sibir' i povolzh'e: zapiska P.A. Stolypina i A.V. Krivosheina*. St. Petersburg: Tip. A.S. Suvorina, 1911.

Tarasov, T.I. *Tserkvi, shkoly i prichtovye doma, sooruzhennye na sredstva fonda imeni imperatora Aleksandra III. Otchet po komandirovke 1903 g. chinovnika kantseliarii kom. ministrov T.I. Tarasova ch.1*. St. Petersburg: Gos. tip., 1904.

— *Tserkvi, shkoly i prichtovye doma, sooruzhennye na sredstva fonda imeni imperatora Aleksandra III. Otchet po komandirovke 1903 g. chinovnika kantseliarii kom. ministrov T.I. Tarasova ch.2.* St. Petersburg: Gos. tip., 1904.

Tregubov, A.L. *Pereselencheskoe delo v Semipalatinskoi i Semirechenskoi oblastiakh.* St. Petersburg, 1910.

— *Po novym mestam: Pereselenie v Sibiri' v 1913 g.* St. Petersburg: Tip. Iu. H. Erlikh, 1913.

United States Government. *The Russian Empire and the Trans-Siberian Railway.* Washington, DC: Government Printing Office, 1899.

Veniamin. *Zhiznennye voprosy pravoslavnoi missii v Sibiri.* St. Petersburg: Tip. A.M. Kotomina, 1885.

Vinogradov, Vasilii. *Poezdka ego preosviashchenstva, preosviashchenneishego Andronika.* Omsk: Tip. K.I. Demidovoi, 1913.

Voshchinin, V.P. *Pereselenie i zemleustroistvo v Aziatskoi Rossii. Sbornik zakonov i rasporiazhenii.* Petrograd, 1915.

Vostorgov, Ioann. *Dobroe slovo pereselentsy.* Moscow: Vernost', 1909.

— *Polnoe sobranie sochinenii.* Vol. 4. Moscow, 1914.

Vsepoddanneishii doklad ministra zemledeliia i gosudarstvennykh' imushchestv [A.S. Ermolova] po poezdke v Sibir' osen'iu 1895 goda. St. Petersburg: Tip. "V. Kirshbauma," 1896.

Zhurnaly s"ezda o.o. deputatov ot dukhovenstva Omskoi eparkhii, proiskhodivshego v 1899 godu v g. Omske Akmolinskoi oblasti. Omsk, 1899.

Zhurnaly 3-go obshcheeparkhial'nogo s"ezda o.o. deputatov ot dukhovenstva Omskoi eparkhii, proizvodivshegosia v 1902 godu v g. Omske Akmolinskoi oblasti. Omsk, 1902.

Zhurnaly 4-go obshcheeparkhial'nogo s"ezda o.o. deputatov ot dukhovenstva, Omskoi eparkhii byvshego v 1905 godu v g. Omske Akmolinskoi oblasti. Omsk, 1905.

Zhurnaly 7-go obshcheeparkhial'nogo s"ezda o.o. deputatov ot dukhovenstva Omskoi eparkhii byvshego v 1912 godu v g. Omske, Akmolinskoi oblasti. Omsk, 1912.

Secondary Sources

Abashin, Sergei, D. Iu. Arapov, and N.E. Bekmakhanova. *Tsentral'naia Aziia v sostave Rossiiskoi imperii.* Moscow: Novoe literaturnoe obozrenie, 2008.

Adamenko, A. *Prikhody Russkoi pravoslavnoi tserkvi na iuge zapadnoi Sibiri v XVII–nachale XX veka.* Kemerovo: Kuzbassvuzizdat, 2004.

Atkin, Nicholas. *Priests, Prelates and People: A History of European Catholicism since 1750.* New York: I.B. Tauris, 2003.

Banivanua-Mar, Tracey, and Penelope Edmonds, eds. *Making Settler Colonial Space: Perspectives on Race, Place and Identity.* New York: Palgrave Macmillan, 2010.

Bassin, Mark. *Imperial Visions: Nationalist Imagination and Geographical Expansion in the Russian Far East, 1840–1865.* Cambridge: Cambridge University Press, 1999.

- "Inventing Siberia: Visions of the Russian East in the Early Nineteenth Century." *American Historical Review* 96, no. 3 (June 1991): 763–94.

Belich, James. *Replenishing the Earth: The Settler Revolution and the Rise of the Anglo-world, 1783–1939*. New York: Oxford University Press, 2009.

Berdinskikh, A. "The Parish Clergy and the Development of Local History in Nineteenth-Century Russia." *Russian Studies in History* 44, no. 4 (Spring 2006): 9–18.

Berkovskaia, Z.N. "Omskaia eparkhiia v kul'turnoi zhizni stepnogo kraia v kontse XIX–nachale XX veka." *Nauchnye soobshchestva istorikov i arkhivistov: intellektual'nye dialogi so vremenem i mirom*. Omsk, 2006.

Breyfogle, Nicholas B. *Heretics and Colonizers: Forging Russia's Empire in the South Caucasus*. Ithaca, NY: Cornell University Press, 2005.

- "Prayer and the Politics of Place: Molokan Church Building, Tsarist Law and the Quest for a Public Sphere in Late Imperial Russia." In *Sacred Stories: Religion and Spirituality in Modern Russia*, edited by Mark D. Steinberg and Heather J. Coleman, 222–52. Bloomington: Indiana University Press, 2007.

Breyfogle, Nicholas B., Abby M. Schrader, and Willard Sunderland, eds. *Peopling the Russian Periphery: Borderland Colonization in Eurasian History*. New York: Routledge, 2007.

Brooks, Jeffrey. *When Russia Learned to Read: Literacy and Popular Literature, 1861–1917*. Evanston, IL: Northwestern University Press, 1985.

Brower, Daniel R. "Islam and Ethnicity: Russian Colonial Policy in Turkestan." In *Russia's Orient: Imperial Borderlands and Peoples, 1700–1917*, edited by Daniel R. Brower and Edward J. Lazzerini, 115–35. Bloomington: Indiana University Press, 1997.

Brown, Kate. "Gridded Lives: Why Kazakhstan and Montana Are Nearly the Same Place." *American Historical Review* 106, no. 1 (2001): 14–48.

Burds, Jeffrey. *Peasant Dreams and Market Politics: Labor Migration and the Russian Village, 1861–1905*. Pittsburgh: University of Pittsburgh Press, 1998.

Cameron, Sarah I. *The Hungry Steppe: Famine, Violence, and the Making of Soviet Kazakhstan*. Ithaca, NY: Cornell University Press, 2018.

Campbell, Elena I. "The Muslim Question in Late Imperial Russia." In *Russian Empire: Space, People, Power, 1700–1930*, edited by Jane Burbank, Mark Von Hagen, and A.V. Remnev, 320–47. Bloomington: Indiana University Press, 2007.

Campbell, Ian W. *Knowledge and the Ends of Empire: Kazak Intermediaries and Russian Rule on the Steppe*. Ithaca, NY: Cornell University Press, 2017.

- "Settlement Promoted, Settlement Contested: The Shcherbina Expedition of 1896–1903." *Central Asian Survey* 30, no. 3–4 (2011): 423–36.

Carey, Hilary M. *God's Empire: Religion and Colonialism in the British World, c.1801–1908*. Cambridge: Cambridge University Press, 2011.

- "Introduction." In *Empires of Religion*, edited by Hilary M. Carey, 1–21. New York: Palgrave Macmillan, 2008.

Carey, Jane. "'Wanted! A Real White Australia': The Women's Movement, Whiteness and the Settler Colonial Project, 1900–1940." In *Studies in Settler Colonialism: Politics, Identity and Culture*, edited by Fiona Bateman and Lionel Pilkington, 122–39. New York: Palgrave Macmillan, 2011.

Chulos, Chris J. *Converging Worlds: Religion and Community in Peasant Russia, 1861–1917*. DeKalb: Northern Illinois University Press, 2003.

Coleman, Heather J. "Defining Heresy: The Fourth Missionary Congress and the Problem of Cultural Power after 1905 in Russia." *Jahrbücher Für Geschichte Osteuropas* 52, no. 1 (2004): 70–91.

– "Introduction." In *Orthodox Christianity in Imperial Russia: A Source Book on Lived Religion*. Bloomington: Indiana University Press, 2014.

– *Russian Baptists and Spiritual Revolution, 1905–1929*. Bloomington: Indiana University Press, 2005.

Cooper, Frederick, and Ann Laura Stoler, eds. *Tensions of Empire: Colonial Cultures in a Bourgeois World*. Berkeley: University of California Press, 1997.

Crews, Robert D. *For Prophet and Tsar: Islam and Empire in Russia and Central Asia*. Cambridge, MA: Harvard University Press, 2009.

Dameshek, L., and A Remnev. *Sibir' v sostave Rossiiskoi imperii*. Moscow: Novoe literaturnoe obozrenie, 2007.

Demko, George. *The Russian Colonization of Kazakhstan, 1896–1916*. Bloomington: Indiana University Press, 1969.

Dolbilov, M. *Russkii krai chuzhaia vera: Etnokonfessional'naia politika imperii v Litve i Belorussii pri Aleksandre II*. Moscow: Novoe literaturnoe obozrenie, 2010.

Emmons, Terence, and Wayne S. Vucinich, eds. *The Zemstvo in Russia: An Experiment in Local Self-Government*. New York: Cambridge University Press, 1982.

Engelstein, Laura. *Castration and the Heavenly Kingdom: A Russian Folktale*. Ithaca, NY: Cornell University Press, 2003.

English, Jim. "Empire Day in Britain, 1904–1958." *Historical Journal* 49, no. 1 (2006): 247–76.

Epp, Petr. *100 let pod krovom Vsevyshnego: istoriia Omskikh obshchin EKhB i ikh ob"edineniia, 1907–2007*. Omsk: Samenkorn, 2007.

Etkind, Aleksandr. *Internal Colonization: Russia's Imperial Experience*. Cambridge, UK: Polity Press, 2011.

Fein, Julia. "Cultural Curators and Provincial Publics: Local Museums and Social Change in Siberia, 1887–1941." PhD diss., University of Chicago, 2012.

Ford, Caroline. "Religion and Popular Culture in Modern Europe." *Journal of Modern History* 65, no. 1 (1993): 152–75.

Forsyth, James. *A History of the Peoples of Siberia: Russia's North Asian Colony, 1581–1990*. Cambridge: Cambridge University Press, 2000.

Frank, Allen J. "Islamic Transformation on the Kazakh Steppe, 1742–1917: Toward an Islamic History of Kazakhstan under Russian Rule." In

The Construction and Deconstruction of National Histories in Slavic Eurasia, edited by Hayashi Tadayuki, 261–89. Sapporo, JP: Hokkaido University Press, 2003.

– *Muslim Religious Institutions in Imperial Russia: The Islamic World of Novouzensk District and the Kazakh Inner Horde, 1780–1910*. Boston: Brill, 2001.

Frank, Allen J., and M.G. Gosmanov, eds. *Materials for the Islamic History of Semipalatinsk: Two Manuscripts by Aḥmad-Walī al-Qazānī and Qurbān'alī Khālidī*. Berlin: Das Arabische Buch, 2001.

Freeze, Gregory L. "All Power to the Parish? The Problems and Politics of Church Reform in Late Imperial Russia." In *Social Identities in Revolutionary Russia*, edited by Madhavan Palat, 174–208. Houndmills, UK: Palgrave, 2001.

– "Institutionalizing Piety: The Church and Popular Religion, 1750–1850." In *Imperial Russia: New Histories for the Empire*, edited by Jane Burbank and David L. Ransel, 210–49. Bloomington: Indiana University Press, 1998.

– *The Parish Clergy in Nineteenth-Century Russia: Crisis, Reform, Counter-Reform*. Princeton: Princeton University Press, 1983.

– "Russian Orthodoxy on the Periphery: Decoding the Raporty Blagochinnykh in Lithuania Diocese." In *Problemy vsemirnoi istorii*, edited by B.V. Anan'ich, 124–31. St. Petersburg: Vilanin, 2000.

Friesen, Aileen. "Building an Orthodox Empire: Archpriest Ioann Vostorgov and Russian Missionary Aspirations in Asia." *Canadian Slavonic Papers* 57, no. 1–2 (2015): 56–75.

Fursova, E.F., and L.I. Vasekha. *Ocherki traditsionnoi kul'tury Ukrainskikh pereselentsev Sibiri XIX–pervoi treti XX veka: po materialam Novosibirskoi oblasti*. Novosibirsk: Agro-Sibir', 2004.

Gaudin, Corinne. *Ruling Peasants: Village and State in Late Imperial Russia*. DeKalb: Northern Illinois University Press, 2007.

Gentes, Andrew. "Review on Siberia as Part of the Russian Empire." *Kritika: Explorations in Russian and Eurasian History* 10, no. 4 (Fall 2009): 963–73.

Geraci, Robert P. "Going Abroad or Going to Russia? Orthodox Missionaries in the Kazakh Steppe, 1881–1917." In *Of Religion and Empire: Missions, Conversion, and Tolerance in Tsarist Russia*, edited by Robert Geraci and Michael Khordarkovsky, 274–310. Ithaca: Cornell University Press, 2001.

– "On 'Colonial' Forms and Functions." *Slavic Review* 69, no. 1 (Spring 2010): 180–84.

– *Window on the East: National and Imperial Identities in Late Tsarist Russia*. Ithaca: Cornell University Press, 2001.

Geraci, Robert P., and Michael Khodarkovsky. "Introduction." *Of Religion and Empire: Missions, Conversion, and Tolerance in Tsarist Russia*, eds. Robert P. Geraci and Michael Khodarkovsky, 1–15. Ithaca: Cornell University Press, 2001.

Golubtsov, S.V. *Istoriia Omskoi eparkhii: obrazovanie Omskoi eparkhii, predstoiatel'stvo preosviashchennogo Grigoriia na Omskoi kafedre (1895–1900 gg.)*. Omsk: Poligraf, 2008.

Goriushkin, L.M. *Krest'ianskoe dvizhenie v Sibiri 1907–1914 gg. Khronika i istoriografiia.* Novosibirsk: Nauka, 1986.

Greene, Robert H. "Bodies in Motion: Steam-Powered Pilgrimages in Late Imperial Russia." *Russian History* 39, no. 1/2 (January 2012): 247–68.

– *Bodies Like Bright Stars: Saints and Relics in Orthodox Russia.* DeKalb: Northern Illinois University Press, 2010.

Hall, David D., ed. *Lived Religion in America: Toward a History of Practice.* Princeton, NJ: Princeton University Press, 1997.

Hartley, Janet M. *Siberia: A History of the People.* New Haven, CT: Yale University Press, 2014.

Hedda, Jennifer. *His Kingdom Come: Orthodox Pastorship and Social Activism in Revolutionary Russia.* DeKalb: Northern Illinois University Press, 2008.

Hoerder, Dirk. *Cultures in Contact: World Migrations in the Second Millennium.* Durham, NC: Duke University Press, 2002.

Holquist, Peter. "'In Accord with State Interests and the People's Wishes': The Technocratic Ideology of Imperial Russia's Resettlement Administration." *Slavic Review* 69, no. 1 (Spring 2010): 151–79.

– "The Shifting Boundary: Regional and Religious Identity among Old Believers and Orthodox Peasants in Western Siberia, 1880s–1914." MA thesis, Columbia University, 1990.

Husband, William. "Happy Birthday, Siberia! Reform and Public Opinion in Russia's 'Colony,' 1881–1882." In *The Human Tradition in Imperial Russia*, edited by Christine Worobec, 85–99. Lanham, MD: Rowman and Littlefield, 2009.

Iadrintsev, N.M. *Sibir' kak koloniia: sovremennoe polozhenie Sibiri, ee nuzhdy i potrebnosti, ee proshloe i budushchee.* St. Petersburg: Tip. M.M. Stasiulevicha, 1882.

Ignatenko, O.V. "Kirgiz dukhovnaia missiia." *Sovremennoe obshchestvo,* vyp.1. Omsk, 1999.

Jacob, W.M. *The Clerical Profession in the Long Eighteenth Century, 1680–1840.* Oxford: Oxford University Press, 2007.

Kan, Sergei. "Russian Orthodox Missionaries at Home and Abroad: The Case of Siberian and Alaskan Indigenous Peoples." In *Of Religion and Empire: Missions, Conversion, and Tolerance in Tsarist Russia,* edited by Robert Geraci and Michael Khordarkovsky, 173–200. Ithaca, NY: Cornell University Press, 2001.

Kappeler, Andreas. *The Russian Empire: A Multiethnic History.* Translated by Alfred Clayton. Harlow: Longman, 2001.

Khodarkovsky, Michael. *Russia's Steppe Frontier: The Making of a Colonial Empire, 1500–1800.* Bloomington: Indiana University Press, 2005.

Kivelson, Valerie A. *Cartographies of Tsardom: The Land and Its Meanings in Seventeenth-Century Russia.* Ithaca, NY: Cornell University Press, 2006.

Kivelson, Valerie A., and Ronald Grigor Suny. *Russia's Empires.* New York: Oxford University Press, 2017.

Kizenko, Nadieszda. *A Prodigal Saint: Father John of Kronstadt and the Russian People*. University Park: Pennsylvania State University Press, 2000.

Kononenko, Natalie. "Folk Orthodoxy: Popular Religion in Contemporary Ukraine." In *Letters from Heaven: Popular Religion in Russia and Ukraine*, edited by John-Paul Himka and Andriy Zayarnyuk, 57–61. Toronto: University of Toronto, 2006.

– "Ukrainian Folklore in Kazakhstan." *Folklorica* 16 (2011): 163–83.

Kovalaschina, Elena, and Alia A. Chaptykova. "The Historical and Cultural Ideals of the Siberian Oblastnichestvo." *Sibirica* 6, no. 2 (October 2007): 87–119.

Kozelsky, Mara. *Christianizing Crimea: Shaping Sacred Space in the Russian Empire and Beyond*. DeKalb: Northern Illinois University Press, 2010.

Kravetskii, Aleksandr. *Tserkovnaia missiia v epokhu peremen*. Moscow: Kruglyi stol po religioznomu obrazovaniiu i diakonii, 2012.

Le Couteur, Howard. "Anglican High Churchmen and the Expansion of Empire." *Journal of Religious History* 32, no. 2 (June 2008): 193–215.

Levin, M.G., and L.P. Potapov, eds. *The Peoples of Siberia*. Translated by Stephen P. Dunn. Chicago: University of Chicago Press, 1964.

Lieven, D.C.B. "Bureaucratic Liberalism in Late Imperial Russia: The Personality, Career and Opinions of A.N. Kulomzin." *Slavonic and East European Review* 60, no. 3 (July 1982): 413–32.

Lincoln, W. Bruce. *The Conquest of a Continent: Siberia and the Russians*. Ithaca, NY: Cornell University Press, 2007.

Lindenmeyr, Adele. "The Ethos of Charity in Imperial Russia." *Journal of Social History* 23, no. 4 (1990): 679–94.

– "Public Life, Private Virtues: Women in Russian Charity, 1762–1914." *Signs* 18, no. 3 (Spring 1993): 562–91.

– "Voluntary Associations and the Russian Autocracy: The Case of Private Charity." *Carl Beck Papers in Russian and East European Studies* no. 807 (June 1990): 1–64.

Lipinskaia, V.A. "Konfessional'nye gruppy pravoslavnogo naseleniia zapadnoi Sibiri (vtoraia polovina XIX–nachalo XX v.)." *Etnograficheskoe obozrenie* 2 (1995): 113–27.

– *Starozhily i pereselentsy: russkie na Altae: XVIII–nachalo XX veka*. Moscow: Nauka, 1996.

Litiagina, Alla Vladimirovna. "Deiatel'nost' Russkoi pravoslavnoi tserkvi v gorodakh zapadnoi Sibiri vo vtoroi polovine XIX – nachale XX v." *Voprosy istorii* 9 (2008): 93–101.

– "Uroven' religioznosti naseleniia zapadnoi Sibiri (1861–1917)." *Voprosy istorii* 9 (2006): 117–24.

Lysenko, Yuliya A. *Missionerstvo Russkoi pravoslavnoi tserkvi v Kazakhstane: vtoraia polovina XIX–nachalo XX v.* Barnaul: Izd-vo Altaiskogo gos. universiteta, 2010.

– *Ocherki istorii Russkoi pravoslavnoi tserkvi v Kazakhstane (XVIII–nachalo XX v.)*. Barnaul: Azbuka, 2011.
– "Pravoslavie i Islam: Praktiki etnokonfessional'noi kommunikatsii na primere Russkikh i Kazakhov verkhnego priirtysh'ia (XIX–nachalo XX V)." *Vestnik arkhelogii, antropologii i etnografii* 15, no. 2 (2011).
– "Stepen' Islamizatsii kazakhskogo obshchestva na rubezhe XIX–XX vv. v otsenke missionerov kirgizskoi dukhovnoi missii." *Izvestiia Altaiskogo gosudarstvennogo universiteta* 4–3 (2008): 149–55.
– "Tserkovnoe stroitel'stvo v stepnom krae." *Mezhdunarodnyi imidzh Rossii* (blog), 9 June 2008. http://image-of-russia.livejournal.com/19208.html.
Malikov, Yuriy Anatolyevich. "Formation of a Borderland Culture: Myths and Realities of Cossack-Kazakh Relations in Northern Kazakhstan in the Eighteenth and Nineteenth Centuries." PhD diss., University of California, Santa Barbara, 2006.
Manchester, Laurie. "Gender and Social Estate as National Identity: The Wives and Daughters of Orthodox Clergymen as Civilizing Agents in Imperial Russia." *Journal of Modern History* 83 (March 2011): 48–77.
– *Holy Fathers, Secular Sons: Clergy, Intelligentsia, and the Modern Self in Revolutionary Russia*. DeKalb: Northern Illinois University Press, 2008.
Manuil (Lemesevskij), Metropolitan. *Die Russischen Orthodoxen Bischöfe von 1893 bis 1965*. Teil II. Erlangen, DE: Erlangen Lehrstuhl für Geschichte u. Theologie d. Christl. Ostens, 1981.
Marks, Steven G. "Conquering the Great East: Kulomzin, Peasant Resettlement, and the Creation of Modern Siberia." In *Rediscovering Russia in Asia: Siberia and the Russian Far East*, edited by Stephen Kotkin and David Wolff, 23–39. Armonk, NY: M.E. Sharpe, 1995.
– *Road to Power: The Trans-Siberian Railroad and the Colonization of Asian Russia, 1850–1917*. Ithaca, NY: Cornell University Press, 1991.
Martin, Virginia. *Law and Custom in the Steppe: The Kazakhs of the Middle Horde and Russian Colonialism in the Nineteenth Century*. Richmond, UK: Routledge Curzon, 2001.
Masoero, Alberto. "Layers of Property in the Tsar's Settlement Colony: Projects of Land Privatization in Siberia in the Late Nineteenth Century." *Central Asian Survey* 29, no. 1 (March 2010): 9–32.
– "Territorial Colonization in Late Imperial Russia: Stages in the Development of a Concept." *Kritika: Explorations in Russian and Eurasian History* 14, no. 1 (Winter 2013): 59–91.
Mavliutova, G. *Missionerskaia deiatel' nost' Russkoi pravoslavnoi tserkvi v severo-zapadnoi Sibiri, XIX – nachalo XX veka*. Tiumen: Izd-vo Tiumenskogo gos. universiteta, 2001.
Mazaev, Gavriel I. *Obrashchenie na istinnyi put' i vospominaniia baptista G.I.M.* Omsk: Board of the Siberian Department of the Baptist Union, 1919.

McGowan, Mark George. *Michael Power: The Struggle to Build the Catholic Church on the Canadian Frontier*. Montreal: McGill-Queen's University Press, 2005.

Michelson, Patrick L., and Judith Deutsch Kornblatt, eds. *Thinking Orthodox in Modern Russia Culture, History, Context*. Madison: University of Wisconsin Press, 2014.

Minenko, N.A. *Russkaia krest'ianskaia sem' ia v zapadnoi Sibiri: XVIII–pervoi polovine XIX v.* Novosibirsk: Nauka, Sibirskoe otd-nie, 1979.

Monahan, Erika. *The Merchants of Siberia: Trade in Early Modern Eurasia*. Ithaca, NY: Cornell University Press, 2016.

Moon, David. "Peasant Migration and the Settlement of Russia's Frontiers, 1550–1897." *Historical Journal* 40, no. 4 (December 1997): 859–93.

– *The Russian Peasantry, 1600–1930: The World the Peasants Made*. New York: Longman, 1999.

Morrison, Alexander. "Peasant Settlers and the 'Civilising Mission' in Russian Turkestan, 1865–1917." *Journal of Imperial and Commonwealth History* 43, no. 3 (May 2015): 387–417.

– *Russian Rule in Samarkand 1868–1910: A Comparison with British India*. New York: Oxford University Press, 2008.

Moss, Walter G. *Russia in the Age of Alexander II, Tolstoy and Dostoevsky*. London: Anthem Press, 2002.

Murray, Jesse D. "Building Empire among the Buryats: Conversion Encounters in Russia's Baikal Region, 1860s–1917." PhD diss., University of Illinois at Urbana-Champaign, 2012.

Neuberger, Joan. *Hooliganism: Crime, Culture, and Power in St. Petersburg, 1900–1914*. Berkeley: University of California Press, 1993.

Olcott, Martha Brill. *The Kazakhs*. Stanford, CA: Hoover Institution Press, Stanford University, 1987.

Osterhammel, Jürgen. *The Transformation of the World: A Global History of the Nineteenth Century*. Translated by Patrick Camiller. Princeton, NJ: Princeton University Press, 2014.

Paert, Irina. "'Two or Twenty Million?' The Languages of Official Statistics and Religious Dissent in Imperial Russia." *Ab Imperio* no. 3 (July 2006): 75–98.

Pasquier, Michael. *Fathers on the Frontier: French Missionaries and the Roman Catholic Priesthood in the United States, 1789–1870*. Oxford: Oxford University Press, 2010.

Payne, Matthew. "Do You Want Me to Exterminate All of Them or Just the Ones Who Oppose Us?" In *Empire and Belonging in the European Borderlands*, edited by Krista A. Goff and Lewis H. Siegelbaum, 65–79. Ithaca, NY: Cornell University Press, 2019.

Peck, Anna. "The Image of Heathens: Archbishop Veniamin Blagonravov's Perception of Religion and Nationality in the Transbaikal." *Sibirica* 10, no. 2 (2011): 50–72.

Pierce, Richard A. *Russian Central Asia, 1867–1917: A Study in Colonial Rule.*
    Berkeley: University of California Press, 1960.
Plamper, Jan. "The Russian Orthodox Episcopate, 1721–1917: A
    Prosopography." *Journal of Social History* 34, no. 1 (Fall 2000): 5–34.
Pokrovskii, N.N. "The Book Registers from the 1722 Tara Revolt." *Russian
    Studies in History* 49, no. 3 (Winter 2010): 8–41.
Polunov, A. Iu. "Konstantin Petrovich Pobedonostsev – Man and Politician."
    Russian Studies in History 39, no. 4 (Spring 2001): 8–32.
– *K.P. Pobedonostsev v obshchestvenno-politicheskoii i dukhovnoii zhizni Rossii.*
    Moscow: Rosspen, 2010.
– "The Religious Department and the Uniate Question, 1881–1894." *Russian
    Studies in History* 39, no. 4 (Spring 2001): 77–85.
Pospielovsky, D. "The Renovationist Movement in the Orthodox Church
    in the Light of Archival Documents." *Journal of Church and State* 39, no. 1
    (1997): 85–105.
Rainbow, David. "Racial 'Degeneration' and Siberian Regionalism in the
    Late Imperial Period." In *Ideologies of Race: Imperial Russia and the Soviet
    Union in Global Context,* edited by David Rainbow. Montreal: McGill-Queen's
    University Press, 2019.
– "Siberian Patriots: Participatory Autocracy and the Cohesion of the Russian
    Imperial State, 1858–1920." PhD diss., New York University, 2013.
Remnev, A.V. "Anatolii Nikolaevich Kulomzin." *Voprosy istorii* 8 (2009): 26–45.
– "Colonization and "Russification" in Asiatic Russia." In *Asiatic Russia:
    Imperial Power in Regional and International Contexts,* edited by Uyama
    Tomohiko. New York: Routledge, 2012.
– "Siberia and the Russian Far East in the Imperial Geography of Power." In
    Russian Empire: Space, People, Power: 1700–1930, edited by Jane Burbank and
    Mark Von Hagen. Bloomington: Indiana University Press, 2007.
Remnev, A.V., and Natal'ia Suvorova. "'Russkoe delo' na aziatskikh
    okrainakh: 'Russkost' pod ugrozoi ili 'somnitel'nye kul'turtregery.'" *Ab
    Imperio* 2 (April 2008): 157–222.
Robbins, Richard G. *The Tsar's Viceroys: Russian Provincial Governors in the Last
    Years of the Empire.* Ithaca, NY: Cornell University Press, 1987.
Romaniello, Matthew P. *The Elusive Empire: Kazan and the Creation of Russia,
    1552–1671.* Madison: University of Wisconsin Press, 2012.
Roslof, Edward. *Red Priests: Renovationism, Russian Orthodoxy, and Revolution,
    1905–1946.* Bloomington: Indiana University Press, 2002.
Ruane, Christine. *The Empire's New Clothes: A History of the Russian Fashion
    Industry, 1700–1917.* New Haven, CT: Yale University Press, 2009.
Sabol, Steven. "Comparing American and Russian Internal Colonization:
    The 'Touch of Civilisation' on the Sioux and Kazakhs." *Western Historical
    Quarterly* 43, no. 1 (Spring 2012): 29–51.

Sahadeo, Jeff. *Russian Colonial Society in Tashkent: 1865–1923*. Bloomington: Indiana University Press, 2007.

– "Visions of Empire: Russia's Place in an Imperial World." *Kritika: Explorations in Russian and Eurasian History* 11, no. 2 (2010): 381–409.

Saler, Bethel. *The Settlers' Empire Colonialism and State Formation in America's Old Northwest*. Philadelphia: University of Pennsylvania Press, 2015.

Scarborough, Daniel L. "The White Priest at Work: Orthodox Pastoral Activism and the Public Sphere in Late Imperial Russia." PhD diss., Georgetown University, 2012.

Schorkowitz, Dittmar. "The Orthodox Church, Lamaism, and Shamanism among the Buriats and Kalmyks, 1825–1925." In *Of Religion and Empire: Missions, Conversion, and Tolerance in Tsarist Russia*, edited by Robert Geraci and Michael Khodarkovsky, 201–26. Ithaca, NY: Cornell University Press, 2001.

Shafiyev, Farid. *Resettling the Borderlands State Relocations and Ethnic Conflict in the South Caucasus*. Montreal: McGill-Queen's University Press, 2018.

Shevzov, Vera. *Russian Orthodoxy on the Eve of Revolution*. Oxford: Oxford University Press, 2004.

– "Scripting the Gaze: Liturgy, Homilies and the Kazan Icon of the Mother of God in Late Imperial Russia." In *Sacred Stories: Religion and Spirituality in Modern Russia*, edited by Mark D. Steinberg and Heather J. Coleman, 61–92. Bloomington: Indiana University Press, 2007.

Shubin, Daniel H. *A History of Russian Christianity*. Vol. 3. New York: Algora Publications, 2005.

"Siberia: Colony and Frontier." *Kritika: Explorations in Russian and Eurasian History* 14, no. 1 (Winter 2013): 1–4.

Siegelbaum, Lewis. "Those Elusive Scouts: Pioneering Peasants and the Russian State, 1870s–1950s." *Kritika: Explorations in Russian and Eurasian History* 14, no. 1 (Winter 2013): 31–58.

Siegelbaum, Lewis, and Leslie Page Moch. *Broad Is My Native Land: Repertoires and Regimes of Migration in Russia's Twentieth Century*. Ithaca, NY: Cornell University Press, 2014.

Skinner, Barbara. *The Western Front of the Eastern Church: Uniate and Orthodox Conflict in 18th-century Poland, Ukraine, Belarus, and Russia*. DeKalb: Northern Illinois University Press, 2009.

Slezkine, Yuri. *Arctic Mirrors: Russia and the Small Peoples of the North*. Ithaca, NY: Cornell University Press, 1994.

Slocum, John W. "Who, and When, Were the Inorodtsy? The Evolution of the Category of 'Aliens' in Imperial Russia." *Russian Review* 57, no. 2 (April 1998): 173–90.

Smillie, Benjamin, ed. *Visions of the New Jerusalem: Religious Settlement on the Prairies*. Edmonton, AB: NeWest Press, 1983.

Smolich, Igor. *Istoriia Russkoi tserkvi*. Vol. 1. Moscow: Izd-vo Spaso-Preobrazhenskogo Valaamskogo monastyria, 1996.

Sofronov, Viacheslav. *Missionerskaia i dukhovno-prosvetitel'skaia deiatel'nost' Russkoi pravoslavnoi tserkvi v zapadnoi Sibiri: konets XVII–nachalo XX vv.* Tobol'sk: GOU VPO Tobol'skii gosudarstvennyi pedagogicheskii institut imeni D.I. Mendeleeva, 2005.

Stavrou, George. *Russian Interests in Palestine, 1882–1914: A Study of Religious and Educational Enterprise*. Thessaloniki, GR: Inst. for Balkan Studies, 1963.

Stebelsky, Ihor. "Ukraine Settlement Patterns in the Kirgiz Steppe Before 1917: Ukrainian Colonies or Russian Integration?" In *Transforming Peasants: Society, State and the Peasantry, 1861–1930*, edited by Judith Pallot, 130–45. New York: Palgrave Macmillan, 1998.

Steinberg, Mark D., and Heather J. Coleman, eds. *Sacred Stories: Religion and Spirituality in Modern Russia*. Bloomington: Indiana University Press, 2007.

Steinwedel, Charles. "Resettling People, Upsetting the Empire: Migration and the Challenges of Governance, 1861–1917." In *Peopling the Russian Periphery: Borderland Colonization in Eurasian History*, edited by Nicholas B. Breyfogle, Abby M. Schrader, and Willard Sunderland, 128–47. New York: Routledge, 2007.

Stolberg, Eva-Maria. "The Siberian Frontier and Russia's Position in World History: A Reply to Aust and Nolte." *Review (Fernand Braudel Center)* 27, no. 3 (January 2004): 243–67.

– *The Siberian Saga: A History of Russia's Wild East*. New York: Peter Lang, 2005.

Strickland, John. *The Making of Holy Russia: The Orthodox Church and Russian Nationalism Before the Revolution*. Jordanville, NY: Holy Trinity Publications, 2013.

Strong, Rowan. "The Reverend John Wollaston and Colonial Christianity in Western Australia, 1840–1863." *Journal of Religious History* 25, no. 3 (October 2001): 261–85.

Sultangalieva, Gulmira. "The Intermediary Role of Tatars in Kazakhstan." In *Asiatic Russia: Imperial Power in Regional and International Contexts*, edited by Tomohiko Uyama, 52–79. New York: Routledge, 2012.

Sunderland, Willard. "The 'Colonization Question': Visions of Colonization in Late Imperial Russia." *Jahrbücher Für Geschichte Osteuropas* 48, no. 2 (May 2000): 210–32.

– "Empire without Imperialism? Ambiguities of Colonization in Tsarist Russia." *Ab Imperio* 2 (April 2003): 101–14.

– "The Ministry of Asiatic Russia: The Colonial Office That Never Was but Might Have Been." *Slavic Review* 69, no. 1 (April 2010): 120–50.

– "Peasant Pioneering: Russian Peasant Settlers Describe Colonization and the Eastern Frontier, 1880s–1910s." *Journal of Social History* 34, no. 4 (Summer 2001): 895–922.

- "Russians into Iakuts? 'Going Native' and Problems of Russian National Identity in the Siberian North, 1870s–1914." *Slavic Review* 55, no. 4 (1996): 806–25.
- *Taming the Wild Field: Colonization and Empire on the Russian Steppe*. Ithaca, NY: Cornell University Press, 2004.

Sushko, A.V. "Religious Seminaries in Russia (to 1917)." *Russian Studies in History* 44, no.4 (Spring 2006): 47–61.

Swyripa, Frances. *Storied Landscapes: Ethno-Religious Identity and the Canadian Prairies*. Winnipeg: University of Manitoba Press, 2010.

Tarasova, V.A. *Vysshaia dukhovnaia shkola v Rossii v kontse XIX–nachale XX veka: Istoriia imperatorskikh pravoslavnykh dukhovnykh akademii*. Moscow: Novyi khronograf, 2005.

Thyrêt, Isolde. "Creating a Religious Community in Siberia: The Cultural Politics of Archbishop Nektarii of Tobol'sk." *Canadian-American Slavic Studies* 51, no. 1 (2017): 87–104.

Treadgold, Donald W. *The Great Siberian Migration: Government and Peasant in Resettlement from Emancipation to the First World War*. Princeton, NJ: Princeton University Press, 1957.

Ushakova, O.V. "K voprosu ob otkrytii dukhovnoi seminarii v Omskoi eparkhii." *Stepnoi krai zona vzaimodeistviia russkogo i kazakhskogo narodov*. Omsk, 1998.
- "Zapadnosibirskii episkopat v 1907–1914 gg: K kharakteristike episkopov Russkoi pravoslavnoi tserkvi kak sotsial'noi gruppy." In *Slavianskoe edinstvo: mezhunarodnaia nauchnaia konferentsiia*, 126–29. Omsk, 2000.

Uyama, Tomohiko. "A Particularist Empire: The Russian Policies of Christianization and Military Conscription in Central Asia." In *Empire, Islam, and Politics in Central Eurasia*, edited by Tomohiko Uyama, 23–63. Sapporo, JP: Slavic Research Center, 2007.

Vasil'eva, Aleksandra. "Sotsiokul'turnyi oblik pravoslavnogo dukhovestva v zapadnoi Sibiri v kontse–nachale XX vv." Candidate diss., Omskii gosudarstvennyi pedagogicheskii universitet, 2015.

Veracini, Lorenzo. "Introducing Settler Colonial Studies." *Settler Colonial Studies* 1, no. 1 (2011): 1–12.
- *Settler Colonialism: A Theoretical Overview*. New York: Palgrave Macmillan, 2010.

Vibe, P.P. *Nemetskie kolonii v Sibiri: sotsial'no-ekonomicheskii aspect*. Omsk: Omskii gos. pedagogicheskii universitet, 2007.

Vinkovetsky, Ilya. "Building a Diocese Overseas: The Orthodox Church in Partnership with the Russian-American Company in Alaska." *Ab Imperio* 3 (July 2010): 152–94.

Volgine, Igor. "Entrepreneurship and the Siberian Peasant Commune." In *Rural Reform in Post-Soviet Russia*, edited by Stephen K. Wegren and David J. O'Brien, 23–41. Washington, DC: Woodrow Wilson Center Press, 2002.

Ware, Timothy. *The Orthodox Church*. 2nd ed. New York: Penguin, 1997.

Weiss, Claudia. "Representing the Empire: The Meaning of Siberia for Russian Imperial Identity." *Nationalities Papers* 35, no. 3 (July 2007): 439–56.

Weissman, Neil B. "Rural Crime in Tsarist Russia: The Question of Hooliganism, 1905–1914." *Slavic Review* 37, no. 2 (June 1978): 228–40.

Welch, Pamela. *Church and Settler in Colonial Zimbabwe: A Study in the History of the Anglican Diocese of Mashonaland/Southern Rhodesia, 1890–1925*. Leiden, NL: Brill, 2008.

Werth, Paul. "Arbiters of the Free Conscience: State, Religion, and the Problem of Confessional Transfer after 1905." In *Sacred Stories: Religion and Spirituality in Modern Russia*, edited by Mark D. Steinberg and Heather J. Coleman, 179–99. Bloomington: Indiana University Press, 2007.

– *At the Margins of Orthodoxy: Mission, Governance, and Confessional Politics in Russia's Volga-Kama Region, 1827–1905*. Ithaca, NY: Cornell University Press, 2002.

– "Lived Orthodoxy and Confessional Diversity: The Last Decade on Religion in Modern Russia." *Kritika: Explorations in Russian and Eurasian History* 12, no. 4 (Fall 2011): 849–65.

– *The Tsar's Foreign Faiths: Toleration and the Fate of Religious Freedom in Imperial Russia*. Oxford: Oxford University Press, 2014.

Withycombe, Robert S.M. "Australian Anglicans and Imperial Identity, 1900–1914." *Journal of Religious History* 25, no. 3 (October 2001): 286–305.

Witzenrath, Christoph. *Cossacks and the Russian Empire, 1598–1725: Manipulation, Rebellion and Expansion into Siberia*. New York: Routledge, 2007.

Wood, Alan. *Russia's Frozen Frontier: A History of Siberia and the Russian Far East 1581–1991*. New York: Bloomsbury Academic, 2011.

Worobec, Christine. "Death Rituals among Russian and Ukrainian Peasants: Linkages between the Living and the Dead." In *Letters from Heaven: Popular Religion in Russia and Ukraine*, edited by John-Paul Himka and Andriy Zayarnyuk, 13–45. Toronto: University of Toronto Press, 2006.

– "Lived Orthodoxy in Imperial Russia." *Kritika: Explorations in Russian and Eurasian History* 7, no. 2 (Spring 2006): 329–50.

Yokoyama, Olga. *Russian Peasant Letters: Life and Times of a 19th-Century Family*. Wiesbaden, DE: Harrassowitz, 2010.

Young, Nicole. "The Arduous Road to Enlightenment: The Development of Primary Education in Tobol'sk Guberniia, 1816–1914." PhD diss., University of Toronto, 1996.

Yuzyk, Paul. "Religious Life." In *A Heritage in Transition: Essays in the History of Ukrainians in Canada*, edited by Manoly R. Lupul, 143–72. Toronto: McClelland and Stewart, 1982.

Index